# LPIC-1®
# Linux Professional Institute Certification

## Practice Tests

### Second Edition

Steven Suehring

A Wiley Brand

# Acknowledgments

Book writing tends to take attention away from other things in life. As I write this and look at the overgrown jungle that is my backyard, it's time to reflect and to find another project so I don't have to deal with whatever type of vine has taken over my shed and is creeping towards the house.

Thank you first to Kenyon Brown and Carole Jelen for this (and other) projects. Thank you also to the editors for this book, Kezia Endsley and David Clinton. Their expertise and diligence is essential in order to make the book the best it can be. Thank you to my family for their continued support. My colleagues at University of Wisconsin- Stevens Point help provide guidance and comic relief at times too.

As is the case for many books now, thank you to Jim, Patti, Tim, and Rob at Partners Pub. Thank you also to Kent Laabs for his generosity and continued help.

# About the Author

**Steve Suehring** is an assistant professor of computing and new media technologies at University of Wisconsin—Stevens Point. Prior to joining the faculty in 2015, Steve gained 20 years of field experience in a variety of technical engineering, system and network administration, and system architectural roles. Steve has written several books and has served as an editor for *LinuxWorld* magazine.

# Contents

# Introduction

This book provides practice questions for the Linux Professional Institute LPIC-1 certification. Specifically, the book has been updated to reflect the objectives for exams 101-500 and 102-500. The book includes numerous multiple-choice questions related to the exam objectives found on the LPI website.

## What Does This Book Cover?

Each chapter of the book connects directly to one of the objectives, and each objective is covered throughout the book. In addition, two practice exams are included in the book that you should find helpful in preparing for the exams.

The book does not require that you start at the beginning and read through in a linear, page-by-page manner. Rather, you may skip to objective areas that might be less familiar, and you can do so without losing any fidelity or missing something from a previous chapter.

## Who Should Read This Book

It is assumed that you would have a companion text for this book in order to obtain deeper information on the given subjects for the exam. However, it is possible to use this book as a stand-alone means for preparation.

Here are some basic assumptions about the audience for this book:

- You have used Linux or are using the book to learn Linux.
- You have used a computer for basic operations.
- You will use the book as a means for practicing for the certification exams.

## How to Use This Book

This book is best used as a tool for testing your knowledge in the objective domains specified for the exam. The book provides explanations for each question, including, where applicable, explanations as to why the other options were incorrect. Ideally, the book is used in conjunction with the companion text in order to fully explain the concepts.

# Certification Exam Policies

The Linux Professional Institute outlines various policies related to certification and other similar matters. In addition, other policies applicable may be through the testing facility or organization. More information on some of the LPI policies can be found at www.lpi.org/policies.

# Exam Objectives

The following lists contain the topics and weights for Exams 101 and 102. This list follows the sequence in which they are covered in the book. You can find more information about what is covered in each topic, including key knowledge areas and files, terms, and utilities, at the start of the applicable chapter.

## Exam 101-500

### Topic 101: System Architecture

- 101.1 Determine and configure hardware settings (weight 2).
- 101.2 Boot the system (weight 3).
- 101.3 Change runlevels/boot targets and shutdown or reboot system (weight 3).

### Topic 102: Linux Installation and Package Management

- 102.1 Design hard disk layout (weight 2).
- 102.2 Install a boot manager (weight 2).
- 102.3 Manage shared libraries (weight 1).
- 102.4 Use Debian package management (weight 3).
- 102.5 Use RPM and YUM package management (weight 3).
- 102.6 Linux as a virtualization guest (weight 1)

### Topic 103: GNU and UNIX Commands

- 103.1 Work on the command line (weight 4).
- 103.2 Process text streams using filters (weight 2).
- 103.3 Perform basic file management (weight 4).
- 103.4 Use streams, pipes, and redirects (weight 4).

- 103.5 Create, monitor, and kill processes (weight 4).
- 103.6 Modify process execution priorities (weight 2).
- 103.7 Search text files using regular expressions (weight 3).
- 103.8 Basic file editing 3

## Topic 104: Devices, Linux Filesystems, Filesystem Hierarchy Standard

- 104.1 Create partitions and filesystems (weight 2).
- 104.2 Maintain the integrity of filesystems (weight 2).
- 104.3 Control mounting and unmounting of filesystems (weight 3).
- *104.4 Removed*
- 104.5 Manage file permissions and ownership (weight 3).
- 104.6 Create and change hard and symbolic links (weight 2).
- 104.7 Find system files and place files in the correct location (weight 2).

# Exam 102-500

## Topic 105: Shells and Shell Scripting

- 105.1 Customize and use the shell environment (weight 4).
- 105.2 Customize or write simple scripts (weight 4).

## Topic 106: User Interfaces and Desktops

- 106.1 Install and configure X11 (weight 2).
- 106.2 Graphical desktops (weight 1)
- 106.3 Accessibility (weight 1)

## Topic 107: Administrative Tasks

- 107.1 Manage user and group accounts and related system files (weight 5).
- 107.2 Automate system administration tasks by scheduling jobs (weight 4).
- 107.3 Localization and internationalization (weight 3)

## Topic 108: Essential System Services

- 108.1 Maintain system time (weight 3).
- 108.2 System logging (weight 4)
- 108.3 Mail Transfer Agent (MTA) Basics (weight 3)
- 108.4 Manage printers and printing (weight 2).

## Topic 109: Networking Fundamentals

- 109.1 Fundamentals of Internet protocols (weight 4)
- 109.2 Persistent network configuration (weight 4)
- 109.3 Basic network troubleshooting (weight 4)
- 109.4 Configure client-side DNS (weight 2).

## Topic 110: Security

- 110.1 Perform security administration tasks (weight 3).
- 110.2 Set up host security (weight 3).
- 110.3 Securing data with encryption (weight 4)

# Exam 101-500

# Chapter

# 1

# Topic 101: System Architecture

## THE FOLLOWING EXAM OBJECTIVES ARE COVERED IN THIS CHAPTER:

✓ **101.1 Determine and configure hardware settings.**

- Key knowledge areas:
  - Enable and disable integrated peripherals.
  - Differentiate between the various types of mass storage devices.
  - Determine hardware resources for devices.
  - Tools and utilities to list various hardware information (e.g. lsusb, lspci, etc.)
  - Tools and utilities to manipulate USB devices
  - Conceptual understanding of sysfs, udev, and dbus
- The following is a partial list of the used files, terms, and utilities:
  - /sys/
  - /proc/
  - /dev/
  - modprobe
  - lsmod
  - lspci
  - lsusb

✓ **101.2 Boot the system.**

- Key knowledge areas:
  - Provide common commands to the boot loader and options to the kernel at boot time.
  - Demonstrate knowledge of the boot sequence from BIOS/UEFI to boot completion.

- Understand SysV init and systemd.
- Awareness of Upstart
- Check book events in the log files.
- The following is a partial list of the used files, terms, and utilities:
  - dmesg
  - journalctl
  - BIOS
  - UEFI
  - bootloader
  - kernel
  - initramfs
  - init
  - SysV init
  - systemd

✓ **101.3  Change runlevels/boot targets and shut down or reboot system.**

- Key knowledge areas:
  - Set the default runlevel or boot target.
  - Change between runlevels/boot targets including single-user mode.
  - Shut down and reboot from the command line.
  - Alert users before switching runlevels/boot targets or other major system events.
  - Properly terminate processes.
  - Awareness of acpid
- The following is a partial list of the used files, terms, and utilities:
  - /etc/inittab
  - shutdown
  - init
  - /etc/init.d/

- telinit
- systemd
- systemctl
- /etc/systemd/
- /usr/lib/systemd/
- wall

1. Which of the following commands is used to view kernel-related udev events in real time?

    **A.** `udevls all`

    **B.** `lsudev -f`

    **C.** `udevmon -a`

    **D.** `udevadm monitor`

2. Which command enables you to view the current interrupt request (IRQ) assignments?

    **A.** `view /proc/irq`

    **B.** `cat /proc/interrupts`

    **C.** `cat /dev/irq`

    **D.** `less /dev/irq`

3. Configuration of udev devices is done by working with files in which directory?

    **A.** `/udev/devices`

    **B.** `/devices/`

    **C.** `/udev/config`

    **D.** `/etc/udev`

4. Which command is used to automatically load a module and its dependencies?

    **A.** `modprobe`

    **B.** `lsmod`

    **C.** `insmod`

    **D.** `rmmod`

5. Which command is used to obtain a list of USB devices?

    **A.** `usb-list`

    **B.** `lsusb`

    **C.** `ls-usb`

    **D.** `ls --usb`

6. When working with hotplug devices, you need to gather more information about them through udevadm. Which udevadm command enables you to query the udev database for information on a device?

    **A.** `query`

    **B.** `info`

    **C.** `getinfo`

    **D.** `devinfo`

**7.** Which command can be used to view the kernel ring buffer in order to troubleshoot the boot process?

**A.** lsboot

**B.** boot-log

**C.** krblog

**D.** dmesg

**8.** During the initialization process for a Linux system using SysV init, which runlevel corresponds to single-user mode?

**A.** Runlevel 5

**B.** Runlevel SU

**C.** Runlevel 1

**D.** Runlevel 6

**9.** On a system using SysV init, in which directory are the startup and shutdown scripts for services stored?

**A.** /etc/init-d

**B.** /etc/init

**C.** /etc/sysV

**D.** /etc/init.d

**10.** Which command can be used to reboot a system?

**A.** init 6

**B.** shutdown -h -t now

**C.** init 1

**D.** refresh-system

**11.** When using an SysV init-based system, which command would you use if you make changes to the /etc/inittab file and want those changes to be reloaded without a reboot?

**A.** init-refresh

**B.** init 6

**C.** telinit

**D.** reload-inittab

**12.** Which command displays the current runlevel for a system?

**A.** show-level

**B.** init --level

**C.** sudo init

**D.** runlevel

**13.** Within which folder are `systemd` unit configuration files stored?

   **A.** `/etc/system.conf.d`

   **B.** `/lib/system.conf.d`

   **C.** `/lib/systemd/system`

   **D.** `/etc/sysconfd`

**14.** Which command is used with `systemd` in order to list the available service units?

   **A.** `systemd list-units`

   **B.** `systemctl list-units`

   **C.** `systemd unit-list`

   **D.** `systemctl show-units`

**15.** Which option to `lspci` is used to display both numeric codes and device names?

   **A.** `-numdev`

   **B.** `-n`

   **C.** `-nn`

   **D.** `-devnum`

**16.** Which command can be used to obtain a list of currently loaded kernel modules?

   **A.** `insmod`

   **B.** `modlist`

   **C.** `ls --modules`

   **D.** `lsmod`

**17.** Which option to the `modprobe` command shows the dependencies for a given module?

   **A.** `--show-options`

   **B.** `--list-deps`

   **C.** `--show-depends`

   **D.** `--list-all`

**18.** Which command can you use to send a message to all users who are currently logged into a system?

   **A.** `cat`

   **B.** `wall`

   **C.** `tee`

   **D.** `ssh`

**19.** Which of the following is a good first troubleshooting step when a hard disk is not detected by the Linux kernel?

   **A.** Unplug the disk.

   **B.** Check the system BIOS.

    **C.**  Restart the web server service.

    **D.**  Run the `disk-detect` command.

**20.** Within which directory is information about USB devices stored?

    **A.**  `/etc/usbdevices`

    **B.**  `/var/usb`

    **C.**  `/lib/sys/usb`

    **D.**  `/sys/bus/usb/devices`

**21.** If the kernel ring buffer has been overwritten, within which file can you look to find boot messages?

    **A.**  `/var/log/bootmessages`

    **B.**  `/var/log/mail.info`

    **C.**  `/var/adm/log/boot.info`

    **D.**  `/var/log/dmesg`

**22.** Which command and option can be used to determine whether a given service is currently loaded?

    **A.**  `systemctl --ls`

    **B.**  `telinit`

    **C.**  `systemctl status`

    **D.**  `sysctl -a`

**23.** Which command on a `systemd`-controlled system would place the system into single-user mode?

    **A.**  `systemctl one`

    **B.**  `systemctl isolate rescue.target`

    **C.**  `systemctl single-user`

    **D.**  `systemctl runlevel one`

**24.** Which command on a system controlled by Upstart will reload the configuration files?

    **A.**  `initctl reload`

    **B.**  `systemd reload`

    **C.**  `upstart --reload`

    **D.**  `ups -reload`

**25.** When working with a SysV system, which option to `chkconfig` will display all services and their runlevels?

    **A.**  `--reload`

    **B.**  `--list`

    **C.**  `--all`

    **D.**  `--ls`

**26.** A drive connected to USB is considered which type of device?

   **A.** Medium

   **B.** Coldplug

   **C.** Hotplug

   **D.** Sideplug

**27.** The system is using a temporary flash USB disk for data mounted at /dev/sda1. You need to remove the disk. Which of the following commands will enable the disk to be safely removed from the system?

   **A.** `usbstop /dev/sda`

   **B.** `umount /dev/sda1`

   **C.** `unmount /dev/sda1`

   **D.** `dev-eject /dev/sda1`

**28.** You have connected a USB disk to the system and need to find out its connection point within the system. Which of the following is the best method for accomplishing this task?

   **A.** Rebooting the system

   **B.** Viewing the contents of /var/log/usb.log

   **C.** Connecting the drive to a USB port that you know the number of

   **D.** Running dmesg and looking for the disk

**29.** Which of the following commands will initiate an immediate shutdown of the system?

   **A.** `shutdown -c`

   **B.** `halt`

   **C.** `systemd stop`

   **D.** `stop-system`

**30.** Which option within a systemd service file indicates the program to execute?

   **A.** `StartProgram`

   **B.** `ShortCut`

   **C.** `ExecStart`

   **D.** `Startup`

**31.** Which command will display the default target on a computer running systemd?

   **A.** `systemctl defaults`

   **B.** `update-rc.d defaults`

   **C.** `systemctl runlevel`

   **D.** `systemctl get-default`

**32.** Which option to the `systemctl` command will change a service so that it runs on the next boot of the system?

 **A.** enable

 **B.** startonboot

 **C.** loadonboot

 **D.** start

**33.** Which of the following best describes the `/proc` filesystem?

 **A.** `/proc` contains information about files to be processed.

 **B.** `/proc` contains configuration files for processes.

 **C.** `/proc` contains information on currently running processes, including the kernel.

 **D.** `/proc` contains variable data such as mail and web files.

**34.** Which command will retrieve information about the USB connections on a computer in a tree-like format?

 **A.** lsusb -tree

 **B.** lsusb --tree

 **C.** lsusb -t

 **D.** usblist --tree

**35.** What is one reason why a device driver does not appear in the output of `lsmod`, even though the device is loaded and working properly?

 **A.** The use of `systemd` means that drivers are not required for most devices.

 **B.** The use of `initramfs` means that support is enabled by default.

 **C.** The system does not need a driver for the device.

 **D.** Support for the device has been compiled directly into the kernel.

**36.** Which option to `rmmod` will cause the module to wait until it's no longer in use to unload the module?

 **A.** -test

 **B.** -f

 **C.** -w

 **D.** -unload

**37.** You are using a storage area network (SAN) that keeps causing errors on your Linux system due to an improper kernel module created by the SAN vendor. When the SAN sends updates, it causes the filesystem to be mounted as read-only. Which command and option can you use to change the behavior of the filesystem to account for the SAN bug?

 **A.** mount --continue

 **B.** tune2fs -e continue

 **C.** mkfs --no-remount

 **D.** mount -o remount

**38.** Within which directory are rules related to udev stored?

    **A.** `/etc/udev.conf`

    **B.** `/etc/udev.conf.d`

    **C.** `/etc/udev/rules.d`

    **D.** `/etc/udev.d`

**39.** Which option to `lspci` displays the kernel driver in use for the given Peripheral Component Interconnect (PCI) device?

    **A.** `-t`

    **B.** `-k`

    **C.** `-n`

    **D.** `-a`

**40.** Within which of the following directories will you find blacklist information for modules loaded with `modprobe`?

    **A.** `/etc/blacklist`

    **B.** `/etc/modprobe.d`

    **C.** `/etc/blacklist.mod`

    **D.** `/etc/modprobe`

**41.** When working with a CentOS 6 system, which command is used to create the initial RAM disk?

    **A.** `mkinit`

    **B.** `dracut`

    **C.** `mkraminit`

    **D.** `mkinitfs`

**42.** Within which file will you find a list of the currently available kernel symbols?

    **A.** `/proc/kernelsyms`

    **B.** `/etc/kernel.conf`

    **C.** `/etc/lsyms`

    **D.** `/proc/kallsyms`

**43.** Which of the following commands can be used to show the various information related to a currently loaded module, including core size and settings for options?

    **A.** `systool -v -m <module>`

    **B.** `modinfo -r <module>`

    **C.** `lsmod <module>`

    **D.** `infmod <module>`

**44.** Which directory contains various elements and configuration information about the kernel such as the release number, domain name, location of modprobe, and other settings?

**A.** /proc/sys/kmod

**B.** /proc/sys/kernel

**C.** /proc/kernel

**D.** /proc/kernel/sys

**45.** Within which directory should systemd unit files that you create be stored?

**A.** /etc/system

**B.** /etc/systemd/system

**C.** /usr/share/systemd

**D.** /usr/share/system

**46.** Which of the following commands should you execute after making changes to systemd service configurations in order for those changes to take effect?

**A.** systemd reload

**B.** reboot

**C.** systemctl daemon-reload

**D.** systemctl reboot

**47.** Which of the following files contains the runlevels for the system along with a reference to the corresponding rc file?

**A.** /etc/runlevels

**B.** /etc/inittab

**C.** /etc/rc

**D.** /etc/runlevel

**48.** Which boot loader can be used for File Allocation Table (FAT) filesystems and might be used for a rescue disk?

**A.** SYSBOOT

**B.** SYSLINUX

**C.** TIELINUX

**D.** FATLINUX

**49.** Which of the following is used to provide an early filesystem-based loading process for key drivers needed to continue the boot process?

**A.** bootrd

**B.** driverload

**C.** initrd

**D.** initdrv

**50.** When booting a system you receive an error similar to "No init found" and are then placed at an initramfs prompt. You need to check the hard drive for errors. Which of the following commands performs an error check on a hard drive partition in Linux?

    **A.** defrag

    **B.** fsck

    **C.** checkfs

    **D.** chkfs

**51.** Which of the following commands places the system in single-user mode?

    **A.** tellinit 1

    **B.** chginit 1

    **C.** telinet 1

    **D.** telinit 1

**52.** Which of the following commands changes the boot order for the next boot?

    **A.** efibootmgr -c

    **B.** efibootmgr -b -B

    **C.** efibootmgr -o

    **D.** efibootmgr -n

**53.** Which boot loader can be used with ISO9660 CD-ROMS?

    **A.** ISOLINUX

    **B.** EFIBOOT

    **C.** ISOFS

    **D.** BOOTISO

**54.** Within which directory are systemd user unit files placed by installed packages?

    **A.** /usr/lib/systemd/user

    **B.** /usr/lib/systemd/system

    **C.** /usr/systemd

    **D.** /usr/system

**55.** When using Unified Extensible Firmware Interface (UEFI), which of the following files can be used as a boot loader?

    **A.** shim.uefi

    **B.** shim.efi

    **C.** shim.fx

    **D.** efi.shim

**56.** Which directory on a SysV `init`-based system contains scripts that are used for starting and stopping services?

    **A.** `/etc/rc.int`

    **B.** `/etc/boot`

    **C.** `/etc/bootscripts`

    **D.** `/etc/init.d`

**57.** Which of the following commands is used to find overriding configuration files on a `systemd`-based system?

    **A.** `diff`

    **B.** `systemctl -diff`

    **C.** `systemd-delta`

    **D.** `systemctl configoverride`

**58.** Which of the following commands on a Red Hat system lists all of the SysV services set to be executed on boot along with their setting for each runlevel?

    **A.** `rlevel`

    **B.** `chkconfig --list`

    **C.** `bootldr --list`

    **D.** `init --bootlist`

**59.** Which of the following commands, executed from within the UEFI shell, controls the boot configuration?

    **A.** `bootcfg`

    **B.** `bcfg`

    **C.** `grub-install`

    **D.** `grcfg`

**60.** Which file must exist within `/tftpboot` on the Trivial File Transfer Protocol (TFTP) server for a system that will use PXELINUX for its boot loader?

    **A.** `pxelinux.tftp`

    **B.** `pxelinux.boot`

    **C.** `pxelinux.conf`

    **D.** `pxelinux.0`

**61.** Which utility can you use on a Debian or Ubuntu system to manage SysV `init` scripts, such as setting them to run on boot?

    **A.** `bootorder`

    **B.** `bootloader`

    **C.** `configchk`

    **D.** `update-rc.d`

**62.** Which key, pressed during the operating system selection menu, is used to enable editing of the parameters related to boot with GRUB?

**A.** v

**B.** e

**C.** r

**D.** y

**63.** Which `systemctl` subcommand is used to switch runlevels?

**A.** switch

**B.** move

**C.** runlevel

**D.** isolate

**64.** When examining the `/etc/inittab` file, which option signifies the default runlevel to which the system will boot?

**A.** default

**B.** defaultboot

**C.** initdefault

**D.** defaultlvl

**65.** Which of the following is used instead of `initrd` to provide an early filesystem for essential drivers?

**A.** initnext

**B.** initramfs

**C.** initialize

**D.** initfs

**66.** Which of the following commands sets the default `systemd` target to multi-user?

**A.** `systemctl set-default multi-user.target`

**B.** `systemd set-default multi-user.target`

**C.** `systemctl set-def muser.target`

**D.** `systemd set-def muser.target`

**67.** When using a shim for booting a UEFI-based system, which of the following files is loaded after `shim.efi`?

**A.** grubx64.cfg

**B.** grub.conf

**C.** grubx64.efi

**D.** efi.boot

**68.** Within which hierarchy are files from /etc/init.d linked so that the files are executed during the various runlevels of a SysV system?

**A.** /etc/rc.S

**B.** /etc/rc

**C.** /etc/boot/rc

**D.** /etc/rc.d

**69.** What is the name of the unit to which a systemd system is booted in order to start other levels?

**A.** default.target

**B.** init.target

**C.** initial.target

**D.** load.target

**70.** When viewing information in /dev/disk/by-path using the command ls -l, which of the following filenames represents a logical unit number (LUN) from Fibre Channel?

**A.** /dev/fc0

**B.** pci-0000:1a:00.0-fc-0x500601653ee0025f:0x0000000000000000

**C.** pci-0000:1a:00.0-scsi-0x500601653ee0025f:0x0000000000000000

**D.** /dev/fibre0

**71.** You have purchased new solid-state drive (SSD) hardware that uses the NVMe (Non-Volatile Memory Express) protocol but cannot find the disks in the normal /dev/sd* location in which you have traditionally found such storage. In which location should you look for these drives?

**A.** /dev/nd*

**B.** /dev/nvme*

**C.** /dev/nv*

**D.** /dev/nvme/*

**72.** Which file contains information about the current md Redundant Array of Inexpensive Disks (RAID) configuration such as the personalities?

**A.** /proc/raidinfo

**B.** /proc/rhyinfo

**C.** /proc/mdraid

**D.** /proc/mdstat

**73.** Which of the following directory hierarchies contains information such as the World Wide Name (WWN) for Fibre Channel?

    **A.** `/sys/class/wwn`

    **B.** `/sys/class/fc_host`

    **C.** `/sys/class/fclist`

    **D.** `/sys/class/fc/wwn`

**74.** Information about logical volumes can be found in which of the following directories?

    **A.** `/dev/lvinfo`

    **B.** `/dev/map`

    **C.** `/dev/mapper`

    **D.** `/dev/lvmap`

**75.** Which of the following commands will examine the PCI subsystem for NVMe-based devices?

    **A.** `psnvme`

    **B.** `lsnvme`

    **C.** `lspci | grep scsi`

    **D.** `lspci | grep -i nvme`

**76.** Which of the following devices is the location of the first Small Computer System Interface (SCSI) tape device detected at boot?

    **A.** `/dev/st1`

    **B.** `/dev/sd0`

    **C.** `/dev/sd1`

    **D.** `/dev/st0`

**77.** Which of the following files should be used to display a message to users prior to logging in locally?

    **A.** `/etc/loginmesg`

    **B.** `/etc/logmessage.txt`

    **C.** `/etc/issue`

    **D.** `/etc/banner`

**78.** Which file contains a message that is displayed after a successful login?

    **A.** `/etc/loginbanner`

    **B.** `/etc/issue`

    **C.** `/etc/motd`

    **D.** `/etc/message`

**79.** Which of the following files can be used to provide a message to users logging in remotely with a protocol such as telnet?

   **A.** `/etc/telnet.msg`

   **B.** `/etc/issue.net`

   **C.** `/etc/login.msg`

   **D.** `/etc/telnet.login`

**80.** Which of the following commands turns off the computer, including removing power, if possible?

   **A.** `systemctl halt`

   **B.** `systemctl reboot`

   **C.** `systemctl stop`

   **D.** `systemctl poweroff`

**81.** Which of the following shutdown commands reboots the system in 15 minutes?

   **A.** `shutdown -r +15`

   **B.** `shutdown +15`

   **C.** `shutdown -15`

   **D.** `shutdown -r 00:15`

**82.** When terminating a process on a SysV `init`-based system, which command can be used to stop the process?

   **A.** `service`

   **B.** `sysv`

   **C.** `syscl`

   **D.** `servc`

**83.** Which of the following commands show the boot messages captured by `systemd`?

   **A.** `journalctl -b`

   **B.** `systemctl -b`

   **C.** `journalctl -bm`

   **D.** `journalctl -l`

**84.** Which option to the `shutdown` command halts or stops the system?

   **A.** `-h`

   **B.** `-s`

   **C.** `-f`

   **D.** `-t`

**85.** Which signal number is used as SIGKILL when used with the `kill` command?

    **A.**  1

    **B.**  4

    **C.**  9

    **D.**  11

**86.** Which directory contains `rc`-related startup scripts on a legacy Debian system?

    **A.**  `/etc/init`

    **B.**  `/etc/inittab`

    **C.**  `/etc/init.d`

    **D.**  `/etc/rc.init`

**87.** When attempting to enable an integrated peripheral on a basic input/output system (BIOS) system, what should be done to determine whether the peripheral has been enabled within the BIOS?

    **A.**  Examine boot messages to determine if the kernel has detected the peripheral.

    **B.**  Examine `/var/log/auth.log` for detection of the peripheral.

    **C.**  Reboot the system to determine if the device works.

    **D.**  Enable the peripheral by removing it from the blacklisted modules.

**88.** Which option to the `wall` command suppresses the `"Broadcast message"` banner that normally displays?

    **A.**  `-b`

    **B.**  `-a`

    **C.**  `-n`

    **D.**  `-d`

# Chapter

# 2

# Topic 102: Linux Installation and Package Management

---

## THE FOLLOWING EXAM OBJECTIVES ARE COVERED IN THIS CHAPTER:

✓ **102.1 Design hard disk layout.**

- Key knowledge areas:
  - Allocate filesystems and swap space to separate partitions or disks.
  - Tailor the design to the intended use of the system.
  - Ensure the /boot partition conforms to the hardware architecture requirements for booting.
  - Knowledge of basic features of LVM
- The following is a partial list of the used files, terms, and utilities:
  - /(root) filesystem
  - /var filesystem
  - /home filesystem
  - /boot filesystem
  - EFI System Partition (ESP)
  - swap space
  - mount points
  - partitions

✓ **102.2 Install a boot manager.**

- Key knowledge areas:
  - Provide alternative boot locations and backup boot options.
  - Install and configure a boot loader such as GRUB Legacy.

- Perform basic configuration changes for GRUB2.

- Interact with the boot loader.

- The following is a partial list of the used files, terms, and utilities:

  - `menu.lst, grub.cfg,` and `grub.conf`

  - `grub-install`

  - `grub-mkconfig`

  - MBR

✓ **102.3   Manage shared libraries.**

- Key knowledge areas:

  - Identify shared libraries.

  - Identify the typical locations of system libraries.

  - Load shared libraries.

- The following is a partial list of the used files, terms, and utilities:

  - `ldd`

  - `ldconfig`

  - `/etc/ld.so.conf`

  - `LD_LIBRARY_PATH`

✓ **102.4   Use Debian package management.**

- Key knowledge areas:

  - Install, upgrade, and uninstall Debian binary packages.

  - Find packages containing specific files or libraries which may or may not be installed.

  - Obtain package information like version, content, dependencies, package integrity, and installation status (whether or not the package is installed).

  - Awareness of apt

- The following is a partial list of the used files, terms, and utilities:

  - `/etc/apt/sources.list`

  - `dpkg`

- dpkg-reconfigure
- apt-get
- apt-cache

## ✓ 102.5 Use RPM and yum package management.

- Key knowledge areas:
  - Install, re-install, upgrade, and remove packages using RPM, yum, and zypper.
  - Obtain information on RPM packages such as version, status, dependencies, integrity, and signatures.
  - Determine what files a package provides, as well as find which package a specific file comes from.
  - Awareness of dnf
- The following is a partial list of the used files, terms, and utilities:
  - rpm
  - rpm2cpio
  - /etc/yum.conf
  - /etc/yum.repos.d/
  - yum
  - zypper

## ✓ 102.6 Linux as a virtualization guest

- Key knowledge areas:
  - Understand the general concept of virtual machines and containers.
  - Understand common elements of virtual machines in an IaaS cloud, such as computing instances, block storage, and networking.
  - Understand unique properties of a Linux system that have to change when a system is cloned or used as a template.
  - Understand how system images are used to deploy virtual machines, cloud instances, and containers.
  - Understand Linux extensions that integrate Linux with a virtualization product.
  - Awareness of cloud-init

- The following is a partial list of the used files, terms, and utilities:
  - Virtual machine
  - Linux container
  - Application container
  - Guest drivers
  - SSH host keys
  - D-Bus machine id

1. A Serial Advanced Technology Attachment (SATA) disk will use which of the following identifiers?

   **A.** /dev/hdX

   **B.** /dev/sataX

   **C.** /dev/sdX

   **D.** /disk/sataX

2. Which option given at boot time within the GRUB configuration will boot the system into single-user mode?

   **A.** single-user

   **B.** su

   **C.** single

   **D.** root

3. During boot of a system with GRUB, which key can be pressed to display the GRUB menu?

   **A.** Shift

   **B.** E

   **C.** V

   **D.** H

4. When booting, which option can be added to a GRUB configuration line to set or change the root partition at boot time to /dev/sda2?

   **A.** rootpartition={hd0,2}

   **B.** root=/dev/sda2

   **C.** root={hd0,3}

   **D.** rootpartition=/dev/sda2

5. Which key combination will enable you to edit the kernel options and then boot when using GRUB Legacy?

   **A.** ESC for editing and then Return to boot

   **B.** v for editing and then Return to boot

   **C.** e for editing and then b to boot

   **D.** v for editing and then b to boot

6. During the boot process for a virtual machine, what is the next step in the boot process after the kernel has taken over the initialization process and initializes devices?

   **A.** The system BIOS initializes devices.

   **B.** The system is placed in multi-user mode.

   **C.** The boot loader initializes the kernel.

   **D.** The root partition is mounted.

**7.** Where in the filesystem will the EFI system partition (ESP) typically be mounted?

    **A.** `/etc/efi`

    **B.** `/efi`

    **C.** `/sys/efi`

    **D.** `/boot/efi`

**8.** When partitioning a disk for a mail server running postfix, which partition/mounted directory should be the largest in order to allow for mail storage?

    **A.** `/etc`

    **B.** `/usr/bin`

    **C.** `/mail`

    **D.** `/var`

**9.** Which option within GRUB Legacy is used to indicate that a root partition contains a non-Linux kernel?

    **A.** `initrd`

    **B.** `non-linux`

    **C.** `rootnoverify`

    **D.** `root-win`

**10.** Which command will output a new GRUB2 configuration file and send the output to the correct location for booting?

    **A.** `update-grub > /boot/grub/grub.cfg`

    **B.** `update-grub boot > /boot/grub/grub.cfg`

    **C.** `grub-rc.d`

    **D.** `grub-boot`

**11.** What is the maximum number of primary partitions available on an MBR partitioning system?

    **A.** 2

    **B.** 4

    **C.** 1

    **D.** 5

**12.** Which command is used to update the links and cache for shared libraries on the system?

    **A.** `ldcache`

    **B.** `cache-update`

    **C.** `link-update`

    **D.** `ldconfig`

**13.** Which command and option is used to update a Debian system to the latest software?

    **A.** apt-update

    **B.** apt-get upgrade

    **C.** dpkg -U

    **D.** apt-cache clean

**14.** Which option given to a yum command will install a given package?

    **A.** update

    **B.** configure

    **C.** install

    **D.** get

**15.** What is the location of the home directory for the root user?

    **A.** /home/root

    **B.** /home/su

    **C.** /root

    **D.** /

**16.** When using rpm2cpio, by default the output is sent to which location?

    **A.** STDOUT

    **B.** The cpio.out file

    **C.** The a.out file

    **D.** The /tmp/cpi.out file

**17.** Which partition or directory structure typically holds most of the programs for a Linux system?

    **A.** /etc

    **B.** /usr

    **C.** /home

    **D.** /var

**18.** Your GRUB Legacy configuration includes a dual-boot option with Linux listed first and another operating system listed second. Which of the following options will boot to the Linux partition by default?

    **A.** default=linux

    **B.** default=0

    **C.** default=1

    **D.** default=other

19. Which file should you edit when using GRUB2 in order to set things like the timeout?

    A. /etc/default/grub

    B. /etc/grub/boot

    C. /etc/boot/grub.d

    D. /grub.d/boot

20. Which yum option displays the dependencies for the package specified?

    A. list

    B. deplist

    C. dependencies

    D. listdeps

21. Which options for an rpm command will display verbose output for an installation along with progress of the installation?

    A. -ivh

    B. -wvh

    C. --avh

    D. --ins-verbose

22. Which of the following commands adds /usr/local/lib to the LD_LIBRARY_PATH when using BASH shell?

    A. set PATH=/usr/local/lib

    B. export LD_LIBRARY_PATH=$LD_LIBRARY_PATH:/usr/local/lib

    C. LD_LIBRARY_PATH=/usr/local/lib

    D. connectpath LD_LIBRARY_PATH=/usr/local/lib

23. Which command can be used to download an RPM package without installing it?

    A. yumdl

    B. yumdownloadonly

    C. yumdown

    D. yumdownloader

24. Which command will search for a package named zsh on a Debian system?

    A. apt-cache search zsh

    B. apt-get search zsh

    C. apt-cache locate zsh

    D. apt search zsh

**25.** Which option within /etc/default/grub is used to configure the default operating system for boot?

    **A.** GRUB_OS

    **B.** GRUB_ON

    **C.** GRUB_DEFAULT

    **D.** DEFAULT_OS

**26.** When found in a GRUB configuration file, what does the ro option indicate?

    **A.** Initially mount the root partition as read-only.

    **B.** Mount the kernel as read-only.

    **C.** Start the init program as read-once.

    **D.** Mount the root partition in Raised Object mode.

**27.** Within which directory will you find the repositories used by yum?

    **A.** /etc/yum.conf

    **B.** /etc/repos

    **C.** /etc/yum.conf.d

    **D.** /etc/yum.repos.d

**28.** Which rpm option can be used to verify that no files have been altered since installation?

    **A.** -V

    **B.** -v

    **C.** --verbose

    **D.** --filesum

**29.** Which option for the grub-mkconfig command sends output to a file instead of STDOUT?

    **A.** -stdout

    **B.** --fileout

    **C.** -o

    **D.** -f

**30.** The presence of menu.lst within the filesystem typically indicates which condition?

    **A.** GRUB Legacy is in use on the system.

    **B.** GRUB2 is in use on the system.

    **C.** An error has occurred creating the output to menu.lst.

    **D.** The options for rescue boot have been changed.

**31.** Which command is used to determine the libraries on which a given command depends?

    **A.** ldconfig

    **B.** librarylist

    **C.** listdeps

    **D.** ldd

**32.** Which of the following is true of Linux swap space?

   **A.**  Swap is used to hold temporary database tables.

   **B.**  Swap is used as additional memory when there is insufficient RAM.

   **C.**  Swap is used by the mail server for security.

   **D.**  Swap is used to scrub data from the network temporarily.

**33.** Which of the following is not typically used to store libraries?

   **A.**  `/lib`

   **B.**  `/etc/lib`

   **C.**  `/usr/lib`

   **D.**  `/usr/local/lib`

**34.** Which of the following commands updates the package cache for a Debian system?

   **A.**  `apt-get cache-update`

   **B.**  `apt-cache update`

   **C.**  `apt-get update`

   **D.**  `apt-get upgrade`

**35.** Within which file are details of the current package repositories stored on a Debian system?

   **A.**  `/etc/apt.list`

   **B.**  `/etc/sources.list`

   **C.**  `/etc/apt/sources.list`

   **D.**  `/etc/apt.d/sources.list`

**36.** Of the following choices, which size would be most appropriate for the `/boot` partition of a Linux system?

   **A.**  Between 100MB and 500MB

   **B.**  Between 1GB and 10GB

   **C.**  `/boot` should not be partitioned separately.

   **D.**  Less than 5MB

**37.** Which of the following commands initializes a physical disk partition for use with Logical Volume Manager (LVM)?

   **A.**  `lvmcreate`

   **B.**  `pvcreate`

   **C.**  `fvcreate`

   **D.**  `lvinit`

**38.** Which of the following commands installs GRUB into the MBR of the second SATA disk?

   **A.**  `grub-install /dev/hdb2`

   **B.**  `grub-install /dev/sda2`

    **C.**  `grub-config /dev/sda`

    **D.**  `grub-install /dev/sdb`

**39.** Which command should be used to make changes to the choices made when a Debian package was installed?

    **A.**  `dpkg-reconfigure`

    **B.**  `dpkg -r`

    **C.**  `dpkg --reconf`

    **D.**  `apt-get reinstall`

**40.** Which command is used to create a logical volume with LVM?

    **A.**  `pvcreate`

    **B.**  `lvmcreate`

    **C.**  `lvcreate`

    **D.**  `volcreate`

**41.** What is the logical order for creation of an LVM logical volume?

    **A.**  Physical volume creation, volume group creation, logical volume creation

    **B.**  Physical volume creation, logical volume creation, volume group creation

    **C.**  Logical volume creation, physical volume creation, volume group creation

    **D.**  LVM creation, format, partition

**42.** Which of the Debian package management tools provides a terminal-based interface for management?

    **A.**  `apt-get`

    **B.**  `dpkg`

    **C.**  `apt-cache`

    **D.**  `aptitude`

**43.** Which option for yum performs a search of the package cache?

    **A.**  `seek`

    **B.**  `query`

    **C.**  `--search`

    **D.**  `search`

**44.** Which command option for rpm can be used to show the version of the kernel?

    **A.**  `rpm kernel`

    **B.**  `rpm -qa kernel`

    **C.**  `rpm search kernel`

    **D.**  `rpm --list kern`

**45.** Assuming a menu entry of Debian in your GRUB configuration, which option in /etc/default/grub would set that as the default operating system to boot?

   **A.** GRUB_OS

   **B.** GRUB_OS_DEF

   **C.** GRUB_DEFAULT

   **D.** GRUB_CONF

**46.** Which option in /etc/yum.conf is used to ensure that the kernel is not updated when the system is updated?

   **A.** exclude=kernel*

   **B.** exclude-kernel

   **C.** updatekernel=false

   **D.** include-except=kernel

**47.** Which command should be run after making a change to the /etc/default/grub file?

   **A.** grub

   **B.** grub-mkconfig

   **C.** grub-inst

   **D.** reboot

**48.** Which command searches for and provides information on a given package on a Debian system, including whether or not the package is currently installed?

   **A.** dpkg -i

   **B.** dpkg -s

   **C.** apt-cache

   **D.** apt-info

**49.** Which command is used to search for physical volumes for use with LVM?

   **A.** lvmcreate

   **B.** pvcreate

   **C.** lvmdiskscan

   **D.** lvmscan

**50.** Which option added to yumdownloader will also download dependencies?

   **A.** --deps

   **B.** --resolve

   **C.** --resdeps

   **D.** -d

**51.** Which of the following installs a previously downloaded Debian package?

    **A.** `dpkg -i <package name>`

    **B.** `apt-install <package name>`

    **C.** `apt-slash <package name>`

    **D.** `dpkg -U <package name>`

**52.** A hard drive is reported as `hd(0,0)` by the GRUB Legacy configuration file. To which of the following disks and partitions does this correspond?

    **A.** `/dev/hdb2`

    **B.** `/dev/hda0`

    **C.** `/dev/disk1`

    **D.** `/dev/sda1`

**53.** Which filesystem format type is used for the EFI System Partition (ESP)?

    **A.** FAT

    **B.** EXT4

    **C.** NTFS

    **D.** EXT3

**54.** Which of the following commands installs `extlinux` into the `/boot` partition?

    **A.** `extlinux --install /boot`

    **B.** `extlinux --inst /boot`

    **C.** `extlinux -boot`

    **D.** `extlinux /boot install`

**55.** Which of the following commands mounts `/dev/sda1` in the `/boot` partition?

    **A.** `mount /dev/sda /boot`

    **B.** `mount /boot /dev/sda1`

    **C.** `mount /dev/sda1 /boot`

    **D.** `mount -dev sda1 /boot`

**56.** Which of the following can be identified as an initial sector on a disk that stores information about the disk partitioning and operating system location?

    **A.** Minimal boot record (MBR)

    **B.** Master boot record (MBR)

    **C.** Init sector

    **D.** Master partition table (MPT)

**57.** Which option to grub-install will place the GRUB images into an alternate directory?

   **A.** --boot-dir

   **B.** -b

   **C.** -boot

   **D.** --boot-directory

**58.** Within which file is a list of the currently mounted filesystems stored?

   **A.** /etc/fstab

   **B.** /etc/curmount

   **C.** /var/spool/files

   **D.** /etc/mtab

**59.** Which command is used to activate swap space on a system?

   **A.** mkswap

   **B.** swapon

   **C.** swapact

   **D.** actswap

**60.** Which of the following commands displays information about a given physical volume in an LVM setup?

   **A.** pvdisp

   **B.** pvlist

   **C.** pvdisplay

   **D.** pvl

**61.** Which of the following commands creates a logical volume with LVM?

   **A.** lvc

   **B.** lvcreate

   **C.** lvlist

   **D.** lvmake

**62.** Which of the following commands looks for LVM physical volumes and volume groups involved in an LVM configuration?

   **A.** vgscan

   **B.** lvmscan

   **C.** lvlist

   **D.** pvlist

**63.** Which of the following commands is used to display a list of physical volumes involved in LVM?

   **A.** pvdisp

   **B.** pvlist

   **C.** pvscan

   **D.** pvmm

**64.** Which option to lvchange sets whether the logical volume is available?

   **A.** -a

   **B.** -b

   **C.** -c

   **D.** -d

**65.** When working with a script to create directories, the script is checking to see if srv/vhosts exists. When doing an ls of the root directory, /, you see that it does exist. However, the script does not. What might be the issue?

   **A.** The script is not executable.

   **B.** The script does not have the setuid bit set.

   **C.** The script is using a relative path.

   **D.** The script is owned by root.

**66.** You are architecting an application and need to choose between application containerization and virtualization. Which of the following describes a difference between application containers and a virtual machine?

   **A.** An application container can contain only one application whereas a virtual machine can contain many.

   **B.** An application container shares the host kernel whereas a virtual machine can have its own kernel.

   **C.** An application container is used for small applications whereas a virtual machine is used for large applications.

   **D.** The use of application containers is for testing only whereas a virtual machine is used for production.

**67.** In addition to including /lib and /usr/lib, where does ldconfig look to find additional directories to incorporate into the library path?

   **A.** /etc/lib.conf

   **B.** /etc/ldconf

   **C.** /etc/lib.cfg

   **D.** /etc/ld.so.conf

**68.** You are working with a cloud instance virtual machine deployed with an Infrastructure-as-a-Service (IaaS) provider. The virtual machine is running slowly. Which type of resource might you add to the cloud instance in order to improve performance?

    **A.** Compute

    **B.** Block storage

    **C.** Networking

    **D.** Disk

**69.** When working with a system to determine if it is using GRUB or GRUB2, the presence of which file indicates that it is GRUB2?

    **A.** `grub.cfg`

    **B.** `grub.conf`

    **C.** `menu.lst`

    **D.** `grub2.conf`

**70.** You are working to create a system image or template from which other virtual machines will be deployed. Which of the following represents a unique item that will change with each deployed virtual host or image?

    **A.** System directories

    **B.** MAC address

    **C.** Guest drivers

    **D.** Pilot homing

**71.** Which program can be used to deploy an Ubuntu image to a remote cloud provider?

    **A.** `dep-image`

    **B.** `cloud-init`

    **C.** `init-cloud`

    **D.** `image-dep`

**72.** Which file is used as the primary configuration file for the yum package manager?

    **A.** `/etc/yum.cfg`

    **B.** `/etc/yum.d`

    **C.** `/etc/yum.conf`

    **D.** `/etc/yum.config`

**73.** Which of the following commands and options lists all of the files included with a package on a Debian system?

    **A.** `apt -L`

    **B.** `dpkg -L`

    **C.** `dpkg -f`

    **D.** `apt-get show`

**74.** When working with SSH (Secure Shell) keys for a virtual machine cloud deployment, which key is deployed to the virtual machine so that you can connect from the host?

**A.** The public key

**B.** The signature file

**C.** The private key

**D.** Both the public and private keys

**75.** When using a GPT disk, which partition needs to be created for a Linux system to boot?

**A.** /boot/efi

**B.** /boot/gpt

**C.** /gpt

**D.** /vmgpt

**76.** Which option to zypper installs a package?

**A.** install

**B.** retr

**C.** get

**D.** ref

**77.** You are working with a Fedora 22 system and need to install a package. Which of the following is the default package manager on this system?

**A.** yum

**B.** apt

**C.** dpkg

**D.** dnf

**78.** You need to list the files available on a package on CentOS. Which of the following commands accomplishes this task?

**A.** repoquery -l

**B.** pkgquery -l

**C.** dpkg -L

**D.** pkglist

**79.** You need to create a backup of user home directories including root. Which directory or directories need to be included in the backup?

**A.** /home

**B.** /home and /home/root

**C.** /home and /root

**D.** /home and /root/home

**80.** In which file can you find the unique D-Bus machine ID for a given system?

   **A.** /etc/machine-id

   **B.** /etc/machineID

   **C.** /etc/mch.conf

   **D.** /etc/machine.id.conf

**81.** Which option to ldconfig can be used to process only those directories given on the command line rather than the directories found in /etc/ld.so.conf?

   **A.** -n

   **B.** -i

   **C.** -v

   **D.** -r

**82.** When working with package caches on Debian, you need to determine if the package list is being updated. Which option to apt-cache shows the number of available packages on the system?

   **A.** packagenum

   **B.** status

   **C.** stats

   **D.** liststatus

**83.** Which option to grub-install specifies the directory in which the EFI partition is located?

   **A.** --boot-dir

   **B.** --efi

   **C.** --efi-boot

   **D.** --efi-directory

**84.** Within which file are mount points for the system stored?

   **A.** /etc/fstab

   **B.** /etc/mtab

   **C.** /etc/partitions.list

   **D.** /etc/disk.conf

**85.** Which of the following option sets for rpm lists the files within the package?

   **A.** lf

   **B.** qlp

   **C.** qf

   **D.** eps

**86.** When working with a CentOS system, you need to determine the release of a certain package. Which command and option will accomplish this task?

    **A.** dpkg -i

    **B.** yum info

    **C.** yum search

    **D.** apt search

**87.** You are using a host machine and are unsure if it supports the extensions to enable virtualization. Which of the following should you look for in /proc/cpuinfo to indicate that the system is ready for virtualization?

    **A.** vmx

    **B.** virt

    **C.** envirt

    **D.** vtcapable

**88.** Within which file can you configure a filter for devices when using vgscan?

    **A.** lvm.conf

    **B.** vg.conf

    **C.** vgscan.conf

    **D.** lv.cfg

**89.** Which of the following swapon options displays information on the size of swap space along with its used space?

    **A.** --list

    **B.** -a

    **C.** --show

    **D.** -h

# Chapter 3

# Topic 103: GNU and UNIX Commands

**THE FOLLOWING EXAM OBJECTIVES ARE COVERED IN THIS CHAPTER:**

✓ **103.1  Work on the command line.**

  ▪ Key knowledge areas:

    ▪ Use single shell commands and one-line command sequences to perform basic tasks on the command line.

    ▪ Use and modify the shell environment including defining, referencing, and exporting environment variables.

    ▪ Use and edit command history.

    ▪ Invoke commands inside and outside the defined path.

  ▪ The following is a partial list of the used files, terms, and utilities:

    ▪ bash

    ▪ echo

    ▪ env

    ▪ export

    ▪ pwd

    ▪ set

    ▪ unset

    ▪ type

    ▪ which

    ▪ man

    ▪ uname

    ▪ history

    ▪ .bash_history

    ▪ Quoting

✓ **103.2   Process text streams using filters.**

- Key knowledge areas:
  - Send text files and output streams through text utility filters to modify the output using standard UNIX commands found in the GNU textutils package.
  - The following is a partial list of the used files, terms, and utilities:
    - bzcat
    - cat
    - cut
    - head
    - less
    - md5sum
    - nl
    - od
    - paste
    - sed
    - sha256sum
    - sha512sum
    - sort
    - split
    - tail
    - tr
    - uniq
    - wc
    - xzcat
    - zcat

✓ **103.3   Perform basic file management.**

- Key knowledge areas:
  - Copy, move, and remove files and directories individually.
  - Copy multiple files and directories recursively.

- Remove files and directories recursively.
- Use simple and advanced wildcard specifications in commands.
- Use find to locate and act on files based on type, size, or time.
- Use tar, cpio, and dd.

- The following is a partial list of the used files, terms, and utilities:
  - cp
  - find
  - mkdir
  - mv
  - ls
  - rm
  - rmdir
  - touch
  - tar
  - cpio
  - dd
  - file
  - gzip
  - gunzip
  - bzip2
  - bunzip2
  - xz
  - unxz
  - file globbing

✓ **103.4 Use streams, pipes, and redirects.**

- Key knowledge areas:
  - Redirect standard input, standard output, and standard error.

- Pipe the output of one command to the input of another command.
- Use the output of one command as arguments to another command.
- Send output to both stdout and a file.
- The following is a partial list of the used files, terms, and utilities:
  - tee
  - xargs

## ✓ 103.5 Create, monitor, and kill processes.

- Key knowledge areas:
  - Run jobs in the foreground and background.
  - Signal a program to continue running after logout.
  - Monitor active processes.
  - Select and sort processes for display.
  - Send signals to processes.
- The following is a partial list of the used files, terms, and utilities:
  - &
  - bg
  - fg
  - jobs
  - kill
  - nohup
  - ps
  - top
  - free
  - uptime
  - pgrep
  - pkill
  - killall

- watch
- screen
- tmux

## ✓ 103.6 Modify process execution priorities.

- Key knowledge areas:
    - Know the default priority of a job that is created.
    - Run a program with higher or lower priority than the default.
    - Change the priority of a running process.
- The following is a partial list of the used files, terms, and utilities:
    - nice
    - ps
    - renice
    - top

## ✓ 103.7 Search text files using regular expressions.

- Key knowledge areas:
    - Create simple regular expressions containing several notational elements.
    - Understand the differences between basic and extended regular expressions.
    - Understand the concepts of special characters, character classes, quantifiers, and anchors.
    - Use regular expression tools to perform searches through a filesystem or file content.
    - Use regular expressions to delete, change, and substitute text.
- The following is a partial list of the used files, terms, and utilities:
    - grep
    - egrep
    - fgrep

- sed
- regex(7)

## ✓ 103.8 Basic file editing

- Key knowledge areas:
  - Navigate a document using vi.
  - Understand and use Vi modes.
  - Insert, edit, delete, copy, and find text in Vi.
  - Be aware of Emacs, nano, and vim.
  - Configure the standard editor.
- The following is a partial list of the used files, terms, and utilities:
  - vi
  - /, ?
  - h,j,k,l
  - i, o, a
  - d, p, y, dd, yy
  - ZZ, :w!, :q!
  - EDITOR

1. Assume that you're using the Bash shell and want to prevent output redirects from accidentally overwriting existing files. Which command and option can be used to invoke this behavior?

   **A.** setoutput -f

   **B.** overwrite=no

   **C.** overwrite -n

   **D.** set -C

2. What command can be used to view the current settings for your environment when using Bash?

   **A.** environment

   **B.** env

   **C.** listenv

   **D.** echoenv

3. Which command is used to access documentation on the Linux computer for a given command?

   **A.** doc

   **B.** heredoc

   **C.** man

   **D.** manual

4. Which of the following commands will print various information about the kernel and architecture, along with other details?

   **A.** info --sys

   **B.** man sys

   **C.** sysinfo

   **D.** uname -a

5. When using sed for a substitution operation, which option must be included so that the substitution applies to the entire line rather than just the first instance?

   **A.** g

   **B.** a

   **C.** r

   **D.** y

6. Which option for the wc command prints the number of lines given as input?

   **A.** -f

   **B.** -a

   **C.** -l

   **D.** -o

**7.** What is the default number of lines printed by the head and `tail` commands, respectively?

   **A.** 10 for head, 5 for tail

   **B.** 5 for head, 10 for tail

   **C.** 10 for both head and tail

   **D.** 3 for both head and tail

**8.** You are attempting to use `rmdir` to remove a directory, but there are still multiple files and other directories contained within it. Assuming that you're sure you want to remove the directory and all of its contents, what is the command and arguments to remove the directory and all of its contents?

   **A.** `rm -f`

   **B.** `rm -rf`

   **C.** `rmdir -a`

   **D.** `rmdir -m`

**9.** Which command will find directories with names beginning with 2014 located beneath the current directory?

   **A.** `find ./ -name "2014"`

   **B.** `find ./ -type d -name "2014"`

   **C.** `find / -type d "2014"`

   **D.** `find ./ -type d -name "2014*"`

**10.** Which of the following commands will provide the usernames in a sorted list gathered from the /etc/passwd file?

   **A.** `cat /etc/passwd | awk -F : '{print $1}' | sort`

   **B.** `sort /etc/passwd | cut`

   **C.** `echo /etc/passwd`

   **D.** `cat /etc/passwd | awk '{print $1}' | sort`

**11.** Which options to `ls` will produce output, including hidden (dot) files, in a list that is ordered such that the newest files are at the end of the output?

   **A.** `-la`

   **B.** `-lat`

   **C.** `-latr`

   **D.** `-ltr`

**12.** What will be the result if the `touch` command is executed on a file that already exists?

   **A.** The access time stamp of the file will change to the current time when the `touch` command was executed.

   **B.** The file will be overwritten.

   **C.** There will be no change.

   **D.** The file will be appended to.

**13.** Which option to both mv and cp will cause the command to prompt before overwriting files that already exist?

- **A.** -f
- **B.** -Z
- **C.** -r
- **D.** -i

**14.** Which of the following commands will send the contents of /etc/passwd to both STDOUT and to a file called passwordfile?

- **A.** cat /etc/passwd > passwordfile
- **B.** var /etc/passwd | passwordfile
- **C.** cat /etc/passwd | tee passwordfile
- **D.** echo /etc/passwd | stdout > passwordfile

**15.** The current hierarchy on the server contains a directory called /usr/local. You need to create additional directories below that are called /usr/local/test/october. Which command will accomplish this task?

- **A.** mkdir -p /usr/local/test/october
- **B.** mkdir /usr/local/test/october
- **C.** mkdir -r /usr/local/test/october
- **D.** mkdir -f /usr/local/test/october

**16.** Which option to the cp command will copy directories in a recursive manner?

- **A.** -v
- **B.** -R
- **C.** -Z
- **D.** -i

**17.** You have received a file that does not have a file extension. Which command can you run to help determine what type of file it might be?

- **A.** grep
- **B.** telnet
- **C.** file
- **D.** export

**18.** Which command will create an image of the /dev/sda1 disk partition and place that image into a file called output.img?

- **A.** dd if=sda of=/dev/sda1
- **B.** dd if=output.img of=/dev/sda1
- **C.** dd if=/dev/sda1 of=output.img
- **D.** echo /dev/sda1 > output.img

**19.** What is the default delimiter used by the cut command?

   **A.** Colon

   **B.** Tab

   **C.** Space

   **D.** Comma

**20.** Which of the following will unzip and extract the contents of a file that has been tarred and gzipped?

   **A.** `tar -zxf <file.tgz>`

   **B.** `tar -xf <file.tgz>`

   **C.** `tar -vz <file.tgz>`

   **D.** `tar -fd <file.tgz>`

**21.** What command is used to bring a command to foreground processing after it has been backgrounded with an &?

   **A.** `bg`

   **B.** `fore`

   **C.** `4g`

   **D.** `fg`

**22.** You need to write a script that gathers all of the process IDs for all instances of Apache running on the system. Which of the following commands will accomplish this task?

   **A.** `ps auwx | grep apache`

   **B.** `pgrep apache`

   **C.** `processlist apache`

   **D.** `ls -p apache`

**23.** Which of the following command lines would monitor a single process called nagios in a continuous manner?

   **A.** `top -n 1`

   **B.** `top -p 23`

   **C.** `ps -nagios`

   **D.** `top -p`pidof nagios``

**24.** Users are reporting that various programs are crashing on the server. By examining logs, you see that certain processes are reporting out-of-memory conditions. Which command can you use to see the overall memory usage, including available swap space?

   **A.** `tree`

   **B.** `pgrep`

   **C.** `uptime`

   **D.** `free`

**25.** You are using the Vi editor for changing a file and need to exit. You receive a notice indicating "No write since last change". Assuming you want to save your work, which of the following commands will save your work and exit Vi?

    **A.** :wq

    **B.** :q!

    **C.** dd

    **D.** x

**26.** What option is used to change the number of lines of output for the head and tail commands?

    **A.** -l

    **B.** -f

    **C.** -g

    **D.** -n

**27.** Which command can be used to determine the current load average along with information on the amount of time since the last boot of the system?

    **A.** uptime

    **B.** sysinfo

    **C.** bash

    **D.** ls -u

**28.** You need to start a long-running process that requires a terminal and foreground processing. However, you cannot leave your terminal window open due to security restrictions. Which command will enable you to start the process and return at a later time to continue the session?

    **A.** fg

    **B.** bg

    **C.** kill

    **D.** screen

**29.** You have attempted to stop a process using its service command and also using the kill command. Which signal can be sent to the process using the kill command in order to force the process to end?

    **A.** -15

    **B.** -f

    **C.** -9

    **D.** -stop

**30.** When working in the Bash shell, you need to redirect both STDOUT and STDERR. Which of the following commands will redirect both STDOUT and STDERR?

  **A.** 1>2

  **B.** >2

  **C.** 2>&1

  **D.** >>

**31.** Which command can be run to determine the default priority for processes spawned by the current user?

  **A.** prio

  **B.** nice

  **C.** renice

  **D.** defpriority

**32.** Which of the following egrep commands will examine /etc/passwd to find users who are using either /bin/bash or /usr/bin/zsh for their shell environment?

  **A.** grep sh /etc/passwd

  **B.** egrep '/*/.sh$' /etc/passwd

  **C.** grep '/*/.=sh$' /etc/passwd

  **D.** egrep '/*/..?sh$' /etc/passwd

**33.** Which option to the man command accesses a different level of documentation, for example, system call documentation?

  **A.** man 2 <argument>

  **B.** progman <argument>

  **C.** man --sys <argument>

  **D.** man --list sys

**34.** When editing with Vi, which command changes to insert mode and opens a new line below the current cursor location?

  **A.** f

  **B.** a

  **C.** o

  **D.** i

**35.** Which kill signal can be sent in order to restart a process?

  **A.** -HUP

  **B.** -RESTART

  **C.** -9

  **D.** -SIG

**36.** Which of the following commands will display the last 50 lines of your command history when using Bash, including commands from the current session?

  **A.** bashhist 50

  **B.** history 50

  **C.** cat .bash_history

  **D.** tail -f .bash_history

**37.** You have backgrounded several tasks using &. Which command can be used to view the current list of running tasks that have been backgrounded?

  **A.** procs

  **B.** plist

  **C.** jobs

  **D.** free

**38.** Which of the following commands searches each user's .bash_history file to determine whether the user has invoked the sudo command?

  **A.** find /home -name "bash_history" | grep sudo

  **B.** find /home -name ".bash_history" | xargs grep sudo

  **C.** find /home/.bash_history | xargs grep sudo

  **D.** find /home -type history | xargs grep sudo

**39.** Which command will watch the Apache log at /var/log/httpd/access.log and continually scroll as new log entries are created?

  **A.** watch /var/log/httpd/access.log

  **B.** tail /var/log/httpd/access.log

  **C.** tail -f /var/log/httpd/access.log

  **D.** mon /var/log/httpd/access.log

**40.** You are debugging a configuration file and the daemon indicates there is a problem on line 932. Which of the following commands will prepend line numbers onto the file?

  **A.** lines

  **B.** wc -l

  **C.** newline

  **D.** nl

**41.** You receive a file with an .lzma extension. Which command can you use to decompress this file?

  **A.** xz

  **B.** lz

  **C.** gz

  **D.** bzip

42. Which `find` command will locate files within the current directory that have been modified within the last 24 hours?

    **A.** `find ./ -type f -mtime 0`

    **B.** `find ./ -type f -mtime 24`

    **C.** `find ./ -type f -mtime +1`

    **D.** `find ./ type -f time 24`

43. Which command will move all files with a `.txt` extension to the `/tmp` directory?

    **A.** `mv txt* tmp`

    **B.** `move *txt /temp`

    **C.** `mv *.txt /tmp`

    **D.** `mv *.txt tmp`

44. Which command prints your current directory?

    **A.** `cwd`

    **B.** `curdur`

    **C.** `cd`

    **D.** `pwd`

45. Assume that you have a file called `zips.txt` that contains several postal ZIP codes and you need to determine how many unique ZIP codes there are in the file. Which of the following commands can be used for that purpose?

    **A.** `sort zips.txt | uniq -c`

    **B.** `uniq zips.txt`

    **C.** `count zips.txt`

    **D.** `cat zips.txt | uniq -c`

46. When using Bash, how would you execute the last command starting with a certain string, even if that command was not the last one that you typed?

    **A.** Precede the command with ! and then the string to search for.

    **B.** Search for the command in history.

    **C.** Precede the command with a ? and then the string to search for.

    **D.** This is not possible with Bash.

47. Which command can be used to kill all processes by using their name?

    **A.** `killproc`

    **B.** `killname`

    **C.** `killall`

    **D.** `kill -f`

**48.** You're working with a large file in Vi and need to search for instances of a string earlier in the file. Which key will search backward in the file?

   **A.** /

   **B.** h

   **C.** ?

   **D.** x

**49.** You need to declare a local environment variable that will then be available to child processes. Which of the following commands accomplishes this task?

   **A.** ex

   **B.** echo

   **C.** dec

   **D.** export

**50.** You are creating a Bash shell script and need to output the current script name to the current terminal. Which of the following commands accomplishes this task?

   **A.** cat <CMD>

   **B.** echo $0

   **C.** echo $SCRIPT

   **D.** echo $PS1

**51.** You have downloaded a file with a .gz extension. What is the most likely command that you will use to decompress this file?

   **A.** unz

   **B.** gunzip

   **C.** hunzip

   **D.** gzunzip

**52.** You need to remove a single file from a directory if it exists but would like to be prompted for confirmation before doing so. Which option to the rm command causes the command to prompt for confirmation?

   **A.** -a

   **B.** -e

   **C.** -i

   **D.** -o

**53.** You need to determine files that are sized above 1GB. Which of the following commands accomplishes this task?

   **A.** find / -size +1G

   **B.** find / -size 10000M

   **C.** find / +1M

   **D.** find / -size +1B

**54.** Which option to cpio lists the files as it is operating on them?

   **A.** -l

   **B.** -v

   **C.** -k

   **D.** -s

**55.** Which command is used to send contents of a bzip2 archive to STDOUT?

   **A.** bzout

   **B.** bzcat

   **C.** bz2cat

   **D.** bz2echo

**56.** You are attempting to find more information about the jobs command; however, an Internet search was not particularly helpful because there are so many Linux-related jobs available. Additionally, you attempted to view the man page for the jobs command but it was not available. Which man page should you use to view more information on jobs?

   **A.** jbs

   **B.** procctl

   **C.** bash

   **D.** ps

**57.** You need to start a process that cannot be sent or will not accept a SIGHUP signal. Which command should be used to start the process?

   **A.** nosig

   **B.** nohup

   **C.** nokill

   **D.** noproc

**58.** You need to run a command periodically and examine its output in real time. Which of the following commands enables this scenario?

   **A.** mon

   **B.** procmon

   **C.** pgrep

   **D.** watch

**59.** You would like to tail a log file to watch entries as they are being added to the log file. In addition, you would also like to work within the same terminal window or SSH (Secure Shell) session to add entries to another file at the same time. Which command can be used to create two sessions within the same terminal window?

   **A.** screen

   **B.** tmux

   **C.** sess

   **D.** termse

**60.** You need to kill several processes at once. Rather than writing a complex ps-based command to do so, you can use which other command?

**A.** pkill

**B.** psk

**C.** pskill

**D.** prock

**61.** You are using `pgrep` to find the process IDs for a given command. However, several other commands seem to also appear. Which option to `pgrep` enables matching against the full path of the process?

**A.** -f

**B.** -d

**C.** -o

**D.** -i

**62.** You need to determine the exact command that will be run based on your current environment settings. Which command is used for this purpose?

**A.** what

**B.** which

**C.** find

**D.** ls

**63.** An environment variable has been set on login, but you need to remove that variable temporarily for the current session. Which shell built-in command can be used for this purpose?

**A.** reset

**B.** unset

**C.** undo

**D.** clear

**64.** You cannot find the man page of a command but you know the command exists. For example, the `alias` command exists but there is no man page for it. Which of the following commands could you execute to determine what type of command `alias` is?

**A.** type

**B.** cmd

**C.** uses

**D.** listr

**65.** Which type of quotes are used so that variables are interpolated within a Bash shell script?

**A.** Escaped quotes

**B.** Single quotes

**C.** Double quotes

**D.** Side quotes

**66.** Which of the following pagers includes the ability to search backward and forward as well as move backward and forward, line-by-line, and page-by-page?

   **A.**  more

   **B.**  mplus

   **C.**  less

   **D.**  catch

**67.** You have a specialized need for outputting a file in octal format. Which command or series of commands can be used for this purpose?

   **A.**  oct

   **B.**  cat <file> | octalf

   **C.**  od

   **D.**  octf

**68.** Which option to sha256sum causes the file to be read in binary mode?

   **A.**  -i

   **B.**  -b

   **C.**  -c

   **D.**  -p

**69.** When operating in command mode, which keys enable you to move the cursor in the Vi editor?

   **A.**  a, s, d, f

   **B.**  h, j, k, l

   **C.**  q, w, e, r

   **D.**  z, x, c, v

**70.** Which options to xz are functionally equivalent to the xzcat program?

   **A.**  decompress and output

   **B.**  output and format

   **C.**  decompress and stdout

   **D.**  stdout and format

**71.** Which environment variable is used to control the default text editor used on a Linux system?

   **A.**  EDITOR

   **B.**  EDIT

   **C.**  TEXTEDITOR

   **D.**  DEFAULT_EDITOR

**72.** You need to examine the seventh section of the manual page for regular expressions, or regex, on a Linux system. Which command displays the seventh section of the manual?

    **A.** `man regex -7`

    **B.** `man regex 7`

    **C.** `man --page 7 regex`

    **D.** `man 7 regex`

**73.** Which of the following commands reprioritizes an already running process?

    **A.** `nice`

    **B.** `renice`

    **C.** `chnice`

    **D.** `altnice`

**74.** The `fgrep` command is equivalent to running the `grep` command with which option?

    **A.** `-f`

    **B.** `-F`

    **C.** `-a`

    **D.** `-E`

**75.** Which of the following regular expressions would find the pattern `Steve` or `steve` in a file when used with grep?

    **A.** `'[sS]teve'`

    **B.** `'[S]*teve'`

    **C.** `'^[Ss]teve'`

    **D.** `'[$Steve]'`

**76.** Which of the following commands shows the currently running processes and their resource usage in real time, updated every few seconds?

    **A.** `nice`

    **B.** `ps`

    **C.** `top`

    **D.** `procs`

**77.** You have been asked to create a compressed file that will be readable by those with other operating systems. Which tool can you use for this purpose?

    **A.** `gzip`

    **B.** `bzip2`

    **C.** `xz`

    **D.** `tar`

**78.** You need to match files that begin with 201, as in 2017, 2018, 2019. Which of the following wildcard specifications can be used?

**A.** 201?

**B.** 201$

**C.** 201@

**D.** 201]

**79.** You need to break a large file into smaller pieces. Which command can be used for this purpose?

**A.** cut

**B.** split

**C.** dice

**D.** rem

**80.** When examining the output from top, you see that a process has a value in the PR column of 20. To what does the PR column refer?

**A.** The process ID

**B.** The process utilization

**C.** The process priority

**D.** The processor core on which the process is executing

**81.** You need to cut or remove eight lines from a file while editing with Vi. Which combination should be used for this purpose?

**A.** d7

**B.** d8

**C.** r8

**D.** x7

**82.** Which command is used in order to decompress a file that has been compressed with xz?

**A.** unxz

**B.** dexz

**C.** xzu

**D.** u2xz

**83.** Which of the following commands uses 128-bit message digests?

**A.** sha256sum

**B.** sha512sum

**C.** sh128sum

**D.** md5sum

**84.** You have several files that need to be combined, with a line from each file being appended onto a single line. Which command can be used for this purpose?

   **A.** paste

   **B.** comb

   **C.** appfile

   **D.** combo

**85.** You need to run a command that is not inside your current path. Which of the following represents the typical method for doing so?

   **A.** Use a fully qualified path for the command.

   **B.** Set the PATH environment variable to include the correct path.

   **C.** Restart the shell environment.

   **D.** Restart the computer for settings to take effect.

**86.** Which signal is used by default by the pkill command?

   **A.** SIGKILL

   **B.** SIGTERM

   **C.** SIGHUP

   **D.** SIGKS

**87.** You are working with the jobs built-in command to display jobs. You would like to see only running jobs. Which option to the jobs built-in command will display only running jobs?

   **A.** -s

   **B.** -a

   **C.** -l

   **D.** -r

**88.** Which option to the bunzip2 command sends output to STDOUT, much like the bzcat command?

   **A.** -s

   **B.** -o

   **C.** -c

   **D.** -d

# Chapter 4

# Topic 104: Devices, Linux Filesystems, Filesystem Hierarchy Standard

---

**THE FOLLOWING EXAM OBJECTIVES ARE COVERED IN THIS CHAPTER:**

✓ **104.1 Create partitions and filesystems.**

- Key knowledge areas:
  - Manage MBR and GPT partition tables.
  - Use various `mkfs` commands to create various filesystems such as:
    - ext2/ext3/ext4
    - XFS
    - VFAT
    - exFAT
  - Basic feature knowledge of Btrfs, including multi-device filesystems, compression, and subvolumes
- The following is a partial list of the used files, terms, and utilities:
  - `fdisk`
  - `gdisk`
  - `parted`
  - `mkfs`
  - `mkswap`

✓ **104.2   Maintain the integrity of filesystems.**

- Key knowledge areas:
  - Verify the integrity of filesystems.
  - Monitor free space and inodes.
  - Repair simply filesystem problems.
- The following is a partial list of the used files, terms, and utilities:
  - du
  - df
  - fsck
  - e2fsck
  - mke2fs
  - tune2fs
  - xfs_repair
  - xfs_fsr
  - xfs_db

✓ **104.3   Control mounting and unmounting of filesystems.**

- Key knowledge areas:
  - Manually mount and unmount filesystems.
  - Configure filesystems mounting on bootup.
  - Configure user mountable removable filesystems.
  - Use labels and UUIDs for identifying and mounting filesystems.
  - Awareness of systemd mount units
- The following is a partial list of the used files, terms, and utilities:
  - /etc/fstab
  - /media/
  - mount
  - umount
  - blkid
  - lsblk

✓ **104.4   Manage file permissions and ownership.**

- Key knowledge areas:
  - Manage access permissions on regular and special files as well as directories.
  - Use access modes such as suid, sgid, and the sticky bit to maintain security.
  - Know how to change the file creation mask.
  - Use the group field to grant file access to group members.
- The following is a partial list of the used files, terms, and utilities:
  - chmod
  - umask
  - chown
  - chgrp

✓ **104.5   Create and change hard and symbolic links.**

- Key knowledge areas:
  - Create links.
  - Identify hard and/or soft links.
  - Copying versus linking files
  - Use links to support system administration tasks.
- The following is a partial list of the used files, terms, and utilities:
  - ln
  - ls

✓ **104.6   Find system files and place files in the correct location.**

- Key knowledge areas:
  - Understand the correct locations of files under the FHS.
  - Find files and commands on a Linux system.
  - Know the location and purpose of important file and directories as defined in the FHS.

- The following is a partial list of the used files, terms, and utilities:
  - find
  - locate
  - updatedb
  - whereis
  - which
  - type
  - /etc/updatedb.conf

1. Which option best describes the following output from the `ls -la` command:
   ```
   lrwxrwxrwx.  1   root   root   35   Jul 8 2014   .fetchmailrc ->
   .configs/fetchmail/.fetchmailrc?
   ```
   **A.** It is a file called `.fetchmailrc` that is linked using a symbolic link.

   **B.** It is a file called `.configs/fetchmail/.fetchmailrc` that is owned by `lrwxrwxrwx`.

   **C.** It is a directory called `.fetchmailrc` that is owned by user `Jul`.

   **D.** It is a local directory called `.configs/fetchmail/.fetchmailrc`.

2. Assuming that a USB disk contains a single partition and is made available on `/dev/sdb`, which command mounts the disk in `/media/usb`?

   **A.** `mount /dev/sdb1 /media/usb`

   **B.** `usbconnect /dev/sdb0 /media/usb`

   **C.** `mount /dev/sdb0 /media/usb`

   **D.** `usbmount /dev/sdb1 /media/usb`

3. Which option within a partition-mounting command will cause the partition to be mounted in such a way as to prevent execution of programs?

   **A.** `execless`

   **B.** `stoprun`

   **C.** `noexec`

   **D.** `norun`

4. When working with partitions on disk, you see the type 0x82. Which type of partition is this?

   **A.** Linux

   **B.** Linux swap

   **C.** NTFS

   **D.** FAT

5. Which partition type should be created for a Linux system, non-swap partition?

   **A.** 82

   **B.** 83

   **C.** 84

   **D.** L

6. Which command can be used to determine the location of a given executable that would be run if typed from your current environment and location?

   **A.** `which`

   **B.** `what`

   **C.** `whatis`

   **D.** `when`

**7.** Which of the following commands will correctly change the group ownership of the file called `a.out` to users?

   **A.**  `chgrp users a.out`

   **B.**  `chgrp a.out users`

   **C.**  `groupchg a.out users`

   **D.**  `grpchg users a.out`

**8.** Another administrator made a change to one of the local scripts used for administrative purposes. The change was also immediately reflected in your copy of the script. However, when examining the file with `ls`, you see that it appears to be a normal file. What is the likely cause of such a scenario?

   **A.**  The file was executed after edit.

   **B.**  The administrator copied the file to yours.

   **C.**  Your file is a hard link to the original.

   **D.**  The file has been restored from backup.

**9.** Which of the following commands shows the usage of inodes across all filesystems?

   **A.**  `df -i`

   **B.**  `ls -i`

   **C.**  `du -i`

   **D.**  `dm -i`

**10.** You're running `fsck` on an ext3 filesystem, and the process is taking longer than expected and requiring input from the administrator to fix issues. What option could be added to `fsck` next time so that the command will automatically attempt to fix errors without intervention?

   **A.**  `-o`

   **B.**  `-V`

   **C.**  `-y`

   **D.**  `-f`

**11.** Which of the following describes a primary difference between ext2 and ext3 filesystems?

   **A.**  ext3 was primarily a bug fix update to ext2.

   **B.**  ext3 includes journaling for the filesystem.

   **C.**  ext3 completely changed the tools needed for management of the disks.

   **D.**  ext3 filesystems have no significant differences.

**12.** Which option to `umask` will display the permissions to be used in a Portable Operating System Interface (POSIX) format?

   **A.**  `-P`

   **B.**  `-p`

   **C.**  `-S`

   **D.**  `-v`

**13.** Which option to `ln` creates a symlink to another file?

  **A.** `-sl`

  **B.** `-s`

  **C.** `-l`

  **D.** `--ln`

**14.** Which of the following commands can be used if you need to locate various elements of a given command, such as its binaries and man pages?

  **A.** `whatis`

  **B.** `find`

  **C.** `whereis`

  **D.** `ls`

**15.** Which option in `/etc/updatedb.conf` will remove a path from inclusion in the results?

  **A.** `PRUNEPATHS`

  **B.** `EXCLUDEPATHS`

  **C.** `INCLUDEEXCLUDE`

  **D.** `SEPARATEPATH`

**16.** According to the filesystem hierarchy standard (FHS), what is the correct location for site-specific data for a server?

  **A.** `/etc`

  **B.** `/var`

  **C.** `/tmp`

  **D.** `/srv`

**17.** Which of the following commands enables the sticky bit for a user on a file called `homescript.sh`?

  **A.** `chmod +sticky homescript.sh`

  **B.** `chmod 755 homescript.sh`

  **C.** `chmod u+s homescript.sh`

  **D.** `chown u+sticky homescript.sh`

**18.** Which option to the `mount` command will mount all filesystems that are currently available in `/etc/fstab`?

  **A.** `-g`

  **B.** `-a`

  **C.** `-r`

  **D.** `-y`

**19.** Which command is used to format a swap partition?

  **A.** fdisk

  **B.** mkswap

  **C.** formatswap

  **D.** format -s

**20.** Which command and option is used to display the number of times that a filesystem has been mounted?

  **A.** tune2fs -l

  **B.** cat /etc/fstab

  **C.** mount -a

  **D.** less /etc/fsmnt

**21.** Which option to xfs_metadump displays a progress indicator?

  **A.** -g

  **B.** -p

  **C.** -f

  **D.** -v

**22.** The system is running out of disk space within the home directory partition and quotas have not been enabled. Which command can you use to determine the directories that might contain large files?

  **A.** du

  **B.** df

  **C.** ls

  **D.** locate

**23.** Which file contains information about the filesystems to mount, their partitions, and the options that should be used to mount them?

  **A.** /etc/filesystems

  **B.** /etc/mounts

  **C.** /etc/fstab

  **D.** /srv/mounts

**24.** According to the FHS, what is the proper mount point for removable media?

  **A.** /etc

  **B.** /srv

  **C.** /tmp

  **D.** /media

**25.** Which file contains information on currently mounted filesystems, including their mount options?

   **A.**  /etc/mtab

   **B.**  /etc/fstab

   **C.**  /tmp/files

   **D.**  /etc/filesystems

**26.** Which option to umount will cause the command to attempt to remount the filesystem in read-only mode if the unmounting process fails?

   **A.**  -o

   **B.**  -r

   **C.**  -f

   **D.**  -v

**27.** The umask reports as 022. What is the permission that will be in effect for a newly nonexecutable created file?

   **A.**  u+rw, g+r, w+r

   **B.**  755

   **C.**  022

   **D.**  a+r

**28.** The locate command is reporting out-of-date information. Which command should be run in order to have the locate command update its database?

   **A.**  locatedb -u

   **B.**  locate -u

   **C.**  updatedb

   **D.**  updatelocate

**29.** Which shell built-in command can be used to determine what command will be run?

   **A.**  type

   **B.**  when

   **C.**  find

   **D.**  help

**30.** Which option to chown recursively changes the ownership?

   **A.**  -f

   **B.**  -R

   **C.**  -a

   **D.**  -m

**31.** Which of the following represents the correct format for the `/etc/fstab` file?

   **A.** `<directory> <device> <type> <options>`

   **B.** `<device> <type> <options>`

   **C.** `<device> <type> <options> <directory> <dump> <fsck>`

   **D.** `<filesystem> <mount point> <type> <options> <dump> <pass>`

**32.** Which of the following commands is used to identify the UUID for partitions?

   **A.** `blkid`

   **B.** `ls`

   **C.** `find`

   **D.** `cat`

**33.** Which of the following describes the priority order for configuration files with systemd?

   **A.** Files in `/etc/`, files in `/run`, and then files in `/lib`

   **B.** Files in `/run`, files in `/etc/`, and then files in `/lib`

   **C.** Files in `/lib`, files in `/run`, and then files in `/etc`

   **D.** Files in `/lib`, files in `/etc`, and then files in `/run`

**34.** Which options to the `fsck` command will find and automatically assume that it should repair errors that it finds?

   **A.** `-y`

   **B.** `-vy`

   **C.** `-my`

   **D.** `-xy`

**35.** Which option to `mke2fs` sets the type of filesystem to be created?

   **A.** `-F`

   **B.** `-a`

   **C.** `-t`

   **D.** `-e`

**36.** Which of the following files is the default configuration file for the `autofs` automounter?

   **A.** `/etc/autofs`

   **B.** `/etc/auto.master`

   **C.** `/etc/autofs.conf`

   **D.** `/etc/automounter.conf`

**37.** Which of the following commands is used to create an ISO filesystem?

   **A.** `mkiso`

   **B.** `mkfsiso`

   **C.** `mkisofs`

   **D.** `isofs-mk`

**38.** Which option to the `tune2fs` command sets the maximum mount count before the system will automatically run `fsck` on the partition on boot?

   **A.**  -b

   **B.**  -c

   **C.**  -C

   **D.**  -a

**39.** Which option to the `mount` command can be used to simulate the mount process without actually mounting the filesystem?

   **A.**  -q

   **B.**  -v

   **C.**  -l

   **D.**  -f

**40.** When viewing `/proc/mounts`, you see a filesystem with the letters `ro` in the fourth column. To what do the letters `ro` refer?

   **A.**  relative option

   **B.**  realtime option

   **C.**  read-only

   **D.**  relative-only

**41.** Which option to `dumpe2fs` displays the bad blocks for a given partition?

   **A.**  -bb

   **B.**  -C

   **C.**  -b

   **D.**  -f

**42.** Which of the following filesystem types features copy-on-write?

   **A.**  ext3

   **B.**  ext4

   **C.**  FAT

   **D.**  Btrfs

**43.** Which of the following commands displays filesystem geometry for an XFS filesystem?

   **A.**  xfsinfo

   **B.**  xfs_info

   **C.**  xfs -info

   **D.**  xfs --info

**44.** Which of the following commands can be used to display information such as the UUID for partitions on a system?

   **A.**  blkid

   **B.**  blockdev

   **C.**  devinfo

   **D.**  uuidinfo

**45.** Which option to the umount command will cause it to unmount only filesystems of the specified type?

   **A.**  -v

   **B.**  -f

   **C.**  -t

   **D.**  -a

**46.** Which command causes unwritten data to be written to disk immediately?

   **A.**  write

   **B.**  wrnow

   **C.**  connwrite

   **D.**  sync

**47.** Which option to xfs_check is used to verify a filesystem that is stored in a file?

   **A.**  -v

   **B.**  -a

   **C.**  -f

   **D.**  -d

**48.** Which option to debugfs causes the filesystem to be opened in read-write mode rather than the default read-only?

   **A.**  -rw

   **B.**  -w

   **C.**  -r

   **D.**  -n

**49.** Which daemon is responsible for monitoring Self-Monitoring, Analysis, and Reporting Technology (SMART)-compatible hard drives?

   **A.**  smartmon

   **B.**  smarty

   **C.**  sartd

   **D.**  smartd

**50.** When checking an ext3 filesystem, which option to the `fsck.ext3` command causes it to run the check even if the filesystem is apparently marked as clean?

   **A.**  -f

   **B.**  -m

   **C.**  -a

   **D.**  -c

**51.** You are performing an `xfsrestore`. The `xfsdump` was executed with a block size of 4MB. Which option do you need to invoke on `xfsrestore` in order for it to successfully use this dump?

   **A.**  -b 4M

   **B.**  -g 1M

   **C.**  -i 1M

   **D.**  -k 1028K

**52.** You see the word *defaults* within `/etc/fstab`. Which options are encompassed within the defaults?

   **A.**  ro, exec, auto

   **B.**  rw, suid, dev, exec, auto, nouser, async

   **C.**  rw, exec, auto, nouser, async

   **D.**  rw, exec, nouser, async, noauto, suid

**53.** Which of the following commands creates a btrfs subvolume?

   **A.**  btrfs create subvolume

   **B.**  btrfs subvolume create

   **C.**  btrfs sv create

   **D.**  btrfs svcreate

**54.** Which of the following options to `xfsdump` sets the maximum size for files to be included in the dump?

   **A.**  -p

   **B.**  -s

   **C.**  -z

   **D.**  -b

**55.** Which option to the `tune2fs` command sets the behavior when a filesystem error occurs?

   **A.**  -f

   **B.**  -d

   **C.**  -e

   **D.**  -k

**56.** The /etc filesystem has been mounted as a read-only for a recovery process. You need to mount another partition. Which option to the mount command causes it to not write to /etc/mtab?

    **A.**  -a

    **B.**  -m

    **C.**  -b

    **D.**  -n

**57.** Which of the following commands deactivates swap space?

    **A.**  swapoff

    **B.**  swap -off

    **C.**  unmountswap

    **D.**  uswap

**58.** Within the [mount] section of a systemd mount unit, which directive specifies the location for mounting the chosen filesystem?

    **A.**  Where=

    **B.**  Location=

    **C.**  List=

    **D.**  Dest=

**59.** Which of the following commands can be used to format a FAT filesystem?

    **A.**  mkfs.fat

    **B.**  mkfs -f

    **C.**  mkfs --fat

    **D.**  mkfat

**60.** Which of the following commands adds a journal to an existing ext2 filesystem?

    **A.**  tune2fs -jrn

    **B.**  e2fs -x

    **C.**  tune3fs

    **D.**  tune2fs -j

**61.** Which of the following commands creates a snapshot of a btrfs subvolume?

    **A.**  btrfs subvolume snapshot

    **B.**  btrfs snapshot --create

    **C.**  btrfs create snapshot

    **D.**  btrfs --create

**62.** Which option to `xfs_repair` will force log zeroing even if there may be metadata within the log?

**A.** -L

**B.** -v

**C.** -d

**D.** -V

**63.** Which of the following commands mounts a filesystem in read-only mode?

**A.** `mount read-only`

**B.** `mount --read`

**C.** `mount -o ro`

**D.** `mount -or`

**64.** When you are using `tune2fs` to set an extended option such as `stripe_width`, which command-line option is needed to signify that an extended option follows?

**A.** `-extend`

**B.** `-E`

**C.** `-e`

**D.** `-f`

**65.** Which utility is used for formatting GPT disks?

**A.** `gdisk`

**B.** `gptdisk`

**C.** `gpdisk`

**D.** `pgdisk`

**66.** What is the maximum size of a partition on an MBR-formatted disk?

**A.** 2TB

**B.** 4TB

**C.** 2MB

**D.** 512TB

**67.** Which option to `mkfs.ext4` can be used to prevent reservation of blocks for system or superuser use?

**A.** `-r 0`

**B.** `-r 0b`

**C.** `-m 0`

**D.** `-m 0b`

**68.** What is the default time in seconds that `xfs_fsr` will use to reorganize a filesystem?

    **A.**  3600

    **B.**  7200

    **C.**  86400

    **D.**  5150

**69.** A user who is a member of the custom `admins` group is attempting to read the contents of a file but is not the owner of the file. Rather than granting `sudo` access to this file, what is another way to grant read access, assuming that the file is currently marked with 640 permissions? Note that you should choose the most appropriate answer to fulfill the need while minimizing additional privileges.

    **A.**  Grant root access to the user.

    **B.**  Run chmod  777 on the file.

    **C.**  Use chgrp to change group ownership to `admins`.

    **D.**  Use chown to change the ownership of the file to the individual user.

**70.** Which option to `lsblk` shows empty devices?

    **A.**  -g

    **B.**  -a

    **C.**  -r

    **D.**  -y

**71.** The `/media/` mount point is used frequently for which types of devices?

    **A.**  Hard drives

    **B.**  SAN

    **C.**  NAS

    **D.**  USB devices

**72.** Which of the following commands is used to format an exFAT filesystem?

    **A.**  mkexfat

    **B.**  mkfat.ex

    **C.**  mkfs.exfat

    **D.**  mkfs2.exf

**73.** Which of the following commands is used for debugging an XFS-formatted filesystem?

    **A.**  debug_xfs

    **B.**  xfs_debug

    **C.**  xfs_db

    **D.**  debugxfs

**74.** You're working with an ext2 filesystem and you suspect the superblock is corrupted. Which option to e2fsck enables you to specify the location of an alternate superblock?

    **A.**  -B

    **B.**  -s

    **C.**  -b

    **D.**  -o

**75.** Which option to df shows the numerical output in larger size increments, like MB, GB, TB, and so on rather than in bytes?

    **A.**  -h

    **B.**  -m

    **C.**  -n

    **D.**  -s

**76.** Assuming the use of Bash for the shell, in which file can the umask be set such that the file creation mask is set automatically on login?

    **A.**  /etc/umask.def

    **B.**  /etc/profile

    **C.**  /etc/bash.d/umask

    **D.**  /etc/bash.umask

**77.** You need to enable two users to edit the same file but keep their own individual changes. Another administrator suggested making a symbolic link for the file. Is a symbolic link the appropriate solution for this scenario and, if not, what is?

    **A.**  A symbolic link is not appropriate because the users cannot keep their own changes. A copy would be a better option.

    **B.**  A symbolic link is appropriate here because each user can access the file, assuming write permissions.

    **C.**  A symbolic link is not appropriate given that the users will not have permissions on symbolic links. Linux cannot meet the scenario described.

    **D.**  A symbolic link is appropriate because symbolic links have the ability to do version control, thus enabling the scenario.

**78.** You have deleted a user from the system and want to determine if this user still has files on the system. Which command will fulfill this scenario?

    **A.**  locate <user>

    **B.**  find -uid <uid>

    **C.**  find -user <user>

    **D.**  fileloc -user <user>

**79.** You need to update the `locate` database. Which of the following commands is used for this purpose?

    **A.** updatedb

    **B.** locatedb

    **C.** updlocdb

    **D.** locdbupd

**80.** Which option to `lsblk` shows the UUID of each filesystem?

    **A.** -u

    **B.** -f

    **C.** -o

    **D.** -a

**81.** Which option to `mkswap` checks the device for bad blocks before formatting?

    **A.** -b

    **B.** -B

    **C.** -c

    **D.** -d

**82.** You are examining output from `ls -la` and one file contains the permissions `-rwSrw-r--`. To what does the *S* refer?

    **A.** Specific execute

    **B.** Source formatting

    **C.** Selective execution

    **D.** Sticky bit

**83.** You need to change file permissions to be `setgid` for a file called `sync.sh`. The file is normally permission 755. Which of the following commands accomplishes this task?

    **A.** chmod 2775 sync.sh

    **B.** chmod u+s sync.sh

    **C.** chmod 2755 sync.sh

    **D.** chmod 4755 sync.sh

**84.** Which of the following commands finds files with a `.sql` extension across the entire filesystem?

    **A.** find . -name "*.sql"

    **B.** find /root -ext sql

    **C.** find / -name "*.sql"

    **D.** find / -exten ".sql"

**85.** When working with /etc/fstab to mount by UUID, which syntax is correct as the first column in /etc/fstab, assuming a UUID denoted by <UUID>?

   **A.** <UUID>

   **B.** UUID=<UUID>

   **C.** ID=<UUID>

   **D.** GPT=<UUID>

**86.** Which option to du displays information on inode usage?

   **A.** -i

   **B.** -h

   **C.** --inodes

   **D.** -d

**87.** Which of the following find commands will look for files that are over 1GB in size?

   **A.** find -size +1G

   **B.** find -size 1GB

   **C.** find -fssize +1GB

   **D.** find -filesize +1G

**88.** You have a set of libraries that were installed into /usr/local/lib and would like to ensure that the libraries are also available in /usr/lib. What is the preferred way to make the libraries available in this location?

   **A.** Copy the libraries.

   **B.** Create a symbolic link.

   **C.** Move the libraries.

   **D.** Create a script to synchronize the libraries between the two locations with rsync.

# Exam 102-500

# Chapter 5

# Topic 105: Shells and Shell Scripting

**THE FOLLOWING EXAM OBJECTIVES ARE COVERED IN THIS CHAPTER:**

✓ **105.1 Customize and use the shell environment.**

- Key knowledge areas:
    - Set environment variables (e.g. PATH) at login or when spawning a new shell.
    - Write bash functions for frequently used sequences of commands.
    - Maintain skeleton directories for new user accounts.
    - Set command search path with the proper directory.
- The following is a partial list of the used files, terms, and utilities:
    - .
    - source
    - /etc/bash.bashrc
    - /etc/profile
    - env
    - export
    - set
    - unset
    - ~/.bash_profile
    - ~/.bash_login
    - ~/.profile
    - ~/.bashrc
    - ~/.bash_logout
    - function
    - alias

✓ **105.2 Customize or write simple scripts.**

- Key knowledge areas:

  - Use standard sh syntax (loops, tests).

  - Use command substitution.

  - Test return values for success or failure or other information provided by a command.

  - Execute chained commands.

  - Perform conditional mailing to the superuser.

  - Correctly select the script interpreter through the shebang (#!) line.

  - Manage the location, ownership, execution, and suid-rights of scripts.

- The following is a partial list of the used files, terms, and utilities:

  - for

  - while

  - test

  - if

  - read

  - seq

  - exec

  - ||

  - &&

**1.** Which of the following best describes the PS1 environment variable?

   **A.** PS1 is used to set the location of the PostScript command.

   **B.** PS1 is used to define the default shell prompt for bash.

   **C.** PS1 is used as a per-system variable.

   **D.** PS1 is user-defined and does not have a default value or setting.

**2.** Which command is used to read and execute commands from a file in the Bash shell?

   **A.** run

   **B.** execute

   **C.** source

   **D.** func

**3.** You need a command to be executed on logout for all users. Within which file should this be placed (assuming all users are using Bash)?

   **A.** ~/.bash_logout

   **B.** /etc/bash.bash_logout

   **C.** /home/.bash_logout

   **D.** /etc/bash_logout

**4.** Which of the following commands removes an environment variable that has been set?

   **A.** profile --unset

   **B.** env -u

   **C.** set -u

   **D.** import

**5.** Which option to the unset command explicitly informs the command that the name given refers to a shell variable and not a function?

   **A.** -a

   **B.** -s

   **C.** -v

   **D.** -e

**6.** Which of the following commands ensures that the -la options are used when the ls command is executed without other options?

   **A.** alias ls="ls -la"

   **B.** ln -s ls ls -la

   **C.** alias "ls -la" = ls

   **D.** set ls

**7.** What is the order in which user configuration files are located on login to a Bash shell?

   **A.** `.bash_login, .profile, /etc/profile`

   **B.** `.bash_profile, .bash_login, .profile`

   **C.** `.profile, .bash_login, .bash_profile`

   **D.** `.bash_login, .bash_profile, .profile`

**8.** Which variable within a Bash script is used to access the first command-line parameter?

   **A.** `$ARG`

   **B.** `$CMD`

   **C.** `$1`

   **D.** `$ARG0`

**9.** Which of the following provides the end for an `if` conditional in a Bash script?

   **A.** `ex`

   **B.** `}`

   **C.** `]`

   **D.** `fi`

**10.** Which of the following commands will print a list of 6 numbers beginning at 0 within a Bash script?

   **A.** `list 0-5`

   **B.** `seq 0 1 5`

   **C.** `echo 0-5`

   **D.** `seq 0 1 6`

**11.** When creating a shell script, which of the following commands is used to display the contents of variables?

   **A.** `var_dump`

   **B.** `echo`

   **C.** `ls`

   **D.** `env`

**12.** A command has the following listing obtained with `ls -la`:

```
-rwsr-xr-x 1 suehring suehring 21 Nov  2 13:53 script.sh
```

What does the s denote within the user permissions in the listing?

   **A.** The `suid` bit has been set for this program.

   **B.** This is a symlink.

   **C.** The file will not be executable.

   **D.** The file is a special system file.

**13.** Which of the following commands will execute a script and then exit the shell?

  **A.** run

  **B.** source

  **C.** ./

  **D.** exec

**14.** Which sequence of characters will execute two commands but only if the first command exits successfully?

  **A.** --

  **B.** &*

  **C.** &&

  **D.** &

**15.** Which command within a shell script awaits user input and places that input into a variable?

  **A.** exec

  **B.** get

  **C.** read

  **D.** prompt

**16.** What characters are used to mark a sequence of commands as a function in a Bash script?

  **A.** Parentheses to declare the function (optional) and curly braces to contain the commands

  **B.** Curly braces to declare the function and parentheses to contain the commands

  **C.** Square brackets to declare the function and curly braces to contain the commands

  **D.** Runquotes to denote the function

**17.** Which character sequences denote an alternate command to execute if the preceding command does not exit successfully?

  **A.** &&

  **B.** --

  **C.** ||

  **D.** EL

**18.** Which keyword(s) is/are used to begin an alternate condition within a Bash script?

  **A.** if

  **B.** else if

  **C.** elif

  **D.** elsif

**19.** Which of the following commands removes a currently defined aliased command?

**A.** remove

**B.** rm

**C.** unalias

**D.** delete

**20.** When sourcing a file in Bash, which chmod command would be necessary to provide the minimum privileges in order for the file to be sourced correctly, assuming that your current user owns the file?

**A.** chmod 600

**B.** chmod 755

**C.** chmod 777

**D.** chmod 400

**21.** Assuming that a space-separated list of values has been defined as LIST="one two three four", which of the following for loop constructs will iterate through the elements in the list?

**A.** for LIST

**B.** for VAR in LIST

**C.** for VAR in $LIST

**D.** for $LIST -> $VAR

**22.** Which test within a shell script while loop will examine one value to see if it is less than another?

**A.** -less

**B.** -lessThan

**C.** -lt

**D.** -lthan

**23.** Which of the following tests will determine if a file exists in the context of a shell script?

**A.** -a

**B.** -e

**C.** -m

**D.** -i

**24.** Within which directory should you place files to have them automatically copied to a user's home directory when the user is created?

**A.** /etc/userhome

**B.** /etc/templateuser

**C.** /etc/skel

**D.** /home/skel

**25.** Which option to bash will cause the shell to be executed without reading the initialization files?

   **A.** `--no-rc`

   **B.** `--no-init`

   **C.** `--norc`

   **D.** `--rc-none`

**26.** Which of the following creates an array in a Bash script?

   **A.** `ARRAY=(val1 val2)`

   **B.** `ARRAY = "val1 val2"`

   **C.** `ARRAY_PUSH($ARRAY,"val1","val2");`

   **D.** `ARRAY{0} = "val1"`

**27.** Which option of `declare` displays output in a way that could then be used as input to another command?

   **A.** `-o`

   **B.** `-n`

   **C.** `-p`

   **D.** `-m`

**28.** You need to create a function that will be available each time that you log in to the system. Within which file should this function be placed?

   **A.** `.bash_profile`

   **B.** `.rc`

   **C.** `/etc/profile`

   **D.** `.bash_run`

**29.** Which shell built-in command is used to display a list of read-only variables?

   **A.** `ro`

   **B.** `readonly`

   **C.** `env-ro`

   **D.** `ro-env`

**30.** Which characters are used to denote the beginning and end of the test portion of a `while` loop in a shell script?

   **A.** Parentheses ( )

   **B.** Curly braces { }

   **C.** Square brackets [ ]

   **D.** Double-quotes " "

31. When using the `test` built-in with one argument, what will be returned if its argument is not null?

    **A.** false

    **B.** true

    **C.** unknown

    **D.** -1

32. Which environment variable is used when changing directory with the tilde character, such as cd ~ ?

    **A.** HOMEDIR

    **B.** HOMEPATH

    **C.** HOME

    **D.** MAILPATH

33. Which environment variable can be set if you want to automatically log users out of their shell after a certain period of inactivity?

    **A.** TIMEOUT

    **B.** TMOUT

    **C.** TO

    **D.** IDLETIME

34. When using a `case` statement within a shell script, which sequence denotes the ending of the `case`/`switch` statement?

    **A.** caseend

    **B.** esac

    **C.** endcase

    **D.** }

35. Which of the following commands will obtain the date in seconds since the epoch and place it into a variable called DATE within a shell script?

    **A.** DATE="$(date +%s)"

    **B.** DATE="date"

    **C.** DATE="$(date)";

    **D.** DATE="$date %s"

36. Assume that you have a variable called $FILEPATH within a Bash shell script. Which characters can be used to ensure that the variable will be interpolated correctly regardless of where the variable appears within the script?

    **A.** Dollar sign: $FILEPATH

    **B.** Curly braces: ${FILEPATH}

    **C.** Parentheses: $(FILEPATH)

    **D.** Square brackets: $[FILEPATH]

**37.** Which sequence is used to mark the beginning and end of the commands to execute within a for loop in a shell script?

  **A.** Curly braces: {   }

  **B.** The keywords do and done

  **C.** Semicolons: ;

  **D.** Tabs

**38.** Which of the following tests will determine if a file exists and can be read by the user executing the test?

  **A.** -e

  **B.** -m

  **C.** -a

  **D.** -r

**39.** Which option of the declare command will create a variable that is read-only?

  **A.** -r

  **B.** -ro

  **C.** -p

  **D.** -x

**40.** Which character sequence is used to provide a default case when used within a case statement in a shell script?

  **A.** default:

  **B.** =)

  **C.** -->

  **D.** *)

**41.** Which character sequence can be used for command substitution in Bash?

  **A.** Backquotes: ` `

  **B.** Single quotes: ' '

  **C.** Double quotes: ""

  **D.** Backslashes: \\

**42.** When using a while loop in Bash, which character sequence marks the end of the loop?

  **A.** elihw

  **B.** done

  **C.** end

  **D.** od

**43.** Which operator is used to test if a value is greater than or equal to something in a Bash script?

    **A.** `!=`

    **B.** `>=`

    **C.** `=>`

    **D.** `>>`

**44.** You are working with a shell script called `listusers` and the script does not execute with the error `"permission denied"`. What could be the possible cause of this issue?

    **A.** The script should have an `.sh` extension.

    **B.** The script contains a syntax error.

    **C.** The script does not have its execute permission set correctly.

    **D.** The script is named with lowercase letters.

**45.** Which option to the `export` built-in command makes names available as functions to child processes?

    **A.** `-m`

    **B.** `-e`

    **C.** `-w`

    **D.** `-f`

**46.** If a variable has been created using the `set` command, which command can be used to remove the variable?

    **A.** `remove`

    **B.** `del`

    **C.** `delete`

    **D.** `unset`

**47.** Which of the following files is a systemwide initialization script for Bash?

    **A.** `/etc/bash.bashrc`

    **B.** `/etc/bash.init`

    **C.** `/etc/bash.cfg`

    **D.** `/etc/bash/bash.init`

**48.** Which option to the `set` command enables debugging output?

    **A.** `-d`

    **B.** `+d`

    **C.** `-x`

    **D.** `+x`

**49.** Which of the following files is executed with every interactive Bash shell invocation?

**A.** /etc/bash.d

**B.** /etc/bash.interactive

**C.** ~/.bash_inter

**D.** ~/.bashrc

**50.** Which keyword declares a block of code to be a function in a Bash script?

**A.** function

**B.** repeat

**C.** func

**D.** block

**51.** Which of the following statements adds the /srv/bin path to the path for a Bash shell?

**A.** PATH=/srv/bin

**B.** PATH=$PATH:/srv/bin

**C.** PATH = /srv/bin

**D.** PATH=/srv/bin;$PATH

**52.** Which variable is available to a Bash script and contains the name of the script itself?

**A.** $SCR

**B.** $SCRIPT

**C.** $CMD

**D.** $0

**53.** Which option to the seq command sets a delimiter of a space between the numbers 1 through 5?

**A.** seq -s ' ' 1 5

**B.** seq -d ' ' 1 5

**C.** seq 1 5

**D.** seq -m 1 5

**54.** Which file test is used to determine if you are the owner of the file being tested?

**A.** -m

**B.** -k

**C.** -w

**D.** -O

**55.** When testing a return value in a Bash script, which exit code indicates success?

**A.** 0

**B.** 1

**C.** 2

**D.** C

**56.** You have created a README file and placed it into /etc/skel so that users get the file in their home directories. The file is missing from some home directories on the system. Which of the following best explains this scenario?

    **A.** The file is not copied automatically for existing users.

    **B.** The file is too big for a user's home directory.

    **C.** The file already exists.

    **D.** The file needs a file extension.

**57.** You have a Bash script that uses the following find command:

```
find . -name ".git" -type d
```

When another administrator uses the script, it does not find all of the indicated directories. Which of the following is the best explanation for this scenario?

    **A.** The find command is tied to specific users.

    **B.** The find command cannot find directories beginning with a dot.

    **C.** The find command begins the search in the current directory.

    **D.** The find command cannot find directories.

**58.** You have specialized software that needs to be installed with an empty environment. Which option to the env command can be used to meet this requirement?

    **A.** -e

    **B.** –i

    **C.** -f

    **D.** -c

**59.** Which option enables debugging when used on the interpreter (#!) line within a Bash script?

    **A.** -x

    **B.** -d

    **C.** -a

    **D.** -f

**60.** Which of the following will output the number 5 as part of a Bash script?

    **A.** echo 2+3

    **B.** echo 2 + 3

    **C.** echo $[2+3]

    **D.** echo ${2+3}

**61.** You need to prompt the user to enter two values in a Bash script and capture them in variables VAL1 and VAL2. Which of the following commands can be used for this purpose?

    **A.** read VAL1 VAL2

    **B.** prompt VAL1 VAL2

    **C.** VAL1=$0 VAL2=$1

    **D.** (VAL1 VAL2) = prompt

**62.** Which option to the `export` built-in command removes a variable from being exported?

   **A.** `-m`

   **B.** `-o`

   **C.** `-r`

   **D.** `-n`

**63.** Which of the following tests the return value from the previous command to see if the command was successful?

   **A.** `if [ $? -eq 0 ];`

   **B.** `if [ $? = 0 ];`

   **C.** `if ($PREV == 0) {`

   **D.** `if [ $RETV === 0 ];`

**64.** You have a file containing bash functions. Which command can be used to add these functions to the current environment?

   **A.** `function`

   **B.** `include`

   **C.** `require`

   **D.** `source`

**65.** Which chmod command grants the user execute permission on a script?

   **A.** `chmod user += exec`

   **B.** `chmod u+x`

   **C.** `chmod 644`

   **D.** `chmod u+all`

**66.** Which `find` command will locate all files named with an `.sh` extension?

   **A.** `find / -name "*.sh"`

   **B.** `find / -name "*.sh" -type f`

   **C.** `find / -name "*.sh" -type d`

   **D.** `find ./ -name "*.sh"`

**67.** Which `unset` option can be used to remove a function from being defined?

   **A.** `-r`

   **B.** `-a`

   **C.** `-f`

   **D.** `-g`

**68.** When setting the shebang line of a shell script, which of the following commands will help to determine the location of the interpreter automatically?

   **A.** `#!/usr/bin/env bash`

   **B.** `#!/bin/bash`

   **C.** `#!env`

   **D.** `/bin/int bash`

**69.** Which mathematical operator is used for division within a Bash script?

   **A.** \

   **B.** /

   **C.** *

   **D.** //

**70.** You need to send an email to the superuser if a command is successful. Which of the following commands will send mail from a Bash script?

   **A.** smtpsend

   **B.** mailx

   **C.** sendm

   **D.** mailsend

**71.** Which file test operator is used to determine if the file is not zero size?

   **A.** -d

   **B.** -e

   **C.** -f

   **D.** -s

**72.** You have created an alias but it is gone the next time you log in. Which of the following best explains this scenario?

   **A.** The alias was not placed into an initialization script.

   **B.** The alias was invalid.

   **C.** The command is not valid for which the alias was created.

   **D.** The alias created an invalid symlink.

**73.** Which of the following is valid syntax to create a variable named FILENAME in a Bash script and set it equal to the second command-line argument?

   **A.** $FILENAME = $2

   **B.** FILENAME=1

   **C.** FILENAME = $(2)

   **D.** FILENAME=$2

**74.** You are working with a user who is reporting that their environment does not have certain variables defined, but other users do have those same variables available within their environment on login. The issue was not corrected by having the user log out and then log in again, and you can see their successful login. What is the most likely explanation for this issue?

   **A.** The user has logged in from the console.

   **B.** The user is using a different shell.

   **C.** The user has removed the environment variables manually.

   **D.** The user is logging in to a different system.

**75.** Which environment variable contains the username of the currently logged-in user?

- **A.** LOGNAME
- **B.** LOGIN
- **C.** LOGGEDIN
- **D.** LOGINUSER

**76.** Which file test operator is used to determine if the file is a symbolic link?

- **A.** -h
- **B.** -p
- **C.** -s
- **D.** -t

**77.** Which option to the readonly command marks a function as being read-only?

- **A.** -a
- **B.** -r
- **C.** -f
- **D.** -p

**78.** Which find command will locate all files where the users have the execute bit set?

- **A.** find ./ -type f -perm 700
- **B.** find / -type f -perm -u+x
- **C.** find / -type f -perm 777
- **D.** find / -type f -perm -execuser

**79.** According to the FHS, which of the following directories is used for local binaries?

- **A.** /usr/local/bin
- **B.** /usr/bin
- **C.** /usr/sbin
- **D.** /home/scripts

**80.** Which key sequence can be used to terminate a Bash script?

- **A.** Ctrl+d
- **B.** Ctrl+l
- **C.** Ctrl+a
- **D.** Ctrl+c

**81.** You need to view the current environment variables in a single line rather than with newlines separating each variable. Which option to the env command can be used for this purpose?

- **A.** -n
- **B.** -0
- **C.** -c
- **D.** -e

**82.** You are attempting to copy several files, but the cp command keeps asking for confirmation before overwriting. Which of the following best describes the most likely cause?

   **A.** The cp command has been compiled to ask for confirmation.

   **B.** The cp command always prompts for confirmation.

   **C.** The cp command cannot be used for the purpose described.

   **D.** The cp command has been aliased to include the -i option.

**83.** You receive an exit code of 1 when working with the grep command in a Bash script. What does exit code 1 mean with grep?

   **A.** Error

   **B.** Success

   **C.** Search pattern not found

   **D.** Search pattern found

**84.** Which of the file test operators is used to determine if a file is a directory?

   **A.** -e

   **B.** -d

   **C.** -w

   **D.** -a

**85.** Which of the following statements prepends the /usr/local/bin path to the path for a Bash shell?

   **A.** $PATH=/usr/local/bin:$PATH

   **B.** PATH=/usr/local/bin:$PATH

   **C.** PATH=$PATH:/usr/local/bin

   **D.** PATH=$PATH;/usr/local/bin

**86.** Which looping construct is executed at least once in a Bash script?

   **A.** while

   **B.** for

   **C.** until

   **D.** case

**87.** Which character or character sequence is equivalent to the source built-in in Bash?

   **A.** <>

   **B.** .

   **C.** ->

   **D.** %

**88.** Which option to the `export` built-in command displays the list of exported variables?

   **A.**  -p

   **B.**  -a

   **C.**  -t

   **D.**  -d

**89.** Which character or character sequence denotes the beginning of a `while` loop in a Bash script?

   **A.**  start

   **B.**  {

   **C.**  >>

   **D.**  do

# Chapter

# 6

# Topic 106: User Interfaces and Desktops

---

## THE FOLLOWING EXAM OBJECTIVES ARE COVERED IN THIS CHAPTER:

✓ **106.1 Install and configure X11.**

- Key knowledge areas:

  - Understanding of the X11 architecture

  - Basic understanding and knowledge of the X Window configuration file

  - Overwrite specific aspects of Xorg configuration, such as keyboard layout.

  - Understand the components of desktop environments, such as display managers and window managers.

  - Manage access to the X server and display applications on remote X servers.

  - Awareness of Wayland

- The following is a partial list of the used files, terms, and utilities:

  - /etc/X11/xorg.conf

  - /etc/X11/xorg.conf.d/

  - ~/.xsession-errors

  - xhost

  - xauth

  - DISPLAY

  - X

## ✓ 106.2 Graphical desktops

- Key knowledge areas:
  - Awareness of major desktop environments
  - Awareness of protocols to access remote desktop sessions
- The following is a partial list of the used files, terms, and utilities:
  - KDE
  - Gnome
  - Xfce
  - X11
  - XDMCP
  - VNC
  - Spice
  - RDP

## ✓ 106.3 Accessibility

- Key knowledge areas:
  - Basic knowledge of visual settings and themes
  - Basic knowledge of assistive technology
- The following is a partial list of the used files, terms, and utilities:
  - High contrast/large print desktop themes
  - Screen reader
  - Braille display
  - Screen magnifier
  - On-screen keyboard
  - Sticky/repeat keys
  - Slow/bounce/toggle keys
  - Mouse keys
  - Gestures
  - Voice recognition

1. Within which configuration file is the greeter configured for LightDM?

   **A.** `/etc/lightdm/lightdm.conf`

   **B.** `/etc/lightdm/greeter.conf`

   **C.** `/etc/lightdm.conf`

   **D.** `/var/lib/lightdm/lightdm.conf`

2. Which section in `/etc/X11/xorg.conf` is used to describe configurations for a given graphics card and monitor pair?

   **A.** `Server`

   **B.** `Screen`

   **C.** `VidMode`

   **D.** `Video`

3. When you're setting the frequency options for a given monitor, which of the following is not an available frequency unit?

   **A.** uHz

   **B.** MHz

   **C.** kHz

   **D.** M

4. Which command on a systemd-based system is used to disable booting into a GUI?

   **A.** `systemctl gui-boot disable`

   **B.** `systemctl set-default boot-gui false`

   **C.** `systemctl set-default multi-user.target`

   **D.** `systemctl set-default-multi false`

5. Assuming X forwarding has been enabled on the SSH server, which environment variable is used to set the location for newly spawned windows from within an SSH session?

   **A.** `DISPLAY`

   **B.** `XTERMINAL`

   **C.** `XTERM`

   **D.** `XDISP`

6. Within the greeter section of a display manager such as GNOME Display Manager (GDM), which option sets the welcome message for users logging in locally?

   **A.** `LoginMessage`

   **B.** `Login`

   **C.** `WinGreet`

   **D.** `Welcome`

7. Within GNOME, enabling sticky keys can be done by pressing which key five times in a row?

   **A.** Ctrl

   **B.** Enter

   **C.** Shift

   **D.** Tab

8. Which option in the Module section of the `xorg.conf` configuration file causes a default module to be unloaded or not loaded by default?

   **A.** `Disable`

   **B.** `Unload`

   **C.** `LoadDisable`

   **D.** `DisableLoad`

9. Which program is used in a GNOME environment as a screen reader?

   **A.** Orca

   **B.** Screed

   **C.** Screen

   **D.** Reader

10. Assuming a monitor that is currently set at 1024×768, which command will change the screen resolution so that icons and other elements appear larger?

    **A.** `xterm -r 0`

    **B.** `xset res 1024x768`

    **C.** `xrandr -s 800x600`

    **D.** `xVGA`

11. LightDM typically allows guest login by default. Which configuration option within `SeatDefaults` changes this to disallow guests?

    **A.** `guest-login=false`

    **B.** `guest=false`

    **C.** `allowg=false`

    **D.** `allow-guest=false`

12. When using XFree86 as the X server, which command will cause the X server to query for hardware and create a new configuration file?

    **A.** `XFree86 --newconfig`

    **B.** `XFree86 --query`

    **C.** `XFree96 -configure`

    **D.** `xf -config`

**13.** Which configuration option for X is used to configure the keyboard model?

    **A.** XkbLayout

    **B.** XkbModel

    **C.** XkbType

    **D.** XkbInput

**14.** Which configuration line with a Monitor section of an X server configuration file will set the vertical refresh rate between 55 and 75 hertz?

    **A.** Vert 55-75

    **B.** VertRefresh 55.0 - 75.0

    **C.** VertSync 55.0 - 75.0

    **D.** RefreshMode 55.0 - 75.0

**15.** Within which file can a user place commands for executing X clients?

    **A.** ~/.xclients

    **B.** ~/.xsess.rc

    **C.** ~/.xsessrc

    **D.** ~/.xsession

**16.** Which AccelerationProfile for an input device such as a mouse enables linear acceleration (more speed and more acceleration)?

    **A.** 0

    **B.** −1

    **C.** 6

    **D.** 7

**17.** Which of the following directories is used by an Xorg-based server for storage of fonts?

    **A.** /usr/share/fonts

    **B.** /usr/X11/fonts

    **C.** /etc/fonts

    **D.** /var/font/xorg

**18.** Native support for a Braille display requires a minimum of which kernel version?

    **A.** 2.2.0

    **B.** 2.4.22

    **C.** 2.6.26

    **D.** 3.2.1

19. Which configuration option in an `xorg.conf` file can be set to prevent a user from changing video modes using the Ctrl+Alt+Keypad-Plus and Ctrl+Alt+Keypad-Minus?

    **A.** `DontZoom`

    **B.** `Modes=No`

    **C.** `NoModeSwitch`

    **D.** `DontZap`

20. In which location does the `xauth` utility look for the X authority file?

    **A.** `~/.Xauth`

    **B.** `~/.xauth.cfg`

    **C.** `~/.Xauthority`

    **D.** `~/.xau`

21. Access to hosts controlled with XDMCP is configured in which file?

    **A.** `xdmcp.access.conf`

    **B.** `XDMCPAccess.cfg`

    **C.** `Xaccess`

    **D.** `XDaccess.conf`

22. When using KDE, which program provides magnification functionality?

    **A.** xmag

    **B.** mag

    **C.** pmag

    **D.** kmag

23. Which signal is used by an X server to cause a clean exit?

    **A.** `SIGTERM`

    **B.** `SIGKILL`

    **C.** `SIGCLEAN`

    **D.** `SIGEX`

24. Within GNOME, which section of GNOME Control Center is used to choose a high-contrast theme?

    **A.** Display

    **B.** Appearance

    **C.** Locale

    **D.** Contrast

25. Which of the following best describes the concept of a mouse gesture?

    **A.** A mouse gesture enables special clicks, such as a right-click context menu.

    **B.** A mouse gesture facilitates the use of programs by moving the mouse in a certain way.

   **C.**  A mouse gesture is used for login purposes.

   **D.**  A mouse gesture is used to capture screenshots.

**26.** In GNOME 3.9 or later, which keyboard shortcut activates the screen reader?

   **A.**  Super+R

   **B.**  Super+S

   **C.**  Ctrl+Super+S

   **D.**  Alt+Super+S

**27.** Assume that the display manager has been disabled on boot. Which command can be used after login to start the X server?

   **A.**  xs

   **B.**  xstart

   **C.**  X -start

   **D.**  startx

**28.** Which option in an xorg.conf file configures the amount of time before the screen goes into blank mode but does not go into standby and is available on non-Display Power Management Signaling (DPMS)-capable monitors?

   **A.**  StandbyTime

   **B.**  BlankTime

   **C.**  SuspendTime

   **D.**  OffTime

**29.** Which of the following commands helps you to determine information about a given window within an X session, including information on the window size and its position?

   **A.**  xkbinfo

   **B.**  xdspy

   **C.**  xwininfo

   **D.**  xver

**30.** Which option/button on the GNOME On-Screen Keyboard (GOK) is used show the keys that would be used in place of a mouse?

   **A.**  Mouse

   **B.**  MouseKeys

   **C.**  Movement

   **D.**  Compose

**31.** Which of the following commands allows a host named cwa to connect to the X server?

   **A.** xconnect cwa

   **B.** xterm +cwa

   **C.** xhost +cwa

   **D.** xf cwa

**32.** Which of the following options in the client SSH configuration file needs to be enabled so that X sessions can be sent over an SSH connection?

   **A.** X11Connect yes

   **B.** ForwardX11 yes

   **C.** ForwardX yes

   **D.** XForward yes

**33.** Which configuration option in a Files section of an xorg.conf configuration file can be used to add a path in which the server will search for fonts?

   **A.** FontSection

   **B.** Fonts

   **C.** FontLoc

   **D.** FontPath

**34.** Which assistive technology is used to provide an input method for users who cannot type but can use a pointer, such as a mouse?

   **A.** Keyboard

   **B.** Sticky keys

   **C.** Mouse keys

   **D.** On-screen keyboard

**35.** Which environment variable can be used to specify the location of a user's xauth authority file?

   **A.** XAUTH

   **B.** USERXAUTH

   **C.** XAUTHORITY

   **D.** xauthloc

**36.** When using LightDM, which key combination is used to revert back to a terminal?

   **A.** Alt+Ctrl+F2

   **B.** Alt+Ctrl+F1

   **C.** Ctrl+F1

   **D.** Ctrl+Esc

**37.** Which option in the LightDM configuration enables automatic login for a specific user?

- **A.** `auto-login`
- **B.** `autologin-user`
- **C.** `autologin`
- **D.** `auto-login-user`

**38.** Which of the following is a legacy utility that can be used to set accessibility options on older systems?

- **A.** Xaccessibility
- **B.** Xas
- **C.** AccessX
- **D.** setX

**39.** Which command, when executed on a remote host, will send the display of X programs to the local client? (Assume Bash is used as the shell.)

- **A.** `export DISPLAY`
- **B.** `env DISPLAY`
- **C.** `setx HOST`
- **D.** `export XHOST`

**40.** Which option in GOK is used to display the keys that correspond to a given application's menu?

- **A.** Menus
- **B.** Activate
- **C.** MenuKeys
- **D.** Keys

**41.** Which directory is used to store individual configuration files related to LightDM?

- **A.** `/etc/light`
- **B.** `/etc/lightdm/lightdm.conf.d`
- **C.** `/usr/lightdm`
- **D.** `/etc/lightdm.conf`

**42.** Which environment variable is used by Xsession to specify the width of a terminal device?

- **A.** `TERMCHAR`
- **B.** `COLUMNS`
- **C.** `CHARACTERWIDTH`
- **D.** `TERMCOL`

**43.** Which option within the `Device` section for a video card will set the amount of RAM available on the card?

    **A.** VRAM

    **B.** RAM

    **C.** VideoRam

    **D.** vRam

**44.** When configuring a `Screen` section in an X configuration file, the `Display` subsection can contain the color depth. What is the name of the option to set the color depth of the given display?

    **A.** ColorDepth

    **B.** Depth

    **C.** CDepth

    **D.** colorDep

**45.** Multiple server layouts may be created within an X configuration file. Which option is used to differentiate between the different server layout options?

    **A.** ID

    **B.** Identifier

    **C.** LayoutName

    **D.** Layout

**46.** Which command can be used to create a `fonts.scale` file definition when executed against the current directory?

    **A.** mkfontsscale

    **B.** mk.fonts

    **C.** mkfontfile

    **D.** fontmk

**47.** What abbreviation used in X signifies a display that utilizes additional capabilities such as extended power-saving capabilities?

    **A.** DPMS

    **B.** XPMS

    **C.** DISPPWR

    **D.** PWRD

**48.** What is the name of the accessibility function that provides an alternative to the Orca program to assist users who have visual impairments?

    **A.** Viz

    **B.** emacspeak

    **C.** Ahleah

    **D.** vAssist

**49.** Which of the following is a reference implementation of the Wayland protocol?

    **A.** Wlnd

    **B.** Weston

    **C.** Wausau

    **D.** Wittenberg

**50.** Within an xorg configuration file, which option sets the inactivity timeout for the suspend mode of a DPMS-capable monitor?

    **A.** InactTimeout

    **B.** InactivityTime

    **C.** SuspendTime

    **D.** InTmout

**51.** When the X server is started as a normal user, configuration files from which directory are also included?

    **A.** /etc/X

    **B.** /etc/X11/UserConfig

    **C.** /etc/X11/xorg.conf.d

    **D.** /etc/X/UserConf.d/

**52.** Which of the following remote desktop protocols uses no compression or transport/session encryption?

    **A.** SSH

    **B.** XDMCP

    **C.** XR

    **D.** RD

**53.** Within which desktop implementation would you find the xfwm4 window manager?

    **A.** XWin

    **B.** KDXF

    **C.** Exf

    **D.** Xfce

**54.** Which option to Spice startup disables simple authentication?

    **A.** disable-auth

    **B.** disable-ticketing

    **C.** disable-authentication

    **D.** disable-simpleauth

**55.** Which speech recognition software is included with the KDE desktop environment?

   **A.** Alvin

   **B.** Simon

   **C.** Theodore

   **D.** Zeppo

**56.** Within the GNOME 3 desktop environment, within which Settings panel are the options for slow keys found?

   **A.** Access

   **B.** Typing Settings

   **C.** Keyboard

   **D.** Universal Access

**57.** When an X session is already running, which command can be used to enable pointer keys?

   **A.** setxkbmap

   **B.** ptrkeys

   **C.** pointerkeys

   **D.** keypad -ptrkeys

**58.** Which of the following provides a server-side implementation of Remote Desktop (RDP) for Linux?

   **A.** lrdp

   **B.** xrdp

   **C.** rdp-linux

   **D.** lindp

**59.** You are attempting to edit the sudoers file with visudo over an SSH connection on a system that has GNOME installed and you receive an error indicating that gedit cannot run. Which of the following commands can be used to solve this issue?

   **A.** export VISUAL="/bin/vim"

   **B.** export DISPLAY

   **C.** subst DISPLAY=local

   **D.** env VISUAL=ssh

**60.** Which option to x11vnc sets the password to be used for clients connecting to the server?

   **A.** -password

   **B.** -passwd

   **C.** -pass

   **D.** -auth

**61.** Which program is used to add entries to the X authority file?

    **A.** xf

    **B.** xauthen

    **C.** authx

    **D.** xauth

**62.** Which assistive technology will ignore keys that are pressed in succession or held down?

    **A.** Sticky keys

    **B.** Mouse keys

    **C.** Bounce keys

    **D.** On-screen keyboard

**63.** Which environment variable is used by Xsession if the Xsession error file cannot be opened in its default location?

    **A.** XLOG

    **B.** TMPDIR

    **C.** SESSLOG

    **D.** LOGTMP

**64.** From within an X session, which of the following commands shows information about the display, including resolution and color depth?

    **A.** xinfo

    **B.** xterm

    **C.** xwin

    **D.** xdpyinfo

**65.** Which of the following files is the configuration file for Weston?

    **A.** ~/.config/weston.cfg

    **B.** ~/.config/weston.ini

    **C.** ~/weston.cfg

    **D.** ~/.westoncfg

**66.** Which of the following remote desktop programs offers transport layer security?

    **A.** x11vnc

    **B.** xrd

    **C.** tls

    **D.** x11rtm

**67.** Which add-on to Orca enables braille display support?

    **A.** `brl`

    **B.** `brltty`

    **C.** `brldis`

    **D.** `dispbrl`

**68.** Which of the following is a screen magnifier program?

    **A.** xmag

    **B.** xzoom

    **C.** xzmag

    **D.** scrmag

**69.** Which GRUB variable can be used to beep when the GRUB prompt is ready to accept input?

    **A.** `GRUB_BEEP`

    **B.** `BEEP_START`

    **C.** `GRUB_START_TONE`

    **D.** `GRUB_INIT_TUNE`

**70.** You need to remove a host from being able to connect to the X server. Which of the following will remove a host named `cwa` from being able to connect?

    **A.** `xrem cwa`

    **B.** `xhost -cwa`

    **C.** `xhost -rem:cwa`

    **D.** `xrem -host cwa`

**71.** The X Display Manager, xdm, runs various scripts as part of the login process. Which of the following scripts is executed as the user logging in?

    **A.** `Xstart`

    **B.** `Xsession`

    **C.** `Xstartup`

    **D.** `Xuser.conf`

**72.** Which option to the X server disables listening for TCP connections?

    **A.** `-nolisten tcp`

    **B.** `-notcp`

    **C.** `-noconn tcp`

    **D.** `-noconnect tcp`

**73.** Which signal is used to close existing connections, free resources, and restore defaults for an X server?

   **A.** SIGKILL

   **B.** SIGHUP

   **C.** SIGN4

   **D.** SIGALL

**74.** Which option in the SeatDefaults section of the lightdm.conf configuration file is used to disable the display of usernames for login?

   **A.** greeter-disable-user

   **B.** greeter-enable-login

   **C.** greeter-show-manual-login

   **D.** greeter-disable-auto-login

**75.** Which option to the xauth program disables hostname resolution?

   **A.** -r

   **B.** -n

   **C.** -h

   **D.** -m

**76.** Which command will switch the system into an init in which the X server is not typically executed?

   **A.** telinit 6

   **B.** telinit 1

   **C.** telinit 3

   **D.** telinit 5

**77.** What is the default location for the error log if the X server is run with xdm?

   **A.** /etc/X11.log

   **B.** /var/log/Xdm.log

   **C.** /usr/lib/X11/xdm/xdm-errors

   **D.** /var/log/xdmerrors

**78.** Which script can be used for per-user initialization of xinit?

   **A.** ~/.xinit.conf

   **B.** ~/.xinitrc

   **C.** ~/.xinit.rc

   **D.** ~/.xinit.cfg

**79.** Which option prevents abstract sockets from listening with X11?

    **A.**  `-nolisten sock`

    **B.**  `-nolisten absock`

    **C.**  `-nolisten local`

    **D.**  `-nolisten socklocal`

**80.** Which option to XDMCP enables sending of BroadcastQuery packets?

    **A.**  `-bcast`

    **B.**  `-bcastQ`

    **C.**  `-broadcastQuery`

    **D.**  `-broadcast`

**81.** When using GDM as the display manager, which GUI program can be used to set options for the login window?

    **A.**  `gdmlogin`

    **B.**  `gdmconfig`

    **C.**  `gdmsetup`

    **D.**  `gdm`

**82.** Within the XDMCP access configuration file, there is a line like the following:

`*.example.com`

Which of the following describes how access will be treated for hosts from `example.com`?

    **A.**  Only the host named `*.example.com` can connect.

    **B.**  No hosts from `example.com` can connect.

    **C.**  Any host within `example.com` can connect.

    **D.**  Hosts that begin with `*` within `example.com` can connect.

**83.** When using xhost, what is the syntax to enable a host named `san` to connect using IPv6?

    **A.**  `xhost +ipv6:san`

    **B.**  `xhost -enablev6 san`

    **C.**  `xhost +inet6:san`

    **D.**  `xhost +enablev6 san`

**84.** Within which file are errors for Xsession and X client processes placed?

    **A.**  `~/.xsession-error.log`

    **B.**  `~/.xsession-errors`

    **C.**  `~/.xclient.log`

    **D.**  `~/.xclient.errorlog`

**85.** GNOME includes native on-screen keyboard functionality. Which of the following commands starts the on-screen keyboard?

- **A.** gok
- **B.** osk
- **C.** kb
- **D.** oskb

**86.** Which option to the xauth program specifies the authority file to use?

- **A.** -a
- **B.** -f
- **C.** -a
- **D.** -v

**87.** Which accessibility option is helpful if several keys are sometimes pressed or if there is difficulty in consistently pressing the correct key on the keyboard?

- **A.** Key toggle
- **B.** Slow keys
- **C.** KeyAssist
- **D.** UniversalKeys

**88.** On which port does RDP listen by default?

- **A.** 389
- **B.** 8080
- **C.** 3389
- **D.** 3306

# Chapter

# 7

# Topic 107: Administrative Tasks

## THE FOLLOWING EXAM OBJECTIVES ARE COVERED IN THIS CHAPTER:

✓ **107.1  Manage user and group accounts and related system files.**

- Key knowledge areas:
  - Add, modify, and remove users and groups.
  - Manage user/group info in password/group databases.
  - Create and manage special purpose and limited accounts.
- The following is a partial list of the used files, terms, and utilities:
  - /etc/passwd
  - /etc/shadow
  - /etc/group
  - /etc/skel/
  - chage
  - getent
  - groupadd
  - groupdel
  - groupmod
  - passwd
  - useradd
  - userdel
  - usermod

✓ **107.2 Automate system administration tasks by scheduling jobs.**

- Key knowledge areas:

  - Manage cron and at jobs.

  - Configure user access to cron and at services.

  - Understand systemd timer units.

- The following is a partial list of the used files, terms, and utilities:

  - /etc/cron.{d,daily,hourly,monthly,weekly}/

  - /etc/at.deny

  - /etc/at.allow

  - /etc/crontab

  - /etc/cron.allow

  - /etc/cron.deny

  - /var/spool/cron

  - crontab

  - at

  - atq

  - atrm

  - systemctl

  - systemd-run

✓ **107.3 Localization and internationalization**

- Key knowledge areas:

  - Configure locale settings and environment variables.

  - Configure time zone settings and environment variables.

- The following is a partial list of the used files, terms, and utilities:

  - /etc/timezone

  - /etc/localtime

  - /usr/share/zoneinfo/

  - LC_*

- LC_ALL
- LANG
- TZ
- /usr/bin/locale
- tzselect
- timedatectl
- date
- iconv
- UTF-8
- ISO-8859
- ASCII
- Unicode

1. You need to enable the web server (running as the www-data user and group) to write into a directory called /home/webfiles. Which commands will accomplish this task in the most secure manner?

   **A.** chgrp  www-data /home/webfiles ; chmod 775 /home/webfiles

   **B.** chmod 777 /home/webfiles

   **C.** chgrp www-data /home/webfiles ; chmod 711 /home/webfiles

   **D.** chmod 707 /home/webfiles

2. Which of the following will execute a job through cron at 12:15 a.m. and 12:15 p.m. every day?

   **A.** 0,12 15 * * *

   **B.** 15 0,12 * * *

   **C.** 15 * * * 0/12

   **D.** */12 * * * 15

3. Which file is used to indicate the local time zone on a Linux server?

   **A.** /etc/timez

   **B.** /etc/timezoneconfig

   **C.** /etc/localtime

   **D.** /etc/localtz

4. When importing entries into the LDAP database using ldapadd -f <filename>, in which format should the file be?

   **A.** LDAP

   **B.** TXT

   **C.** CSV

   **D.** LDIF

5. Which of the following commands removes an expiration from an account?

   **A.** sudo chage -l username

   **B.** sudo chage -E -1 username

   **C.** sudo chage -E now username

   **D.** sudo chage --noexpire username

6. Within which directory will you find files related to the time zone for various regions?

   **A.** /etc/timezoneinfo

   **B.** /etc/zoneinfo

   **C.** /var/zoneinfo

   **D.** /usr/share/zoneinfo

**7.** Which of the following commands schedules a series of commands to execute 1 hour from now?

   **A.** atq +1hr

   **B.** at now + 1 hour

   **C.** atq

   **D.** at -1

**8.** You need to delete a user from the system, including their home directory. Which of the following commands accomplishes this task?

   **A.** userdel

   **B.** userdel -r

   **C.** userdel -R

   **D.** deluser

**9.** Which file contains a list of usernames, UIDs, and encrypted passwords?

   **A.** /etc/passwd

   **B.** /etc/shadow

   **C.** /etc/encpass

   **D.** /etc/grouppass

**10.** Which job scheduler should you use if the computer on which you need to schedule the job is powered down at various times?

   **A.** cron.d

   **B.** cron.hourly

   **C.** anacron

   **D.** at

**11.** Which of the following commands provides the current date and time in a format of seconds since the epoch?

   **A.** date +%seconds

   **B.** date +%s

   **C.** date --seconds

   **D.** date --now

**12.** Which option to the iconv command shows the available character sets on a given system?

   **A.** --showchar

   **B.** --show

   **C.** --list

   **D.** --all

**13.** Which environment variable controls the format of dates and times, such as a 12-hour or 24-hour formatted clock?

    **A.** LOCALE_DATE

    **B.** DATE_FORMAT

    **C.** LC_TIME

    **D.** LC_DATE

**14.** Which command is recommended for configuration of slapd for OpenLDAP versions 2.3 and later?

    **A.** slapd-conf

    **B.** config-slapd

    **C.** openldap-config

    **D.** slapd-config

**15.** Which shortcut within cron enables running of a task every day at midnight?

    **A.** @daily

    **B.** @daybegin

    **C.** @topday

    **D.** @beginday

**16.** Which of the following encoding provides a multibyte representation of characters?

    **A.** ISO-8859

    **B.** UTF-8

    **C.** ISO-L

    **D.** UFTMulti

**17.** Which of the following commands changes a group called DomainAdmins to DomainUsers?

    **A.** groupmod -n DomainAdmins DomainUsers

    **B.** groupchg DomainAdmins DomainUsers

    **C.** chgroup DomainAdmins DomainUsers

    **D.** group -N DomainAdmins DomainUsers

**18.** Which file stores group information on a Linux server?

    **A.** /etc/groupinfo

    **B.** /etc/groups

    **C.** /etc/roles

    **D.** /etc/group

**19.** Which command can be used to create an LDIF file from the current LDAP database?

    **A.** slapdump

    **B.** ldapdump

    **C.** slapcat

    **D.** catldap

**20.** You are looking for a scheduled job that is not found in /etc/crontab, through systemd timers, or within /var/spool/cron. What is another location in which the scheduled job might be stored?

    **A.** /etc/crontabs

    **B.** /etc/cron.conf

    **C.** /etc/cron.d/

    **D.** /etc/sked

**21.** You need to determine if LDAP integration is working correctly. In order to do so, you would like to obtain a list of users, as read by /etc/nsswitch.conf. Which command can be used for this purpose?

    **A.** getuser

    **B.** getent

    **C.** usermod

    **D.** userlist

**22.** What is the name of the configuration file that contains information about group and user addition, such as the maximum and minimum user and group IDs, to be used when adding users and groups?

    **A.** /etc/groupinfo

    **B.** /etc/login.defs

    **C.** /etc/login.info

    **D.** /etc/loginlist

**23.** Which environment variable is used for localization related to measurement units such as metric?

    **A.** LC_METRIC

    **B.** LC_MEASURE

    **C.** LC_MEASUREMENT

    **D.** LC_MEASUREUNITS

**24.** Which of the following lines added to .profile in a user's home directory will set their time zone to Central time?

    **A.** TZ=/Central ; export TZ

    **B.** TIMEZONE='America/Chicago' ; export TIMEZONE

    **C.** set TZ=/Central

    **D.** TZ='America/Chicago'; export TZ

**25.** Within which directory will you find scripts that are scheduled to run through `cron` every 24 hours?

**A.** `/etc/cron.daily`

**B.** `/etc/cron.weekly`

**C.** `/etc/cron.hourly24`

**D.** `/etc/crontab`

**26.** Which of the following values for the LANG variable will configure the system to bypass locale translations where possible?

**A.** `LANG=COMPAT`

**B.** `LANG=NONE`

**C.** `LANG=C`

**D.** `LANG=END`

**27.** When running `useradd`, which option needs to be specified in order for the user's home directory to be created?

**A.** `-h`

**B.** `-m`

**C.** `-x`

**D.** `-a`

**28.** Which of the following commands locks out password-based login for a user but does not prevent other forms of login?

**A.** `usermod -L`

**B.** `userdel -r`

**C.** `useradd -h`

**D.** `userlock`

**29.** If you need to temporarily reconfigure all locale variables and settings for a given session, which environment variable can be used?

**A.** `LC_LIST`

**B.** `LC_GLOBAL`

**C.** `LC_ALL`

**D.** `ALL_LOCALE`

**30.** Which of the following will run a command called /usr/local/bin/changehome.sh as the www-data user when placed in /etc/crontab?

**A.** `1 1 * * * www-data /usr/local/bin/changehome.sh`

**B.** `www-data changehome.sh`

**C.** `*/1 www-data changehome.sh`

**D.** `* * */www-data /usr/local/bin/changehome.sh`

**31.** Which of the following commands produces a report listing the last password change date for all users on the system?

    **A.** passwd -a

    **B.** passwd -S

    **C.** passwd -a -S

    **D.** passwd --all

**32.** Assume that passwords must be changed every 60 days. Which command will change the date of the user's last password change without the user actually changing the account password?

    **A.** chage -f

    **B.** chage -W

    **C.** chage -l

    **D.** chage -d

**33.** Which of the following files is used by anacron for reading configuration information related to jobs?

    **A.** /etc/anacron.d

    **B.** /etc/anacrontab

    **C.** /etc/anacron.config

    **D.** /etc/anacron.conf

**34.** Which of the following commands is used to add entries to the OpenLDAP database?

    **A.** ldapd

    **B.** adduser

    **C.** addldap

    **D.** ldapadd

**35.** Which file contains a list of users who are not allowed to create cron scheduled tasks?

    **A.** /etc/cron.users

    **B.** /etc/cron.deny

    **C.** /etc/cron.denyusers

    **D.** /etc/cron.userlist

**36.** You are viewing the /etc/passwd file and see a * where the password should be. What does the presence of a * indicate within the password file?

    **A.** The system uses forward password aging.

    **B.** The system uses shadow passwords.

    **C.** The system has been compromised.

    **D.** Users have a * for their passwords.

**37.** Which of the following best describes the relationship between UIDs and GIDs on a Linux system?

**A.** The UID and GID are the same across the system for a given user.

**B.** Each user has a UID and GID that are the same and are created when the user is created.

**C.** The UID represents the user whereas the GID is a globally unique user ID.

**D.** There is no direct relationship between UID and GID.

**38.** Which of the following commands is used to re-create indexes based on existing `slapd` databases?

**A.** `ldapind`

**B.** `ldapindex`

**C.** `slapindex`

**D.** `indexldap`

**39.** Which command is used to change a user's home directory to `/srv/data/username` and move the contents at the same time?

**A.** `usermod -md /srv/data/username <username>`

**B.** `homedir -m /srv/data/username <username>`

**C.** `userex -m /srv/data/username <username>`

**D.** `userchg /m /srv/data/username -d <username>`

**40.** Which option to `useradd` will add groups for a user?

**A.** `-g`

**B.** `-x`

**C.** `-l`

**D.** `-G`

**41.** Which command will list the `cron` entries for a given user as denoted by `<username>`?

**A.** `crontab -l -u <username>`

**B.** `crontab -u <username>`

**C.** `cron -u <username>`

**D.** `cronent -u <username>`

**42.** Which option to `useradd` creates a system user rather than a normal user?

**A.** `-r`

**B.** `-s`

**C.** `-a`

**D.** `-S`

**43.** Which file contains encrypted password information for groups?

    **A.** /etc/group

    **B.** /etc/gshadow

    **C.** /etc/gsecure

    **D.** /etc/group.conf

**44.** Which of the following commands can be used to help with recovery of a corrupted OpenLDAP database?

    **A.** openldap-recover

    **B.** oreco

    **C.** slapd-recover

    **D.** slapd_db_recover

**45.** Which of the following best describes the use of the groupdel command?

    **A.** You may force group deletion with the -f option.

    **B.** If a user's primary group is to be deleted, that user must be deleted first or have their primary group changed.

    **C.** groupdel can be run at any time, regardless of group membership.

    **D.** The -r option for groupdel will recursively change user's GIDs after group deletion.

**46.** Which of the following commands displays the UID, primary group, and supplemental groups for a given user?

    **A.** id

    **B.** getid

    **C.** passwd

    **D.** chage

**47.** Which option to the usermod command is used to change a given user's real name?

    **A.** -R

    **B.** -n

    **C.** -d

    **D.** -c

**48.** Assume that you have deleted a user account with UID 1501, including the -r option. Which command should you also run to look for other files that might have been owned by the user?

    **A.** find -id 1501

    **B.** grep 1501 *

    **C.** grep -u 1501 *

    **D.** find / -uid 1501

**49.** On which port does the slapd LDAP daemon listen for connections?

    **A.** 389

    **B.** 3389

    **C.** 3306

    **D.** 110

**50.** Which of the following commands will set the systemwide time zone to America/Los_Angeles?

    **A.** ln -sf /usr/share/zoneinfo/America/Los_Angeles /etc/localtime

    **B.** ln -sf America/Los_Angeles ; /etc/localtime

    **C.** ln -sd /etc/localtime /usr/share/timezone/America/Los_Angeles

    **D.** ln -sf /etc/localtime /usr/share/zoneinfo/America/Los_Angeles

**51.** Which locale-related variable is used for currency-related localization?

    **A.** LC_MONE

    **B.** LC_CURRENCY

    **C.** LC_MONETARY

    **D.** LC_CURR

**52.** Which option to systemd-run adds a timed event?

    **A.** --timed

    **B.** --add-timer

    **C.** --on-calendar

    **D.** --on-time

**53.** Which file is used to provide a list of users who can add and delete cron jobs?

    **A.** /etc/cron.job

    **B.** /etc/cron.allow

    **C.** /etc/cron.users

    **D.** /etc/crontab

**54.** Which debug level for slapd is used to provide debugging of configuration file processing?

    **A.** 1

    **B.** 64

    **C.** 8

    **D.** 0

**55.** Which command deletes an at job with an ID of 3?

    **A.** atdt

    **B.** at -l

    **C.** atrm 3

    **D.** rmat 3

**56.** Which command on a Debian-based system can be used to change the time zone using the package-based tools?

   **A.** dpkg-reconfigure time

   **B.** dpkg-reconfigure tzdata

   **C.** apt-select tzdata

   **D.** apt-config timezone

**57.** What will be logged with the loglevel set to 0x10 in a slapd.conf configuration file?

   **A.** No debugging

   **B.** Trace debugging

   **C.** Stats logging

   **D.** Packets sent and received

**58.** Within which directory should you place files in order for the files to be copied to a user's home directory when the user is created?

   **A.** /etc/skel

   **B.** /etc/homedir

   **C.** /home/usertemplate

   **D.** /etc/template

**59.** Which command displays a list of jobs currently scheduled with at?

   **A.** atlist

   **B.** atq

   **C.** atl

   **D.** at --jobs

**60.** On which port does LDAP over SSL listen for connections?

   **A.** 389

   **B.** 443

   **C.** 636

   **D.** 3128

**61.** Which scheduler can be used to schedule a command to run once at a certain time?

   **A.** at

   **B.** cron

   **C.** job

   **D.** jobctl

**62.** Which file provides a list of users who are allowed to create at jobs?

   **A.** /etc/at.users

   **B.** /etc/at.scheduler

   **C.** /etc/at.conf

   **D.** /etc/at.allow

**63.** Which file extension is used for `systemd` timer units?

   **A.** `.conf`

   **B.** `.timer`

   **C.** `.timerd`

   **D.** `.timeevent`

**64.** Within which directory would you find a list of files corresponding to the users who have current `cron` jobs on the system?

   **A.** `/var/spool/cron/crontabs`

   **B.** `/var/spool/jobs`

   **C.** `/etc/cron`

   **D.** `/etc/cron.users`

**65.** When using `slapadd` for a large import, an error occurs at roughly 90 percent completion. Which option to `slapadd` enables specification of a line number from which the import will be restarted?

   **A.** `-l`

   **B.** `-f`

   **C.** `-q`

   **D.** `-j`

**66.** Which argument to the `locale` command displays currently available locales for a given system?

   **A.** `-c`

   **B.** `-a`

   **C.** `-p`

   **D.** `-s`

**67.** Which option to `timedatectl` sets the system clock?

   **A.** `--adjust-system-clock`

   **B.** `-s`

   **C.** `-c`

   **D.** `-a`

**68.** Which option to the `file` command displays information on the MIME type of the file being interrogated?

   **A.** `-i`

   **B.** `-m`

   **C.** `-l`

   **D.** `-a`

**69.** Which environment variable is used to set the paper size?

**A.** LC_PAPERSIZE

**B.** LC_PAPER

**C.** LC_PRINTERQ

**D.** LC_PRINTSIZE

**70.** Which of the following is used as a systemwide cron file?

**A.** /etc/cron.d

**B.** /etc/cron.sys

**C.** /etc/crontab

**D.** /etc/cron.tab

**71.** Which command can be used to view the available timezones on a system and obtain output that can be used in scripts for setting the time zone?

**A.** tzd

**B.** /etc/locale

**C.** tzdata

**D.** tzselect

**72.** Which option within a systemd timer unit will start a timer 90 minutes after boot?

**A.** OnBootSec=90min

**B.** OnBoot=90min

**C.** OnBootHour=1.5

**D.** StartOnBoot=90min

**73.** Which abbreviation is another name for information like the user's full name, telephone number, and other contact information found in /etc/passwd?

**A.** USERINFO

**B.** GECOS

**C.** HOMEINFO

**D.** CDATA

**74.** Which option to the groupadd command specifies the GID for the group?

**A.** -g

**B.** -a

**C.** -h

**D.** -k

**75.** When working with `systemd` timer units, which option to `systemctl` displays the active timers?

   **A.** `list-timerunits`

   **B.** `show-timers`

   **C.** `list-timers`

   **D.** `list-activetimers`

**76.** Which shortcut to the OnCalendar `systemd` timer function indicates that the timer unit should run once a week?

   **A.** OnceAWeek

   **B.** weekly

   **C.** everyweek

   **D.** oneperweek

**77.** Which option to the `crontab` command removes the current `crontab`?

   **A.** `-r`

   **B.** `-l`

   **C.** `-g`

   **D.** `-f`

**78.** Which variable in `/etc/default/useradd` controls the location of the skeleton home directory?

   **A.** `SKELETON`

   **B.** `SKEL`

   **C.** `SKELDIR`

   **D.** `SKELLOC`

**79.** Which option to `getent` enumerates the password database for a given system?

   **A.** `password`

   **B.** `listpass`

   **C.** `passwd`

   **D.** `showpassdb`

**80.** Which directory contains the jobs scheduled with `at`?

   **A.** `/var/spool/cron/atjobs`

   **B.** `/var/spool/at`

   **C.** `/var/spool/cron/at`

   **D.** `/var/spool/atjobs`

**81.** Which variable in /etc/login.defs controls the minimum group ID to use on the system?

   **A.** GIDMIN

   **B.** GROUPID_MIN

   **C.** GID_MIN

   **D.** MIN_GID

**82.** Which variable in /etc/login.defs contains the location of a user's email directory for use by programs such as userdel?

   **A.** EMAILDIR

   **B.** DIR_EMAIL

   **C.** MAILDIR

   **D.** MAIL_DIR

**83.** Which file contains user information such as username and real name and is readable by all users of the system?

   **A.** /etc/pass

   **B.** /etc/shadow

   **C.** /etc/passwd

   **D.** /etc/userinfo

**84.** Which shortcut can be used to indicate that a cron job should be executed on restart?

   **A.** @restart

   **B.** @startup

   **C.** @reboot

   **D.** @onboot

**85.** Which option to groupadd specifies that the group will be a system group?

   **A.** -r

   **B.** -m

   **C.** -j

   **D.** -b

**86.** Within which directory are databases stored for OpenLDAP?

   **A.** /var/lib/ldap

   **B.** /var/cache/openldap

   **C.** /var/share/ldap

   **D.** /usr/share/openldap

**87.** When listing systemd timer units, which option to `list-timers` shows both active and inactive units?

    **A.** `--all`

    **B.** `--active-and-inactive`

    **C.** `--inactive`

    **D.** All are shown by default.

**88.** Which file provides a list of users who are not allowed to create at jobs?

    **A.** `/etc/at.allow`

    **B.** `/etc/at.deny`

    **C.** `/etc/at.denyusers`

    **D.** `/etc/at.conf.deny`

# Chapter

# 8

# Topic 108: Essential System Services

---

## THE FOLLOWING EXAM OBJECTIVES ARE COVERED IN THIS CHAPTER:

✓ **108.1 Maintain system time.**

- ▪ Key knowledge areas:
  - ▪ Set the system date and time.
  - ▪ Set the hardware clock to the correct time in UTC.
  - ▪ Configure the correct timezone.
  - ▪ Basic NTP configuration using ntpd and chrony
  - ▪ Knowledge of using the pool.ntp.org service
  - ▪ Awareness of the ntpq command
- ▪ The following is a partial list of the used files, terms, and utilities:
  - ▪ /usr/share/zoneinfo/
  - ▪ /etc/timezone
  - ▪ /etc/localtime
  - ▪ /etc/ntp.conf
  - ▪ /etc/chrony.conf
  - ▪ date
  - ▪ hwclock
  - ▪ timedatectl
  - ▪ ntpd
  - ▪ ntpdate
  - ▪ chronyc
  - ▪ pool.ntp.org

## ✓ 108.2  System logging

- Key knowledge areas:

  - Basic configuration of `rsyslog`

  - Understanding of standard facilities, priorities, and actions

  - Query the `systemd` journal.

  - Filter systemd journal data by criteria such as date, service, or priority.

  - Configure persistent systemd journal storage and journal size.

  - Delete old systemd journal data.

  - Retrieve systemd journal data from a rescue system or filesystem copy.

  - Understand interaction of `rsyslog` with `systemd-journald`.

  - Configuration of `logrotate`

  - Awareness of `syslog` and `syslog-ng`

- The following is a partial list of the used files, terms, and utilities:

  - `/etc/rsyslog.conf`

  - `/var/log/`

  - `logger`

  - `logrotate`

  - `/etc/logrotate.conf`

  - `/etc/logrotate.d/`

  - `journalctl`

  - `systemd-cat`

  - `/etc/systemd/journald.conf`

  - `/var/log/journal/`

## ✓ 108.3  Mail Transfer Agent (MTA) basics

- Key knowledge areas:

  - Create email aliases.

- Configure email forwarding.
- Knowledge of commonly available MTA programs (Postfix, sendmail, Exim) (no configuration)
- The following is a partial list of the used files, terms, and utilities:
  - `~/.forward`
  - sendmail emulation layer commands
  - `newaliases`
  - `mail`
  - `mailq`
  - Postfix
  - `sendmail`
  - Exim

## ✓ 108.4 Manage printers and printing.

- Key knowledge areas:
  - Basic CUPS configuration (for local and remote printers)
  - Manage user print queues.
  - Troubleshoot general printing problems.
  - Add and remove jobs from configured printer queues.
- The following is a partial list of the used files, terms, and utilities:
  - CUPS configuration files, tools, and utilities
  - `/etc/cups/`
  - lpd legacy interface (`lpr`, `lprm`, `lpq`)

1. Which of the following commands is used to examine the `systemd` journal or log file?

   **A.** `journallist`

   **B.** `ctlj`

   **C.** `journalctl`

   **D.** `jctl`

2. Which system logging facility is used for messages from the kernel?

   **A.** syslog

   **B.** kernel

   **C.** kern

   **D.** system

3. To what server address can you set a Network Time Protocol (NTP) client in order to receive time from a regionally local server?

   **A.** 127.0.0.1

   **B.** 192.168.1.100

   **C.** `ntp.example.com`

   **D.** `pool.ntp.org`

4. What is the name of the `systemd` service that provides logging facilities?

   **A.** `systemd-journald`

   **B.** `systemd-loggingd`

   **C.** `systemd-syslog`

   **D.** `journalctl`

5. Which option within a `logrotate` configuration stanza informs `logrotate` to create a new log file owned by the user and group `www-data` and with permission 600?

   **A.** `new www-data.www-data mode 600`

   **B.** `create 600 www-data www-data`

   **C.** `new 600 www-data`

   **D.** `createlog mode 600 user www-data group www-data`

6. Within which directory hierarchy will you find configuration files related to printing with the Common UNIX Printing System (CUPS) printing system?

   **A.** `/etc/cupsd`

   **B.** `/etc/cups.d`

   **C.** `/etc/CUPS`

   **D.** `/etc/cups`

**7.** Which access control directive in a CUPS configuration file configures the system to accept connections from the local network with addresses from 192.168.1.1 through 192.168.1.127?

**A.** `Allow 192.168.1.0/25`

**B.** `Allow 192.168.1.0/24`

**C.** `Allow 127.0.0.0/8`

**D.** `AllowHosts 192.168.1.0`

**8.** Which of the following commands will set the date immediately and can be used from the command line in a script?

**A.** `ntpd`

**B.** `ntpdate pool.ntp.org`

**C.** `settime`

**D.** `time`

**9.** When executing the `ntpq` command, you receive a message like `read: Connection refused`. What would this typically indicate?

**A.** The network is down.

**B.** The NTP daemon is not running.

**C.** The use of NTP is administratively prohibited.

**D.** The current user does not have permission to execute `ntpq`.

**10.** Which command is used to query and work with the hardware clock on the system?

**A.** `hwc`

**B.** `ntpdate`

**C.** `systime`

**D.** `hwclock`

**11.** Which directory contains a listing of available time zones on a Linux system?

**A.** `/etc/timezones`

**B.** `/etc/tzdata`

**C.** `/usr/share/zoneinfo`

**D.** `/usr/share/timezones`

**12.** Which syslog level is used to provide informational messages?

**A.** `kern`

**B.** `emerg`

**C.** `debug`

**D.** `info`

13. Within /etc/ntp.conf, which of the following configuration lines sets the location of the drift file?

    **A.** `drift /var/lib/ntp/drift`

    **B.** `driftfile /var/lib/ntp/drift`

    **C.** `drift-file /var/lib/ntp/drift`

    **D.** `driftconfig /var/lib/ntp/drift`

14. Which configuration option in /etc/logrotate.conf will cause the log to be emailed to admin@example.com when the logrotation process runs for the selected log?

    **A.** `mailadmin@example.com`

    **B.** `sendmailadmin@example.com`

    **C.** `maillogadmin@example.com`

    **D.** `logmailadmin@example.com`

15. Which of the following commands is used to determine the amount of disk space used by systemd journal logfiles?

    **A.** `journalctl --disk`

    **B.** `journalctl -du`

    **C.** `journalctl --disk-usage`

    **D.** `journalctl -ls`

16. Which of the following commands displays the current mail queue on a Postfix server?

    **A.** `qmail`

    **B.** `mailqueue`

    **C.** `mail -q`

    **D.** `mailq`

17. When you're running the NTP daemon, which command can you execute to work with the NTP server in an interactive mode?

    **A.** `ntpd`

    **B.** `ntpdate`

    **C.** `ntpq`

    **D.** `ntp-interactive`

18. Assume that you want all email for the root user to be sent to admin@example.com. Which of the following lines in /etc/aliases will accomplish this task?

    **A.** `admin@example.com -> root`

    **B.** `root ->admin@example.com`

    **C.** `root,admin@example.com`

    **D.** `root:admin@example.com`

19. When you're working with klogd, which option can be used to control the file to which messages are logged?

    **A.** -d

    **B.** -f

    **C.** -v

    **D.** -l

20. Which set of programs or packages can be used for setting the system time on a device that is offline frequently?

    **A.** chrony

    **B.** htpoffline

    **C.** ntpd-off

    **D.** chrondate

21. Which of the following commands places a file into the print queue?

    **A.** lpr

    **B.** lpd

    **C.** lpq

    **D.** lpx

22. Which of the following options to the sendmail command will print information about the mail queue?

    **A.** -bi

    **B.** -queue

    **C.** -bp

    **D.** -f

23. Which function of the hwclock command will set the hardware clock to the current system time?

    **A.** -w

    **B.** -s

    **C.** -a

    **D.** -m

24. What is the default port for the CUPS administrative web interface?

    **A.** tcp/53

    **B.** tcp/8080

    **C.** udp/456

    **D.** tcp/631

**25.** Which of the following commands causes `sendmail` to attempt to deliver the messages in its queue?

   **A.** `sendmail -q`

   **B.** `sendmail -b`

   **C.** `sendmail -f`

   **D.** `sendmail -v`

**26.** You need to create an email address to accept email for abuse@example.com. However, you would like abuse reports sent to multiple email addresses within your organization. Which of the following will send email destined for the abuse account to admin@example.com and security@example.com?

   **A.** Create a `.forward` in the home directory for the abuse user and forward email accordingly.

   **B.** Within /etc/aliases, add this: `abuse:admin@example.com,security@example.com`.

   **C.** Create a `.forward` file for root and forward email accordingly.

   **D.** Within /etc/aliases, add this: `abuse:admin@example.com\tsecurity@example.com`.

**27.** Which of the following commands sets the hardware clock to Coordinated Universal Time (UTC) based on the current system time?

   **A.** `hwclock --systohc --utc`

   **B.** `hwclock --systohc --localtime`

   **C.** `hwclock --systohc`

   **D.** `hwclock --systoutc`

**28.** You need to delete all messages from the queue on a Postfix server. Which of the following commands will perform this action?

   **A.** `postqueue -remove`

   **B.** `rm -rf`

   **C.** `postfix -f`

   **D.** `postsuper -d ALL`

**29.** Which of the following URLs can be used to view a list of completed print jobs in CUPS?

   **A.** `http://localhost:631/jobs?which_jobs=completed`

   **B.** `http://localhost:631?completed`

   **C.** `http://localhost:631/?completed`

   **D.** `http://cups/jobs=completed`

**30.** Which option to the `journalctl` command will continuously update the display as new log entries are created?

   **A.** `-tail`

   **B.** `-t`

   **C.** `-f`

   **D.** `-l`

**31.** Assuming that the `$ModLoad imudp` configuration option has been set in the configuration for `rsyslogd`, which of the following additional options is necessary to configure the port on which the server will listen?

   **A.** `$Port 514`

   **B.** `$UDPServerRun 514`

   **C.** `$Listen 514`

   **D.** `$UDPListen 514`

**32.** Which of the following commands causes the mail queue to be processed on a Postfix server?

   **A.** `postqueue -f`

   **B.** `postqueue -D`

   **C.** `postfix -q`

   **D.** `postsuper -q`

**33.** When running `ntpd`, the server will not adjust or synchronize if the time is skewed from the NTP server by a significant amount of time. Which option to `ntpd` disables this and causes the synchronization process to continue even if there is a large skew?

   **A.** `ntpd -noskew`

   **B.** `ntpd -skewcheck=off`

   **C.** `ntpd -g 0`

   **D.** `ntpd -s 0`

**34.** Which option in `journald.conf` controls the maximum file size for individual journal logs?

   **A.** `SystemMaxFileSize`

   **B.** `MaxFile`

   **C.** `LogFileSize`

   **D.** `LogSize`

**35.** Which command can be executed to view completed print jobs?

   **A.** `lpstat -q`

   **B.** `lpq`

   **C.** `lpstat -W completed`

   **D.** `lpqueue -c`

**36.** When configuring a log file for rotation, you need to execute a command to run a script after log file rotation. Which option within the `logrotate.conf` configuration file can be used to facilitate this behavior?

    **A.** after-rotate

    **B.** run-script

    **C.** rotatecomplete

    **D.** postrotate

**37.** You are deploying an Exim server and need to work with the firewall to ensure the proper incoming ports are open. Which protocol and port should you allow inbound for normal Simple Mail Transfer Protocol (SMTP) traffic?

    **A.** TCP/23

    **B.** TCP/25

    **C.** TCP/110

    **D.** TCP/143

**38.** Which command should be executed after making a change to the `sendmail` access database /etc/access?

    **A.** makemap

    **B.** makedb

    **C.** newaccess

    **D.** rebuilddb

**39.** When working with `syslog-ng`, which of the following is the correct path and filename for the primary configuration file?

    **A.** /etc/syslog-ng/syslog-ng.conf

    **B.** /etc/syslog/syslog-ng.conf

    **C.** /etc/syslog-ng/ng.conf

    **D.** /etc/syslog-ng/ngd.conf

**40.** A developer has created an application and wants to take advantage of syslog for logging to a custom log file. Which facility should be used for an application such as this?

    **A.** syslog

    **B.** kern

    **C.** local#

    **D.** user

**41.** A user needs to work with printer-related items. Which of the following commands adds the user (called `username` in the options) to the appropriate group for this purpose?

    **A.** usermod -aG printerusers username

    **B.** usermod -aG lpadmin username

**C.** usermod -gA lpadm username

**D.** usermod -a lpadm username

42. Which option within a logrotate configuration file disables compression of the log file?

**A.** compressoff

**B.** limitcompress

**C.** nocompression

**D.** nocompress

43. Which command should be used to enable printer sharing through CUPS?

**A.** cupsctl --enable-sharing

**B.** cupsc --share

**C.** cupsctl --share-printers

**D.** cupsc --printer-sharing

44. Which command can be used to gather and display statistics about mail processed on a server running sendmail?

**A.** mailq

**B.** mailstats

**C.** statmail

**D.** sendmailstats

45. You need to determine the size of the systemd journals on the system. Which option to journalctl is used for this purpose?

**A.** --disk-use

**B.** --disk-usage

**C.** --disk-space

**D.** --disk-used

46. You are troubleshooting a problem with printing and believe the CUPS service needs to be restarted. Which of the following commands can be used to restart CUPS on a server running systemd?

**A.** systemctl restart cups.service

**B.** systemctl restart cups-service

**C.** systemctl reboot cups.target

**D.** systemctl restart cups.target

47. You are working with journalctl and need to see only messages that are at a debug priority. Which of the following options enables this scenario?

**A.** -pri debug

**B.** -prior debug

**C.** -d debug

**D.** -p debug

**48.** Which option in a CUPS configuration file causes the daemon to listen on all interfaces on port 631?

   **A.** `Port 631`

   **B.** `Listen All:631`

   **C.** `Listen 127.0.0.1:631`

   **D.** `Port All:631`

**49.** Which command is used to remove an email from the mail queue with Postfix?

   **A.** `postsuper -d`

   **B.** `postmaster`

   **C.** `postfix -d`

   **D.** `postdel`

**50.** Which option to `journalctl` will clear logs older than five days?

   **A.** `--clear=5d`

   **B.** `--vacuum-time=5d`

   **C.** `--delete-older=5d`

   **D.** `--clear-time=5d`

**51.** When configuring email forwarding with Procmail, which of the following files is used as a user-based configuration file for Procmail?

   **A.** `/home/procmail.conf`

   **B.** `~/.procmailrc`

   **C.** `/etc/procmail.conf`

   **D.** `~/procmail.conf`

**52.** Which of the following definitions in `/etc/aliases` will deliver mail destined to root to two email addresses, admin@example.com and webmaster@example.com?

   **A.** `[root] =admin@example.com, webmaster@example.com`

   **B.** `root: admin webmaster`

   **C.** `root: admin, webmaster`

   **D.** `root:admin@example.com, webmaster@example.com`

**53.** Which of the following commands views the contents of a message that exists in the Postfix queue?

   **A.** `postshow`

   **B.** `postless`

   **C.** `postmore`

   **D.** `postcat`

**54.** Within which file will you find errors related to delivery of mail on a Postfix server?

    **A.** /var/log/mail

    **B.** /var/log/postfix.log

    **C.** /var/log/mail.err

    **D.** /var/log/postfix.err

**55.** When testing SMTP communications between a client and a server, you need to begin the conversation. Which of the following lines shows the beginning of an SMTP conversation using Extended Hello syntax from mail.example.com?

    **A.** BEGIN mail.example.com

    **B.** SMTP mail.example.com

    **C.** HELO mail.example.com

    **D.** EHLO mail.example.com

**56.** Which option to timedatectl shows the available time zones?

    **A.** list-timezones

    **B.** show-tz

    **C.** --tzinfo

    **D.** --timezones

**57.** You are viewing a directory listing of the /etc/localtime file and it looks like the following:

```
lrwxrwxrwx 1 root root 35 Oct 30  2018 /etc/localtime ->
/usr/share/zoneinfo/America/Chicago
```

From that directory listing, what can you tell about the file?

    **A.** The file is a symlink to a timezone in /usr/share/zoneinfo.

    **B.** The /usr/share/zoneinfo file is a symlink to /etc/localtime.

    **C.** The /etc/localtime file is a hard link to /usr/share/zoneinfo.

    **D.** The time zone cannot be set because the file must exist as its own separate file.

**58.** You need to set the correct time zone on a server. How can you tell what the current time zone is set to?

    **A.** Run the date command.

    **B.** Run the tzdata command.

    **C.** Examine /proc/timezone.

    **D.** Examine /etc/tzdata.

59. Which of the following is the configuration file used by the Chrony package?

    **A.** `/etc/chrony.cfg`

    **B.** `/etc/chrony/default.cfg`

    **C.** `/etc/chrony.conf`

    **D.** `/etc/chrony.d/chrony.cf`

60. Which option to `journalctl` queries for only kernel messages?

    **A.** `-ok`

    **B.** `-okern`

    **C.** `-k`

    **D.** `-limitk`

61. Which command must you run after making a change to email aliases on a server running Postfix?

    **A.** `service postfix restart`

    **B.** `newaliases`

    **C.** `alias -n`

    **D.** `postfix -e`

62. You need to log output to the `systemd` journal from a script. Which of the following commands facilitates this scenario?

    **A.** `systemd-log`

    **B.** `systemd-logger`

    **C.** `systemd-logm`

    **D.** `systemd-cat`

63. Which command can be used to remove print jobs from the queue?

    **A.** `lprm`

    **B.** `lpdel`

    **C.** `lpqman`

    **D.** `lprmj`

64. When running from a shell script, which command enables logging to syslog?

    **A.** `logd`

    **B.** `login`

    **C.** `logit`

    **D.** `logger`

65. You need to find the mail queue path on a Postfix server. You're using `postconf -d` to view all parameters. Which parameter contains the mail queue path on a Postfix server?

    **A.** `mqueue`

    **B.** `queue_dir`

**C.** `mailq_path`

**D.** `mqueue_path`

**66.** Which of the following options can be given to `journalctl` in order to filter based on a service name?

**A.** `_SYSTEMD-SERVICE`

**B.** `_SERVICENAME`

**C.** `_SYSTEMD_SERVICE`

**D.** `_SYSTEMD_UNIT`

**67.** Which command can be used to add a job to a print queue?

**A.** `lpadd`

**B.** `lkp`

**C.** `lp`

**D.** `lpprint`

**68.** Which of the following files enables per-user email forwarding?

**A.** `~/.mailforward`

**B.** `~/.forward`

**C.** `~/.formail`

**D.** `~/.forwardmail`

**69.** Which argument to the `mail` command sets the subject for the email to be sent?

**A.** `-E`

**B.** `-s`

**C.** `-c`

**D.** `-f`

**70.** Which option to the `date` command can be used to set the date and time?

**A.** `date -f`

**B.** `date -t`

**C.** `date --change`

**D.** `date -s`

**71.** Which option to `journalctl` will trim the journal data size so that it consumes the amount specified?

**A.** `--clear-size`

**B.** `--vacuum-size`

**C.** `--delete-size`

**D.** `--consume-max`

**72.** Which option to `journalctl` filters based on time?

   **A.** `--since`

   **B.** `--time`

   **C.** `--time-t`

   **D.** `--filter-time`

**73.** When viewing the syslog configuration, you notice a minus sign (–) preceding several log files. What is the significance of the – sign in the configuration?

   **A.** The use of – indicates that the log may be rotated any time.

   **B.** The use of – indicates that the system can utilize other logging facilities when appropriate.

   **C.** The use of – omits the disk sync process for every entry into the log.

   **D.** The use of – comments out the line.

**74.** Which option to `lpr` sends a print job to a given destination?

   **A.** `-P`

   **B.** `-a`

   **C.** `-p`

   **D.** `-h`

**75.** Which Postfix-related command is used to provide an overview of the number of messages in the incoming and active queues arranged by age?

   **A.** `queuelist`

   **B.** `postq`

   **C.** `qshape`

   **D.** `queueshow`

**76.** Within the `journald` configuration file, which option is used to configure the maximum space used by journal files?

   **A.** `SystemFileSizeLimit`

   **B.** `SystemMaxFile`

   **C.** `SystemMaxSize`

   **D.** `SystemMaxUse`

**77.** Within which directory hierarchy are queue-related messages stored for Postfix?

   **A.** `/var/mqueue`

   **B.** `/var/spool/mailq`

   **C.** `/var/spool/postfix`

   **D.** `/var/postfix`

**78.** Which option to `journalctl` can be used to specify an alternate location for journal data, such as might be the case when retrieving journal data from a rescue system or a filesystem copy?

    **A.**  `--alt`

    **B.**  `--journal-location`

    **C.**  `--journal-dir`

    **D.**  `--directory`

**79.** Within which directory are system logs normally kept on a Linux system?

    **A.**  `/etc/logs/`

    **B.**  `/var/logs/`

    **C.**  `/var/log/`

    **D.**  `/tmp/log/`

**80.** Which shortcut can be used as the destination in an Exim alias to prevent Exim from delivering mail to a certain address, such as when you want to essentially delete the mail rather than deliver it?

    **A.**  `:del:`

    **B.**  `:block:`

    **C.**  `:blackhole:`

    **D.**  `:deletemail:`

**81.** Which stanza within a CUPS `printers.conf` configuration file is used to configure a default local printer with CUPS?

    **A.**  `<LOCAL printerName>`

    **B.**  `<Printer printerName>`

    **C.**  `<DefaultPrinter printerName>`

    **D.**  `<PrintDefault printerName>`

**82.** Which of the following commands can be used to remove all jobs queued for printing?

    **A.**  `lprm --all`

    **B.**  `lprm --del A`

    **C.**  `lprm -`

    **D.**  `lprm --remove ALL`

**83.** When using the `mail` command, which option enables setting the From header?

    **A.**  `-f`

    **B.**  `-r`

    **C.**  `-o`

    **D.**  `-m`

**84.** Which character sequence is used to precede the host or IP in order to specify that TCP should be used for remote system logging in /etc/rsyslog.conf?

    **A.** @TCP

    **B.** @@

    **C.** @

    **D.** :tcp@

**85.** Within the /etc/systemd/journald.conf file, which key/value pair will enable the journal to be persistent?

    **A.** Keep=All

    **B.** Store=Persistence

    **C.** Storage=Persistent

    **D.** Keep=Persist

**86.** Which command can be used to monitor the status of chronyd?

    **A.** chronyc

    **B.** chronystat

    **C.** chrony-stats

    **D.** chronyd-stat

**87.** Within which directory will you find configuration files for various logs that are to be rotated with logrotate?

    **A.** /etc/logrotate

    **B.** /etc/logs

    **C.** /etc/logrotate.d

    **D.** /var/spool/logrotate

**88.** Which of the following commands is used to view the pending messages queue on a Postfix server?

    **A.** postqueue -p

    **B.** postconf -pending

    **C.** postqueue -f

    **D.** postsuper pending

# Chapter

# 9

# Topic 109: Networking Fundamentals

---

## THE FOLLOWING EXAM OBJECTIVES ARE COVERED IN THIS CHAPTER:

✓ **109.1 Fundamentals of Internet protocols**

- Key knowledge areas:

  - Demonstrate an understanding of network masks and CIDR notation.

  - Knowledge of differences between private and public "dotted quad" IP addresses

  - Knowledge about common TCP and UDP ports and services (20, 21, 22, 23, 25, 53, 80, 110, 123, 139, 143, 161, 162, 389, 443, 465, 514, 636, 993, 995)

  - Knowledge about the differences and major features of UDP, TCP, and ICMP

  - Knowledge of the major differences between IPv4 and IPv6

  - Knowledge of the basic features of IPv6

- The following is a partial list of the used files, terms, and utilities:

  - /etc/services

  - IPv4, IPv6

  - Subnetting

  - TCP, UDP, ICMP

✓ **109.2 Persistent network configuration**

- Key knowledge areas:

  - Understand basic TCP/IP host configuration.

- Configure ethernet and Wi-Fi network configuration using NetworkManager.
  - Awareness of `systemd-networkd`
- The following is a partial list of the used files, terms, and utilities:
  - `/etc/hostname`
  - `/etc/hosts`
  - `/etc/nsswitch.conf`
  - `/etc/resolv.conf`
  - `nmcli`
  - `hostnamectl`
  - `ifup`
  - `ifdown`

## ✓ 109.3  Basic network troubleshooting

- Key knowledge areas:
  - Manually configure network interfaces, including viewing and changing the configuration of network interfaces using `iproute2`.
  - Manually configure routing, including viewing and changing routing tables and setting the default route using `iproute2`.
  - Debug problems associated with the network configuration.
  - Awareness of legacy net-tools commands
- The following is a partial list of the used files, terms, and utilities:
  - `ip`
  - `hostname`
  - `ss`
  - `ping`
  - `ping6`
  - `traceroute`

- traceroute6
- tracepath
- tracepath6
- netcat
- ifconfig
- netstat
- route

## ✓ 109.4 Configure client-side DNS.

- Key knowledge areas:
  - Query remote DNS servers.
  - Configure local name resolution and use remote DNS servers.
  - Modify the order in which name resolution is done.
  - Debug errors related to name resolution.
  - Awareness of systemd-resolved.
- The following is a partial list of the used files, terms, and utilities:
  - /etc/hosts
  - /etc/resolv.conf
  - /etc/nsswitch.conf
  - host
  - dig
  - getent

1. Which of the following commands shows the current default route without performing Domain Name System (DNS) lookups on the IP address(es) involved?

   **A.** `netstat -rn`

   **B.** `netstat -n`

   **C.** `netstat -r`

   **D.** `netstat -f`

2. You are having difficulty with an interface on the server and it is currently down. Assuming that there is no hardware failure on the device itself, which command and option can you use to display information about the interface?

   **A.** `ifconfig -a`

   **B.** `ifup`

   **C.** `netstat -n`

   **D.** `ifconfig`

3. Which of the following is not used as a private address for internal, non-Internet, use?

   **A.** 172.16.4.2

   **B.** 192.168.40.3

   **C.** 10.74.5.244

   **D.** 143.236.32.231

4. Which of the following commands adds a default gateway of 192.168.1.1 for interface eth0?

   **A.** `route add default gateway 192.168.1.1 eth0`

   **B.** `eth0 --dg 192.168.1.1`

   **C.** `route add default gw 192.168.1.1 eth0`

   **D.** `route define eth0 192.168.1.1`

5. Which option for the `host` command will query for the authoritative name servers for a given domain?

   **A.** `-t ns`

   **B.** `-t all`

   **C.** `-ns`

   **D.** `-named`

6. Which port(s) and protocol(s) should be opened in a firewall in order for the primary and secondary name servers to communicate for a given domain?

   **A.** `udp/53`

   **B.** Both `tcp/53` and `udp/53`

   **C.** `tcp/53`

   **D.** `udp/53` and `tcp/503`

7.  Which option for the ping command enables you to choose the interface from which the Internet Control Message Protocol (ICMP) packets will be generated?

   **A.**  -i

   **B.**  -I

   **C.**  -t

   **D.**  -a

8.  You need to split a subnet to enable four subnets with up to 30 hosts each. Which subnet mask, in Classless Inter-Domain Routing (CIDR) notation, facilitates this scenario?

   **A.**  /25

   **B.**  /24

   **C.**  /32

   **D.**  /27

9.  Which of the following commands queries for the mail servers for the domain example.com?

   **A.**  dig example.com mx

   **B.**  dig example.com

   **C.**  host -t smtp example.com

   **D.**  dig example.com smtp

10. Which of the following addresses represents the localhost in IPv6?

   **A.**  0:1

   **B.**  ::1

   **C.**  127:0:1

   **D.**  :127:0:0:1

11. Which option to the traceroute command will use TCP SYN packets for the path trace?

   **A.**  -T

   **B.**  -t

   **C.**  -s

   **D.**  -i

12. Which of the following commands will attempt to bring online all interfaces marked as auto within the networking configuration?

   **A.**  ifconfig -a

   **B.**  ifup auto

   **C.**  ifup -a

   **D.**  ifstat

**13.** In a scripting scenario, which command will return the domain name configured for the server?

   **A.** dnsname

   **B.** fqdn

   **C.** hostname

   **D.** hostname -d

**14.** Which command can be used to listen for netlink messages on a network?

   **A.** ip monitor

   **B.** netlink -a

   **C.** ip netlink

   **D.** route

**15.** If the traceroute6 command is not available, which option to the traceroute command can be used for an IPv6 traceroute?

   **A.** -ipv6

   **B.** -net6

   **C.** -v6

   **D.** -6

**16.** Which of the following configuration lines in /etc/nsswitch.conf causes a lookup for group information to first use local files and then use LDAP?

   **A.** group: files ldap

   **B.** lookup: group [local ldap]

   **C.** group: [local ldap]

   **D.** group: localfiles ldap

**17.** Which of the following dig commands sends the query for example.com directly to the server at 192.168.2.5 rather than to a locally configured resolver?

   **A.** dig example.com @192.168.2.5

   **B.** dig -t 192.168.2.5 example.com

   **C.** dig -s 192.168.2.5 example.com

   **D.** dig server=192.168.2.5 example.com

**18.** Which ports need to be allowed through the firewall for Simple Network Management Protocol (SNMP) traffic?

   **A.** Ports 23 and 25

   **B.** Ports 110 and 143

   **C.** Ports 80 and 443

   **D.** Ports 161 and 162

**19.** Which of the following commands will enumerate the hosts database?

 **A.** getent hosts

 **B.** gethosts

 **C.** nslookup

 **D.** host

**20.** Which of the following netmasks is used for a subnet described with a /25 in CIDR notation?

 **A.** 255.255.255.0

 **B.** 255.255.0.0

 **C.** 255.255.255.192

 **D.** 255.255.255.128

**21.** Which of the following configuration lines will set the DNS server to 192.168.1.4 using /etc/resolv.conf?

 **A.** dns 192.168.1.4

 **B.** dns-server 192.168.1.4

 **C.** nameserver 192.168.1.4

 **D.** name-server 192.168.1.4

**22.** When examining open ports on the server, you see that TCP port 3000 is listed with no corresponding protocol name, such as SMTP, IMAP over SSL (IMAPS), and so on. In which file would you find a list of port-to-protocol translations that could be customized to add this new port?

 **A.** /etc/ports

 **B.** /etc/p2p

 **C.** /etc/ppp

 **D.** /etc/services

**23.** Which of the following commands adds a route to the server for the network 192.168.51.0/24 through its gateway of 192.168.51.1?

 **A.** route add -net 192.168.51.0 netmask 255.255.255.0 gw 192.168.51.1

 **B.** route add -net 192.168.51/24 gw 192.168.1.51

 **C.** route -net 192.168.51.0/24 192.168.51.1

 **D.** route add 192.168.51.1 -n 192.168.51.0//255.255.255.0

**24.** Which of the following netstat options displays the send and receive queues for each socket?

 **A.** -r

 **B.** -M

 **C.** -a

 **D.** -v

**25.** Which of the following represents a correct configuration line for /etc/hosts?

    **A.**  `192.168.1.4 cwa.braingia.org cwa`

    **B.**  `cwa.braingia.org cwa 192.168.1.4`

    **C.**  `cwa.braingia.org 192.168.1.8 alias cwa`

    **D.**  `alias cwa.braingia.org cwa 192.168.1.4`

**26.** Which of the following commands configures the eth0 device with an IP address of 192.168.1.1 in a /24 network?

    **A.**  `ifconfig eth0 192.168.1.1/24`

    **B.**  `ifconfig eth0 192.168.1.1/255.255.255.0`

    **C.**  `ifconfig eth0 192.168.1.1 netmask 255.255.255.0`

    **D.**  `ifconfig 192.168.1.1 netmask 255.255.255.0 eth0`

**27.** Which of the following describes a primary difference between IPv4 and IPv6?

    **A.**  IPv4 is for internal networks only, whereas IPv6 is for public networks.

    **B.**  IPv4 is for public networks, whereas IPv6 is for internal networks.

    **C.**  IPv4 uses a 32-bit address, whereas IPv6 uses a 128-bit address.

    **D.**  With IPv6, no subnetting is necessary.

**28.** On which port does ICMP operate?

    **A.**  TCP/43

    **B.**  UDP/111

    **C.**  UDP/69

    **D.**  ICMP does not use ports.

**29.** Which of the following commands will change the default gateway to 192.168.1.1 using eth0?

    **A.**  `ip route default gw 192.168.1.1`

    **B.**  `ip route change default via 192.168.1.1 dev eth0`

    **C.**  `ip route default gw update 192.168.1.1`

    **D.**  `ip route update default 192.168.1.1 eth0`

**30.** Which of the following ports is used for Secure Shell communication?

    **A.**  TCP/23

    **B.**  TCP/25

    **C.**  TCP/22

    **D.**  TCP/2200

**31.** Which options for netcat will create a server listening on port 8080?

   **A.** netcat -p 8080

   **B.** nc -l -p 8080

   **C.** nc -p 8080

   **D.** nc -s 8080

**32.** Which of the following commands displays the Start of Authority information for the domain example.com?

   **A.** dig example.com soa

   **B.** dig example.com authority

   **C.** dig example.com -auth

   **D.** dig -t auth example.com

**33.** Assume that you want to enable local client services to go to hosts on the network without needing to fully qualify the name by adding the domain for either example.com or example.org. Which option in /etc/resolv.conf will provide this functionality?

   **A.** search

   **B.** domain

   **C.** local-domain

   **D.** local-order

**34.** Which of the following commands sends an IPv6 ping to a unique local address?

   **A.** ping -6 127.0.0.1

   **B.** ping6 fddi/128

   **C.** ping6 fdd6:551:b09f::

   **D.** ping -6 fdd6:551:b09f::

**35.** Which of the following commands prevents traffic from reaching the host 192.168.1.3?

   **A.** route add -host 192.168.1.3 reject

   **B.** route -nullroute 192.168.1.3

   **C.** route add -null 192.168.1.3

   **D.** route add -block 192.168.1.3

**36.** Which of the following describes a primary difference between traceroute and tracepath?

   **A.** The traceroute command requires root privileges.

   **B.** The tracepath command provides the MTU for each hop, whereas traceroute does not.

   **C.** The tracepath command cannot be used for tracing a path on an external network.

   **D.** The traceroute command is not compatible with IPv6.

**37.** Which of the following commands will emulate the ping command in Microsoft Windows, where the ping is sent for four packets and then the command exits?

   **A.** ping -n 4

   **B.** ping -t 4

   **C.** ping -p 4

   **D.** ping -c 4

**38.** Which command provides an interface into NetworkManager that works from a terminal window?

   **A.** nmcli

   **B.** nmui

   **C.** nm

   **D.** nman

**39.** Which of the following commands configures eth1 with an additional IPv6 address of fdd6:551:b09e::?

   **A.** ifconfig eth1 inet6 add fdd6:551:b09e::/128

   **B.** ifconfig add fdd6:551:b09e::

   **C.** ifconfig fdd6:551:b09e:: eth1

   **D.** ifconfig eth1 fdd6:551:b09e

**40.** On which port does LDAP over SSL operate?

   **A.** Port 53

   **B.** Port 389

   **C.** Port 636

   **D.** Port 443

**41.** You need to prevent local clients from going to a certain host, www.example.com, and instead redirect them to localhost. Which of the following is a method to override DNS lookups for the specified host?

   **A.** Add a firewall entry for the IP address of www.example.com to prevent traffic from passing through it.

   **B.** Delete www.example.com from the route table using the route command.

   **C.** Add a null route to prevent access to the IP address for www.example.com.

   **D.** Add an entry for www.example.com in /etc/hosts to point to 127.0.0.1.

**42.** Which of the following commands should be executed after running ip route change?

   **A.** ip route flush cache

   **B.** ip route reload

   **C.** ip route cache reload

   **D.** ip route restart

**43.** Which option should be used to send a DNS query for a Sender Policy Framework (SPF) record with dig?

   **A.**  -t txt

   **B.**  -t spf

   **C.**  -t mx

   **D.**  -t mailspf

**44.** Which of the following protocols uses a three-way handshake?

   **A.**  ICMP

   **B.**  TCP

   **C.**  UDP

   **D.**  IP

**45.** How many IP addresses are available in the 172.16.0.0 private range in IPv4?

   **A.**  /32

   **B.**  16,777,216

   **C.**  65,536

   **D.**  1,048,576

**46.** When troubleshooting a connectivity issue, you have found that you can reach a server via the web but cannot ping it. Which of the following best describes a possible cause for this scenario?

   **A.**  TCP traffic has been blocked at the firewall.

   **B.**  The DNS lookup is failing.

   **C.**  ICMP traffic has been blocked.

   **D.**  There is a reject route in place.

**47.** When viewing the available routes using the route command, one route contains UG flags and the others contain U flags. What do the letters UG signify in the route table?

   **A.**  The G signifies that the route is good.

   **B.**  The G signifies that the route is unavailable.

   **C.**  The G signifies that this is a gateway.

   **D.**  The G signifies that the route is an aggregate.

**48.** Which of the following commands requests a zone transfer of example.org from the server at 192.168.1.4?

   **A.**  dig example.org @192.168.1.4 axfr

   **B.**  dig example.org @192.168.1.4

   **C.**  dig example.org @192.168.1.4 xfer

   **D.**  dig example.org #192.168.1.4 xfer

**49.** Which of the following commands displays the number of packets forwarded by the kernel?

   **A.** ls

   **B.** ipstat

   **C.** ifconfig -a

   **D.** netstat -s

**50.** When using the ip command, which protocol family is used as the default if not otherwise specified?

   **A.** tcpip

   **B.** ip

   **C.** inet

   **D.** arp

**51.** Which of the following commands changes the Media Access Control (MAC) address of eth0?

   **A.** ifmac eth0

   **B.** ifconfig eth0 hw ether

   **C.** ifconfig eth0 mac

   **D.** ifconfig eth0 hw mac

**52.** You are using the route command to view routes. However, name resolution is taking a long time and causing delay in the response from the route command. Which option to route can be added to cause it to not perform name resolution?

   **A.** -d

   **B.** -e

   **C.** -f

   **D.** -n

**53.** You have replaced a device on the network but used the IP from another active device. Which command can be run to remove the MAC address entry from your computer so that it performs the address resolution again?

   **A.** arp -d

   **B.** netstat -rn

   **C.** hostname

   **D.** dig

**54.** Which of the following commands displays information such as link status about the wireless device wlan0?

   **A.** iw dev wlan0 link

   **B.** wlan0 list

   **C.** iw wlan0 -l

   **D.** iw dev link

**55.** Which command is used for setting parameters such as the `essid`, `channel`, and other related options for a wireless device?

   **A.** `ifconfig`

   **B.** `iwconfig`

   **C.** `wlancfg`

   **D.** `iconf`

**56.** Which of the following commands can be used to scan for available wireless networks?

   **A.** `iwlist get`

   **B.** `iwconfig scan`

   **C.** `iwlist scan`

   **D.** `iw-scan`

**57.** You need to offer internally facing NTP services. On which protocol and port does NTP listen?

   **A.** TCP/20 and TCP/21

   **B.** UDP/123

   **C.** TCP/139

   **D.** UDP/5150

**58.** You need to set the MTU to a specific value for a network interface. Which option to `ifconfig` facilitates this?

   **A.** `-mtu`

   **B.** `mtu`

   **C.** `metric`

   **D.** `addrmtu`

**59.** Which option to the `arp` command creates a new entry for a given IP address-to-MAC address pair?

   **A.** `-s`

   **B.** `-c`

   **C.** `-d`

   **D.** `--add`

**60.** Which of the following commands shows network sockets and their allocated memory?

   **A.** `ss -m`

   **B.** `mpas`

   **C.** `mem`

   **D.** `free`

**61.** When troubleshooting a potential hardware problem, you need to determine which physical interface is being used for a certain address. One way to accomplish this is with the ping command in order to monitor the activity lights on the device. Which of the following options to ping will flood the interface with ECHO_REQUEST packets?

   **A.** -e

   **B.** -a

   **C.** -c

   **D.** -f

**62.** Which of the following commands can be used to test network connectivity at the TCP level instead of telnet?

   **A.** netstat

   **B.** nc

   **C.** nettest

   **D.** ping

**63.** Which option to tcpdump displays a list of available interfaces on which tcpdump can operate?

   **A.** -a

   **B.** -d

   **C.** -D

   **D.** -i

**64.** Which command provides a method for sending ICMP requests for IPv6?

   **A.** ping6

   **B.** pingv6

   **C.** tracert

   **D.** 6ping

**65.** Which of the following commands displays information about addresses, specifically only IPv6 addresses, currently in use on the computer?

   **A.** ip addr

   **B.** ip -6 addr

   **C.** ip6add

   **D.** ipv6addr

**66.** Which of the following commands will disable ARP on the interface eth0?

   **A.** ifconfig eth0 -arp

   **B.** ip eth0 noarp

   **C.** ifconfig eth0 noarp

   **D.** if eth0 disable arp

**67.** Which option to the `route` command forces the kernel to use the specified device for the route rather than attempting to determine the correct device?

    **A.** `inet`

    **B.** `addr`

    **C.** `dev`

    **D.** `device`

**68.** Which option to the `ss` command shows the process IDs associated with the socket?

    **A.** `-l`

    **B.** `-a`

    **C.** `-p`

    **D.** `-f`

**69.** Which option to `traceroute` causes the command to use ICMP for requests?

    **A.** `-T`

    **B.** `-A`

    **C.** `-I`

    **D.** `-i`

**70.** Which programmatic function is used by the `hostname` command internally?

    **A.** `getaddr`

    **B.** `gethost`

    **C.** `gethostname`

    **D.** `getname`

**71.** Which of the following commands will examine the system log for information regarding DHCP activity?

    **A.** `grep -i dhcp /var/log/syslog`

    **B.** `grep -v dhcp /var/log/syslog`

    **C.** `grep -vi dhcp /var/log/kern.log`

    **D.** `dmesg | grep dhcp`

**72.** Which of the following characters are valid for hostnames in `/etc/hosts`?

    **A.** Alphanumerics, minus, underscore, and dot

    **B.** Alphanumerics, minus, and dot

    **C.** Alphanumerics and dot

    **D.** Alphanumerics

**73.** Which of the following configuration lines in /etc/resolv.conf enables debugging?

   **A.** debug

   **B.** options debug

   **C.** option debug

   **D.** enable-debug

**74.** Which of the following commands views systemd journal entries for the NetworkManager unit?

   **A.** systemd NetworkManager

   **B.** systemd NetworkCtl

   **C.** systemctl NetworkManager

   **D.** journalctl -u NetworkManager

**75.** Which file is read at boot to set the local computer's hostname?

   **A.** /etc/hostname

   **B.** /etc/hosts

   **C.** /etc/localhost

   **D.** /etc/networkhost

**76.** Which traceroute command is used exclusively for IPv6 route traces?

   **A.** trace6

   **B.** traceroute6

   **C.** tracert6

   **D.** 6trace

**77.** Which type can be used with the dig command to test a zone transfer?

   **A.** xfr

   **B.** transfer

   **C.** zxfr

   **D.** axfr

**78.** Which option to the host command sets the query type to ANY?

   **A.** -a

   **B.** -b

   **C.** -c

   **D.** -d

**79.** Within which file can per-user default settings be created for the dig command?

  **A.** /etc/dig.cfg

  **B.** /etc/dig.conf

  **C.** ~/.digrc

  **D.** ~/.dig.conf

**80.** Which type of DNS record is used for specifying a POP3 server?

  **A.** POP

  **B.** PO

  **C.** MX

  **D.** There is no specific type for POP3 servers.

**81.** Which of the following iproute2 commands changes the address of device eth0 to 192.168.1.1 with netmask 255.255.255.0?

  **A.** ip addr add 192.168.1.1/24 dev eth0

  **B.** ip addr eth0 192.168.1.1 255.255.255.0

  **C.** ip addr dev eth0 192.168.1.1 255.255.255.0

  **D.** ip addr 192.168.1.1/255.255.255.0 eth0

**82.** Which command is used to show the settings for DNS resolution with systemd-resolved?

  **A.** systemctl resolvers

  **B.** resolvectl status

  **C.** systemctl --resolvers

  **D.** resolvectl --view-status

**83.** Which of the following commands enables NetworkManager so that it can be used to configure Ethernet and Wi-Fi network devices?

  **A.** nmcli networking on

  **B.** netman enable

  **C.** NetworkManager --enable

  **D.** nmti --enable networking

**84.** You are troubleshooting a DNS problem using the dig command and receive a status: NXDOMAIN message. Which of the following best describes what NXDOMAIN means?

  **A.** NXDOMAIN means that you have received a nonauthoritative answer for the query.

  **B.** NXDOMAIN means that the domain or host is not found.

  **C.** NXDOMAIN indicates a successful query.

  **D.** NXDOMAIN signifies a new domain record has been added.

**85.** Which systemd daemon can be used to manage network interfaces through systemd?

   **A.** networker

   **B.** networked

   **C.** networkd

   **D.** netwrkd

**86.** Which command for hostnamectl can be used to set the hostname?

   **A.** set-host

   **B.** set-hostname

   **C.** set-name

   **D.** hostname

**87.** On which port does IMAP over SSL (IMAPS) listen?

   **A.** 993

   **B.** 995

   **C.** 465

   **D.** 514

**88.** When you're looking to parse the output of the ip command, which option can you set to remove newlines so that the output can be piped to the grep command?

   **A.** -n

   **B.** -o

   **C.** -l

   **D.** -f

# Chapter

# 10

# Topic 110: Security

## THE FOLLOWING EXAM OBJECTIVES ARE COVERED IN THIS CHAPTER:

✓ **110.1  Perform security administration tasks.**

- ▪ Key knowledge areas:
  - ▪ Audit a system to find files with suid/sgid bit set.
  - ▪ Set or change user passwords and password aging information.
  - ▪ Be able to use nmap and netstat to discover open ports on a system.
  - ▪ Set up limits on user logins, processes, and memory usage.
  - ▪ Determine which users have logged in to the system or are currently logged in.
  - ▪ Basic sudo configuration and usage
- ▪ The following is a partial list of the used files, terms, and utilities:
  - ▪ find
  - ▪ passwd
  - ▪ fuser
  - ▪ lsof
  - ▪ nmap
  - ▪ chage
  - ▪ netstat
  - ▪ sudo
  - ▪ /etc/sudoers
  - ▪ su
  - ▪ usermod
  - ▪ ulimit
  - ▪ who,w,last

✓ **110.2   Setup host security.**

- Key knowledge areas:

  - Awareness of shadow passwords and how they work

  - Turn off network services not in use.

  - Understand the role of TCP wrappers.

- The following is a partial list of the used files, terms, and utilities:

  - `/etc/nologin`

  - `/etc/passwd`

  - `/etc/shadow`

  - `/etc/xinetd.d/`

  - `/etc/xinetd.conf`

  - `systemd.socket`

  - `/etc/inittab`

  - `/etc/init.d/`

  - `/etc/hosts.allow`

  - `/etc/hosts.deny`

✓ **110.3   Securing data with encryption**

- Key knowledge areas:

  - Perform basic OpenSSH 2 client configuration and usage.

  - Understand the role of OpenSSH 2 server host keys.

  - Perform basic GnuPG configuration, usage, and revocation.

  - Use GPG to encrypt, decrypt, sign, and verify files.

  - Understand SSH port tunnels (including X11 tunnels).

- The following is a partial list of the used files, terms, and utilities:

  - `ssh`

  - `ssh-keygen`

  - `ssh-agent`

  - `ssh-add`

- ~/.ssh/id_rsa and id_rsa.pub
- ~/.ssh/id_dsa and id_dsa.pub
- ~/.ssh/id_ecdsa and id_ecdsa.pub
- ~/.ssh/id_ed25519 and id_ed25519.pub
- /etc/ssh/ssh_host_rsa_key and ssh_host_rsa_key.pub
- /etc/ssh/ssh_host_dsa_key and ssh_host_dsa_key.pub
- /etc/ssh/ssh_host_ecdsa_key and ssh_host_ecdsa_key.pub
- /etc/ssh/ssh_host_ed25519_key and ssh_host_ed25519_key.pub
- ~/.ssh/authorized_keys
- ssh_known_hosts
- gpg
- gpg-agent
- ~/.gnupg/

1.  You need to temporarily prevent users from logging in to the system using ssh or another means. Which of the following describes one method for accomplishing this task?

    **A.**  touch /etc/nologin

    **B.**  Disable sshd.

    **C.**  Remove /etc/login.

    **D.**  Add a shadow file.

2.  Which of the following commands searches the entire filesystem for files with the setuid bit set?

    **A.**  find ./ -perm suid

    **B.**  find / -perm 4000

    **C.**  find / -type suid

    **D.**  find / -type f -perm setuid

3.  Which of the following commands displays the currently open ports and the process that is using the port?

    **A.**  netstat -a

    **B.**  lsof -i

    **C.**  ps auwx

    **D.**  netlist

4.  You are attempting to unmount a filesystem using the umount command. However, when you do so you receive a message indicating that the filesystem is in use. Which of the following commands can be used determine which process is keeping a filesystem open?

    **A.**  fuser

    **B.**  ls

    **C.**  find

    **D.**  ps

5.  Which of the following commands displays account information such as expiration date, last password change, and other related details?

    **A.**  usermod -l

    **B.**  userinfo -a

    **C.**  chageuser -l

    **D.**  chage -l

6.  Which of the following commands scans the IP address 192.168.1.154 for open ports?

    **A.**  nmap 192.168.1.154

    **B.**  lsof 192.168.1.154

    **C.**  netstat 192.168.1.154

    **D.**  netmap 192.168.1.154

**7.** Which command is used to create a public/private key pair for use with `ssh`?

   **A.** `ssh -k`

   **B.** `ssh-keygen`

   **C.** `ssh-genkey`

   **D.** `ssh -key`

**8.** Which of the following configuration options sets a hard limit of 25 processes for a user called suehring in `/etc/security/limits.conf`?

   **A.** `suehring hard proc 25`

   **B.** `suehring hard nproc 25`

   **C.** `suehring proc 25 hard-limit`

   **D.** `proc 25 suehring hard`

**9.** Within which file should you place public keys for servers from which you will accept key-based `ssh` authentication?

   **A.** `~/.ssh/authorized_keys`

   **B.** `~/.ssh/keys`

   **C.** `~/.ssh/keyauth`

   **D.** `~/.sshd/authkeys`

**10.** The system on which you are working does not have the `lsof` command installed, and you are not allowed to install software without going through four levels of approval and scheduling the installation weeks in advance. However, the `netstat` command is available. Which option to `netstat` will show the process ID to which a given network port is connected?

   **A.** `-a`

   **B.** `-n`

   **C.** `-p`

   **D.** `-l`

**11.** You need to look at information on logins beyond that which is captured by the current log file for the last command. Which option to the last command can be used to load information from an alternate file?

   **A.** `-a`

   **B.** `-t`

   **C.** `-e`

   **D.** `-f`

**12.** You need to examine who is currently logged in to the system. Which of the following commands will display this information?

   **A.** `listuser`

   **B.** `fuser`

   **C.** `ls -u`

   **D.** `w`

**13.** You need to execute a command as a specific user. Which of the following commands enables this to occur?

   **A.** `sudo -u`

   **B.** `sudo -U`

   **C.** `sudo -s`

   **D.** `sudo -H`

**14.** Which option in `/etc/sudoers` will cause the specified command to not prompt for a password?

   **A.** `PASSWORD=NO`

   **B.** `NOPASSWD`

   **C.** `NOPASSWORD`

   **D.** `NOPROMPT`

**15.** Which of the following commands will display the CPU time, memory, and other limits for the currently logged-in user?

   **A.** `reslimit`

   **B.** `limitres -a`

   **C.** `ulimit -a`

   **D.** `proclimit -n`

**16.** Which line in the `/etc/hosts.deny` file will prevent any host within the 192.168.1.0/24 network from accessing services that operate from `xinetd`?

   **A.** `BLOCK: 192.168.1.0/24`

   **B.** `REJECT: 192.168.1.0`

   **C.** `ALL: 192.168.1.0/255.255.255.0`

   **D.** `NONE: 192.168.1/255.255.255.0`

**17.** When expiring a user account with `usermod -e`, which of the following represents the correct date format?

   **A.** YYYY-MM-DD

   **B.** MM/DD/YYYY

   **C.** DD/MM/YY

   **D.** MM/DD/YY HH:MM:SS

**18.** Which of the following directives in a configuration file found within /etc/xinetd.d will prevent the service from starting?

- **A.** enable no
- **B.** start no
- **C.** disable yes
- **D.** boot no

**19.** You are using an RSA-based key pair for SSH. By default, what is the name of the private key file in ~/.ssh?

- **A.** id_rsa
- **B.** id_rsa.priv
- **C.** id_rsa.key
- **D.** rsa_key.priv

**20.** Which option to the su command will execute a single command with a noninteractive session?

- **A.** -s
- **B.** -u
- **C.** -c
- **D.** -e

**21.** Which file is used to enable the setting of limits for things like logins, processes, memory, and the like for users?

- **A.** /etc/security/limits.conf
- **B.** /etc/userlimits.conf
- **C.** /etc/security/userlimits.conf
- **D.** /etc/security/procmem.conf

**22.** Which of the following best describes the method to use with ssh in order to execute a single command on a remote server?

- **A.** Use the -e option followed by the command.
- **B.** Send the command after the other options as part of the command line.
- **C.** Use the --execute option followed by the command.
- **D.** Use the -s option followed by the command.

**23.** When you're using ssh-agent, which command and option lists the currently loaded keys?

- **A.** ssh-agent -l
- **B.** ssh -l
- **C.** ssh-list-keys
- **D.** ssh-add -l

**24.** Which of the following commands should be used to edit the /etc/sudoers file?

   **A.** Any text editor such as vi or emacs

   **B.** editsudo

   **C.** visudo

   **D.** visudoers

**25.** Which of the following commands can be used to stop a given service, such as httpd.service, from starting on boot with a systemd-based system?

   **A.** systemctl disable httpdservice

   **B.** systemctl stop httpd.service

   **C.** systemd disable httpd.service

   **D.** systemd enable httpd.service boot=no

**26.** Which of the following commands will set an account to expire based on the number of days elapsed since January 1, 1970?

   **A.** passwd -e

   **B.** chage -E

   **C.** usermod -l

   **D.** chguser

**27.** You need to specify a list of known hosts for SSH for certain hosts within your organization rather than each user needing to accept those keys individually. Which option within a server-wide SSH client configuration file enables this scenario?

   **A.** KnownHosts

   **B.** PerMachineKnownHosts

   **C.** GlobalKnownHostsFile

   **D.** ServerKnownHostsFile

**28.** Which option within /etc/security/limits.conf is used to control the number of times that a given account can log in simultaneously?

   **A.** nlogins

   **B.** loginmax

   **C.** maxlogins

   **D.** loginlimit

**29.** Which file can be used to store a server-wide cache of hosts whose keys are known for ssh?

   **A.** /etc/sshd_known_hosts

   **B.** /etc/ssh_known_hosts

   **C.** ~/.ssh/known_hosts

   **D.** /root/ssh_known_hosts

**30.** Within the following entry in /etc/shadow, to what does the number 15853 refer?

mail:*:15853:0:99999:7:::

**A.** The UID of the mail user

**B.** The number of files owned by mail

**C.** The date of the last password change (since 1/1/1970)

**D.** The number of days until the account expires

**31.** Which of the following commands sets up a local port-forwarding session on local port 5150 to remote port 80 of www.example.com?

**A.** ssh -L 5150:www.example.com:80

**B.** ssh 5150:www.example.com

**C.** ssh -p 5150 www.example.com

**D.** ssh -e 5150 www.example.com:80

**32.** Which option must be enabled in /etc/sshd_config on the destination server in order for X11 forwarding to work?

**A.** XForward yes

**B.** Xenable yes

**C.** X11Forwarding yes

**D.** Xconnection yes

**33.** Which of the following commands generates a GnuPG key pair?

**A.** gpg --gen-key

**B.** gpg --key

**C.** gpg --send-key

**D.** gpg --create-key

**34.** Signatures with gpg can be generated by using which option on the gpg command line?

**A.** --sign

**B.** --signature

**C.** --si

**D.** --dsign

**35.** Which option to ssh is used to set the port for the remote host?

**A.** -p

**B.** -P

**C.** -l

**D.** @

**36.** Which option to nmap sets the scan to use TCP SYN packets for finding open ports?

    **A.**   -sS

    **B.**   -sT

    **C.**   -sY

    **D.**   -type SYN

**37.** Which of the following logs is used by the last command for detailing recent logins?

    **A.**   /var/log/last

    **B.**   /var/log/all.log

    **C.**   /var/log/wtmp

    **D.**   /var/log/logins

**38.** Which option to ssh enables the use of a key for authentication?

    **A.**   -i

    **B.**   -k

    **C.**   -f

    **D.**   --key

**39.** In a scripting scenario, you need to prevent sudo from prompting for credentials or for any other reason. Which option to sudo is used to indicate this?

    **A.**   -n

    **B.**   --noprompt

    **C.**   -i

    **D.**   -q

**40.** Which of the following commands generates an RSA key for use with ssh?

    **A.**   ssh -key rsa

    **B.**   ssh --gen-key rsa

    **C.**   ssh-keygen -t rsa

    **D.**   ssh-keygen rsa

**41.** You need to disable a service found in /etc/inetd.conf. Which of the following is used as a comment character in that file?

    **A.**   -

    **B.**   #

    **C.**   /

    **D.**   %

**42.** Which of the following commands can be used to lock an account?

   **A.** usermod -L

   **B.** usermod -l

   **C.** passwdlock

   **D.** lockacct

**43.** Which file is used as the default storage for public keyrings for gpg?

   **A.** publickeys.gpg

   **B.** pubring.gpg

   **C.** public.gpg

   **D.** pubkeys.gpg

**44.** Which file in ~/.gnupg/, if present, indicates that files have been migrated to gpg version 2.1 or later?

   **A.** .gpg-v21

   **B.** .gpg-updated

   **C.** .gpg-v21-migrated

   **D.** .gpg-files-v21

**45.** Which of the following commands searches a server for files with the setgid bit enabled?

   **A.** find / -perm 4000

   **B.** find ./ -perm setgid

   **C.** grep setgid *

   **D.** find / -perm 2000

**46.** Which of the following commands creates links within /etc/rc.d/* for starting and stopping services on a Debian system?

   **A.** createsym

   **B.** startstop-service

   **C.** update-rc.d

   **D.** createconfig

**47.** Which runlevel is typically used for single-user mode, as indicated in /etc/inittab?

   **A.** 1

   **B.** 2

   **C.** 5

   **D.** 6

**48.** Which option to the su command is used to obtain the normal login environment?

    **A.** -u

    **B.** -U

    **C.** -

    **D.** -login

**49.** Which of the following commands shows network services or sockets that are currently listening along with sockets that are not listening?

    **A.** netstat -a

    **B.** netlink -a

    **C.** sockets -f

    **D.** opensock -l

**50.** Which of the following commands lists open files belonging to all processes except those owned by the user bind?

    **A.** lsof -i

    **B.** lsof -u bind

    **C.** lsof -u ^bind

    **D.** lsof | grep bind

**51.** Which option to nmap will cause it to always perform name resolution?

    **A.** -n

    **B.** -R

    **C.** -b

    **D.** -a

**52.** Which wildcard can be used in /etc/hosts.allow to specify a match for a host whose name does not match its IP address?

    **A.** *

    **B.** ALL

    **C.** PARANOID

    **D.** NAMEMATCH

**53.** Which of the following options within an OpenSSH server configuration is used to determine whether the root user can log in directly with an SSH client?

    **A.** PermitRootLogin

    **B.** AllowRoot

    **C.** RootLogin

    **D.** PermitDirectRootLogin

**54.** Which of the following commands executes a port scan using TCP connect to the host 192.168.2.3?

   **A.** `portscan 192.168.2.3`

   **B.** `nmap -sT 192.168.2.3`

   **C.** `maphost 192.168.2.3`

   **D.** `tcpscan -C 192.168.2.3`

**55.** Which option to the `ssh` command is used for X11 application forwarding?

   **A.** `-X11`

   **B.** `-A`

   **C.** `-X`

   **D.** `-F`

**56.** Which option to gpg should be used in order to specify the destination for the encrypted file?

   **A.** `--dest`

   **B.** `--output`

   **C.** `--destination`

   **D.** `--out`

**57.** Which command is used to add keys to the SSH agent?

   **A.** `ssh-keyadd`

   **B.** `ssh-add`

   **C.** `ssh-ed`

   **D.** `ssh-cat`

**58.** Which option to the `passwd` command sets the maximum password age until the password needs to be changed?

   **A.** `-a`

   **B.** `-x`

   **C.** `-l`

   **D.** `-r`

**59.** Which option to the `ulimit` command enables setting of a limit on memory that can be locked?

   **A.** `-l`

   **B.** `-x`

   **C.** `-b`

   **D.** `-t`

**60.** Which of the following commands prints a list of existing users from the password file?

    **A.** `passwd --list`

    **B.** `cat /etc/passwd | cut -d':' -f1`

    **C.** `grep "USERS" /etc/passwd`

    **D.** `lookup --user`

**61.** You are defining a service in `/etc/xinetd.conf`. Which option is used to configure the times that access to the service is allowed?

    **A.** `time_allowed`

    **B.** `access_times`

    **C.** `timed_access`

    **D.** `access_when`

**62.** What file extension is used for interprocess communication service units that are controlled by systemd?

    **A.** `.socket`

    **B.** `.ipc`

    **C.** `.comm`

    **D.** `.intercom`

**63.** You are generating a host key for the SSH server with `ssh-keygen` and want to ensure that the key does not require a password when the SSH server starts. Which command-line option accomplishes this task?

    **A.** `-p`

    **B.** `-P`

    **C.** `-N`

    **D.** `-d`

**64.** When working with the `/etc/shadow` password file, you see passwords beginning with $1$. What algorithm does $1$ indicate has been used for password storage?

    **A.** MD5

    **B.** Blowfish

    **C.** RIN

    **D.** PIK

**65.** Which option to gpg creates a detached signature?

    **A.** `--sig`

    **B.** `--detach-sig`

    **C.** `--det-sig`

    **D.** `--sgn-det`

**66.** Which of the following best describes the role of server host keys for SSH?

**A.** The server host key is used to connect to remote servers.

**B.** The server host key is used for encrypting SSL communications.

**C.** The server host key is used for client connections and provides a means by which the client can verify that the server has not changed.

**D.** The server host key provides secure DNS resolution.

**67.** When using a custom client configuration for SSH, which option specifies the key that will be used to connect to the host?

**A.** KeyFile

**B.** IdentityFile

**C.** Key

**D.** HostKey

**68.** Which of the following commands is used as a daemon process to manage private keys for GnuPG?

**A.** gpgpkd

**B.** gpg_pkd

**C.** gpg-agent

**D.** gpg-pkagent

**69.** You need to enable editing of certain files with root privileges but do not want to grant sudo access to an editor such as vim due to the possibility of a shell escaping. Which command can be used in place of vim to provide privileged editing of files?

**A.** suvim

**B.** nano

**C.** sudon

**D.** sudoedit

**70.** Which option to the ssh command enables changing the login name for a given host?

**A.** -l

**B.** -u

**C.** -a

**D.** -m

**71.** Which option to the usermod command changes a username?

**A.** -l

**B.** -u

**C.** -a

**D.** -m

**72.** After specifying the key server, which option to gpg is used to specify the key to send to the key server?

    **A.**  key-name

    **B.**  keyname

    **C.**  send-keys

    **D.**  sendkey

**73.** Which of the following represents a group called admins within /etc/sudoers?

    **A.**  @admins

    **B.**  admins

    **C.**  -admins

    **D.**  %admins

**74.** Which limits-related option is used to control the maximum file size that a user can create?

    **A.**  filesize

    **B.**  maxfile

    **C.**  fsmax

    **D.**  fsize

**75.** You are using an SSH server over a poor network connection but would like to maintain the connection in the event of keepalive messages being lost. Which client option can be set to set the number of keepalive messages that can be lost before the client will terminate the connection?

    **A.**  ServerTerminateCount

    **B.**  ServerAliveCountMax

    **C.**  ServerKeepAliveCount

    **D.**  ServerClientKeepAliveCount

**76.** If the /etc/nologin file exists and is in use preventing users from logging in, which file can be used to provide a message to those users who are refused a login?

    **A.**  /etc/login.mesg

    **B.**  /etc/login.disabled

    **C.**  /etc/nologin

    **D.**  /etc/nologin.message

**77.** Which option to ssh-add specifies the lifetime that a key is held in the agent?

    **A.**  -t

    **B.**  -a

    **C.**  -l

    **D.**  -c

**78.** Which option for an SSH connection sets up a remote forwarding scenario?

  **A.**  -R

  **B.**  -r

  **C.**  -e

  **D.**  -d

**79.** Which option to chage sets the number of days that a user will be warned before they need to change their password?

  **A.**  -w

  **B.**  -W

  **C.**  -t

  **D.**  -a

**80.** Another administrator made a change on the system that resulted in the /etc/shadow file becoming corrupted. Which of the following can be used to recover quickly?

  **A.**  The /etc/shadow.bak file

  **B.**  The /etc/shadow- file

  **C.**  The latest backup in /var/backups/

  **D.**  Single-user mode

**81.** When examining the documentation for a service, you notice that it can use libwrap. What functionality does libwrap enable?

  **A.**  Start/stop from remote

  **B.**  TCP wrappers

  **C.**  DNS resolution

  **D.**  Shadow passwords

**82.** Which option within /etc/sudoers enables the use of an alias for a group of users?

  **A.**  User_Alias

  **B.**  User_Group

  **C.**  User_List

  **D.**  User_Spec

**83.** You are using nmap to scan a host for open ports. However, the server is blocking ICMP echo requests. Which option to nmap can you set in order to continue the scan?

  **A.**  -P0

  **B.**  -no-ping

  **C.**  -s0

  **D.**  -ping-0

**84.** Which option within a server-wide SSH client configuration specifies the name and location of the known hosts file to use?

**A.** KnownHosts

**B.** UserKnownHosts

**C.** UserKnownHostsFile

**D.** UserKnownHostsFilePath

**85.** You need to generate a host key for SSH using ssh-keygen that has been generated with DSA rather than RSA. Which option and argument to that option will create a DSA key?

**A.** -k dsa

**B.** -a DSA

**C.** -t dsa

**D.** -h dsa

**86.** The total number of users logged in can be found with which argument to the who command?

**A.** -t

**B.** -e

**C.** -q

**D.** -l

**87.** Which option to the passwd command unlocks an account?

**A.** -t

**B.** -u

**C.** -r

**D.** -l

**88.** Which option for user limits sets the maximum number of logins that a user can have on the system?

**A.** maxsyslogins

**B.** maxuserlogins

**C.** maxlogins

**D.** kennyloggins

# Practice Exams

# Chapter

# 11

# Practice Exam 1

1.  Which filesystem is used to store information about current running processes?

    **A.** /environment

    **B.** /proc

    **C.** /etc

    **D.** /dev

2.  What is the default directory for configuration information related to the modprobe command?

    **A.** /etc/modprobe.conf

    **B.** /etc/modprobe

    **C.** /etc/modprobe.d

    **D.** /var/modprobe

3.  Which of the following wall commands send the message "Please Log Off" to users in the operator group?

    **A.** wall -g operator "Please Log Off"

    **B.** wall "Please Log Off"

    **C.** wall -operator "Please Log Off"

    **D.** echo "Please Log Off" | group operator

4.  Which option to dmesg displays the time in local time?

    **A.** -rel

    **B.** -e

    **C.** -f

    **D.** -t

5.  Which process ID is typically associated with the init process?

    **A.** 0

    **B.** 1

    **C.** 5

    **D.** 100

6.  You have been troubleshooting a system issue that may be related to the driver in use for a PCI device in the system. Which command and option will display the PCI devices and the drivers being used for those devices?

    **A.** lsusb -v

    **B.** ls -pci

    **C.** lspci -k

    **D.** showpci

**7.** Which option to the `telinit` command will cause the operation to not send any notice to logged-on users?

 **A.** `-q`

 **B.** `-v`

 **C.** `--no-wall`

 **D.** `-l`

**8.** Which file in the `sysfs` filesystem could you view in order to see the MAC address of `eth0`?

 **A.** `/sys/class/net/eth0/address`

 **B.** `/sys/devices/eth0`

 **C.** `/sysfs/devices/eth0`

 **D.** `/sys/net/eth0`

**9.** When using `systemctl` to kill a process, what is the default signal sent to a process?

 **A.** `SIGKILL`

 **B.** `SIGTERM`

 **C.** `SIGINT`

 **D.** `SIGCALL`

**10.** A newly added Serial ATA (SATA) disk is not showing up during the boot process. Where can you check to begin troubleshooting this issue?

 **A.** Using system logging

 **B.** Using debugfs

 **C.** Within the `fdisk` utility

 **D.** Within the computer BIOS

**11.** Which command can be used to monitor communication taking place with dbus?

 **A.** `dbus-mon`

 **B.** `dbus -m`

 **C.** `dbus-monitor`

 **D.** `dbus-debug`

**12.** Within a systemd environment, which service manages udev?

 **A.** `systemd-udevd.service`

 **B.** `systemd-udev.service`

 **C.** `udevd-service`

 **D.** `systemd.udevd-service`

13. What is the correct syntax to indicate that the system should shut down at 8 p.m.?

    **A.**  `shutdown 20:00`

    **B.**  `shutdown 8pm`

    **C.**  `shutdown +20:00`

    **D.**  `halt 20`

14. Which option to the `systemctl kill` command will change the signal sent to the process to be killed?

    **A.**  `-k`

    **B.**  `-f`

    **C.**  `-s`

    **D.**  `-d`

15. Which systemd command and option is equivalent to the `chkconfig --list` command in a SysVinit environment?

    **A.**  `systemctl list-unit-files`

    **B.**  `systemctl list-service`

    **C.**  `systemctl --list`

    **D.**  `systemctl list-unit-files --type=service`

16. Which option to `ldconfig` is used to change the location of the cache to be updated?

    **A.**  `-C`

    **B.**  `-c`

    **C.**  `--f`

    **D.**  `-v`

17. Which of the following commands will remove all files for a package in Debian, including configuration files?

    **A.**  `apt-get remove`

    **B.**  `apt-cache clean`

    **C.**  `dpkg -P`

    **D.**  `apt-get conf-remove`

18. What is the prefix used to denote a Debian source repository in `/etc/apt/sources.list`?

    **A.**  `deb`

    **B.**  `source`

    **C.**  `deb-src`

    **D.**  `debsrc`

**19.** Which options to `rpm` will upgrade a package while displaying progress and other additional information about the operation?

   **A.** `-Iv`

   **B.** `-Uvh`

   **C.** `-U`

   **D.** `-vh`

**20.** Which option to a yum install command will cause yum to assume yes and therefore not prompt for verification when performing actions deemed critical?

   **A.** `-y`

   **B.** `-f`

   **C.** `-p`

   **D.** `-m`

**21.** When working with a yum-based system, you need to create a configuration to ensure that certain packages are not upgraded or installed. Which option can you set in `/etc/yum .conf` to facilitate this behavior?

   **A.** `exclude`

   **B.** `noupdate`

   **C.** `assumeupdate`

   **D.** `clearupdate`

**22.** You are having difficulty with shared libraries on the system. Which of the following commands will print the current directories and libraries in the cache?

   **A.** `ldconfig -C`

   **B.** `ldd -f`

   **C.** `ldconfig -p`

   **D.** `ldd -b`

**23.** Which option within a `.repo` file in `/etc/yum.repos.d/` is used to set the URL for the repository?

   **A.** `url`

   **B.** `repourl`

   **C.** `httpurl`

   **D.** `baseurl`

**24.** Which command and option is used to display basic information about each available package and its dependencies on a Debian system?

   **A.** `apt-get list`

   **B.** `apt-cache dump`

   **C.** `apt-get list-all`

   **D.** `apt-cache list`

**25.** When running the `lsblk` command, there is no separate partition listed for /boot. From which partition is the system likely booted?

   **A.** There is a /boot directory under the / partition.

   **B.** The /boot partition is hidden.

   **C.** The system has not yet built the /boot partition.

   **D.** The /boot partition does not show up with `lsblk`.

**26.** Within which hierarchy is cached data stored for both yum- and apt-style systems?

   **A.** /etc

   **B.** /var/cache

   **C.** /usr/lib

   **D.** /tmp

**27.** On a BIOS-based system, within which region of the disk is the boot loader typically installed?

   **A.** MBR

   **B.** /boot

   **C.** Sector 8192

   **D.** Front

**28.** Which of the following best describes the contents of the / filesystem within Linux?

   **A.** The / filesystem is the root filesystem and contains temporary files.

   **B.** The / filesystem is root's home directory.

   **C.** The / filesystem is used for storage of device and swap information.

   **D.** The / filesystem is the root filesystem and is the logical root of the hierarchy within Linux.

**29.** Which of the following commands will send the output of the `grub-mkconfig` command to the correct location for booting?

   **A.** `grub-mkconfig --output=/boot/grub2/grub.cfg`

   **B.** `grub-mkconfig --file=/boot/grub2.menu`

   **C.** `grub-mkconfig --file=/boot/grub.lst`

   **D.** `grub-mkconfig --output=/boot/menu.lst`

**30.** Which of the following commands writes an image called from the current directory called raspbian.img to the SD card mounted at /dev/sdc?

   **A.** `dd if=raspbian.img of=/dev/sdc bs=1M`

   **B.** `imgwrite raspbian.img > /dev/sdc`

   **C.** `imgw raspbian.img | cat /dev/sdc`

   **D.** `dd raspbian.img > /dev/sdc`

**31.** When troubleshooting a problem, you look through .bash_history to determine commands that you've recently executed. However, the file does not contain information from your current session. Which command can you use to view the commands that have been executed during the current session?

**A.** cmdhist

**B.** cmds

**C.** pwd

**D.** history

**32.** Which option should be sent to grub-install if you want to install the boot images within a directory other than /boot?

**A.** --boot

**B.** --image

**C.** --boot-directory

**D.** --b

**33.** Which command should be run in order to make changes take effect for a GRUB2 configuration change?

**A.** update-grub

**B.** grub-update

**C.** grub-config

**D.** grub-ins

**34.** Which of the following commands will set the environment variable JAVA_PATH equal to /home/user/java2 when using the Bash shell?

**A.** invoke JAVA_PATH=/home/user/java2

**B.** export JAVA_PATH=/home/user/java2

**C.** envvar JAVA_PATH=/home/user/java2

**D.** echo JAVA_PATH=/home/user/java2

**35.** Which option in the .bashrc sets the number of commands to keep in the .bash_history file?

**A.** HISTLIMIT

**B.** HISTORYFILE

**C.** HISTFILESIZE

**D.** HISTNUM

**36.** Which of the following commands will cause nl to number all lines, including blank lines, for a file called code.php?

**A.** nl code.php

**B.** nl -a code.php

**C.** nl -n code.php

**D.** nl -b a code.php

**37.** Which command can be used to create an octal representation of a given plaintext file?

    **A.** oct

    **B.** cat

    **C.** list

    **D.** od

**38.** Which command and option can be used to format text with pagination in a double-space format, including page numbers?

    **A.** pr -d

    **B.** pag -db

    **C.** cat -pd

    **D.** print -d

**39.** Of the following options for the `tail` command, which option outputs the last lines beginning at the 30th line from the start of the file rather than the end of the file?

    **A.** -n +30

    **B.** -n 30

    **C.** -30

    **D.** +30

**40.** Which option to the `uniq` command causes the matching to be done in a case-insensitive manner?

    **A.** -c

    **B.** -f

    **C.** -i

    **D.** -n

**41.** Which of the following commands prints the username and real name of all users in /etc/passwd in a tab-separated format?

    **A.** cut -d: -f 1,6 /etc/passwd

    **B.** sed 's/://' /etc/passwd

    **C.** awk -F: '{print $1,$5}' OFS="\t" /etc/passwd

    **D.** cat -o "\t" /etc/passwd

**42.** Which option to `cp` will preserve symlinks in a recursive copy?

    **A.** -f

    **B.** -d

    **C.** -a

    **D.** -b

43. Which of the following key combinations is a technique for moving to the 23rd line of a file in Vi?

    **A.**  23G

    **B.**  /23

    **C.**  i23

    **D.**  ZZ

44. Which option to the top command changes the update interval?

    **A.**  -d

    **B.**  -t

    **C.**  -n

    **D.**  -f

45. Which of the following commands will display the process ID, the real user ID, the filesystem access user ID, and command for processes on the system?

    **A.**  listproc -uf

    **B.**  ps -eo pid,euser,fuser,comm

    **C.**  ps -e pid,user,comm

    **D.**  ps -fa

46. Which command can be used to search the contents of all files below your current location for files that contain the characters DB?

    **A.**  grep -r "DB" *

    **B.**  grep -ri "DB" *

    **C.**  cat * | less

    **D.**  cat *.txt | grep DB

47. Which of the following commands will locate all files that begin with the name DB, starting from the current directory?

    **A.**  locate "DB*"

    **B.**  find ./ -name "DB*"

    **C.**  whereis "DB*"

    **D.**  find "DB*"

48. Which of the following files is the location used to gather information about load average for use in the uptime command?

    **A.**  /proc/uptime

    **B.**  /proc/loadavg

    **C.**  /proc/load

    **D.**  /proc/utime

49. When running `fsck` on an EXT3 filesystem, which option to `fsck` causes the operation to prompt when attempting a repair action?

    **A.** -y

    **B.** -f

    **C.** -a

    **D.** No option required

50. Which of the following files is updated dynamically with information about currently mounted filesystems?

    **A.** /etc/fstab

    **B.** /etc/files

    **C.** /boot/fstab

    **D.** /etc/mtab

51. When running the `df` command, you need to change the scale so that the report shows tera-bytes instead of bytes. Which option will accomplish this task?

    **A.** -ST

    **B.** -BT

    **C.** -j

    **D.** -T

52. What command can be used to create an image of important metadata for an ext3 filesystem?

    **A.** e2image

    **B.** e3image

    **C.** dumpe2fs

    **D.** dumpe3fs

53. Which option to `mke2fs` is used to check for bad blocks during filesystem creation?

    **A.** -a

    **B.** -b

    **C.** -c

    **D.** -d

54. Which of the following commands changes the ownership of the file called `Class.java` to the user `steve` and the group `developers`?

    **A.** chgrp steve:developers Class.java

    **B.** chown steve.developers Class.java

    **C.** chown developers.steve Class.java

    **D.** chown Class.java steve.developers

**55.** When bootstrapping a virtual machine, which command can be used to add the fingerprint of a server to the known_hosts file?

**A.** ssh-keyscan

**B.** ssh-keyadd

**C.** ssh-keylist

**D.** ssh-getkey

**56.** Which configuration option can be set within /etc/default/grub to affect the behavior of the system after a failed boot?

**A.** GRUB_RECOVER

**B.** GRUB_NOFAIL

**C.** GRUB_RECORDFAIL_TIMEOUT

**D.** GRUB_RECOVER_TIMEOUT

**57.** Which options to du will print a summary of information in a human-readable format?

**A.** -sh

**B.** -h

**C.** -s

**D.** -su

**58.** Which option to the find command causes it to follow symbolic links?

**A.** -S

**B.** -H

**C.** -P

**D.** -L

**59.** Which option to the tee command enables appending to the destination files rather than overwriting?

**A.** -a

**B.** -m

**C.** -g

**D.** -d

**60.** When creating a backup for a system, which directory should be included so that most configuration files will be backed up?

**A.** /var

**B.** /opt

**C.** /etc

**D.** /bin

# Chapter

# 12

# Practice Exam 2

1.  To which file should you add an entry in order for a host to be blocked using TCP wrappers?

    **A.** /etc/hosts.deny

    **B.** /etc/tcp.wrappers

    **C.** /etc/wrap.config

    **D.** /etc/tcpwrap.conf

2.  Which of the following commands creates an alias for the ps command such that the options auwx are included when the user types psa?

    **A.** alias "ps auwx" = "psa"

    **B.** alias psa=ps uawx

    **C.** alias psa="ps auwx"

    **D.** psa="ps auwx"

3.  Which of the following conditionals in a Bash script will test if the variable DAY is equal to SUNDAY?

    **A.** if ($DAY == "SUNDAY")

    **B.** if ($DAY -eq "SUNDAY")

    **C.** if [[ $DAY == "SUNDAY" ]]

    **D.** if [ DAY = "SUNDAY" ]

4.  Which of the following commands is necessary for making a variable defined in your current shell available to child processes?

    **A.** export

    **B.** source

    **C.** let

    **D.** def

5.  You are watching another administrator perform some work on a server. As part of that work, the admin uses the following command:

    . variables.sh

    Which of the following is the equivalent of . variables.sh?

    **A.** let variables.sh

    **B.** set variables.sh

    **C.** source variables.sh

    **D.** var variables.sh

6.  Which of the following commands adds ~/code/bin to the path?

    **A.** PATH=~/code/bin:$PATH

    **B.** PATH=/code/bin:$PATH

    **C.**  `PATH=/home/code/bin:$PATH`

    **D.**  `PATH=PATH:~/code/bin`

**7.** Which of the following shows a valid Bash function called `sayHello`?

    **A.**  `function sayHello () {  echo "hello";  }`

    **B.**  `function sayHello{}`

    **C.**  `function sayHello() { echo Hello }`

    **D.**  `function sayHello() { echo Hello } ;`

**8.** Which of the following commands sends an email to root with the subject of `Update` and the content of the `/etc/hostname` file?

    **A.**  `mail root > /etc/hostname`

    **B.**  `mail -s Update root > /etc/hostname`

    **C.**  `mail -s Update root < /etc/hostname`

    **D.**  `mail root -s Update /etc/hostname`

**9.** Files that should be copied to a user's home directory when their account is created should be placed in which of the following directories?

    **A.**  `/etc/usertemplate`

    **B.**  `/etc/template`

    **C.**  `/etc/skel`

    **D.**  `/etc/userskel`

**10.** Which of the following areas within an Ubuntu system contains information and settings for accessibility?

    **A.**  Accessibility

    **B.**  Access and Help

    **C.**  Universal Use

    **D.**  Universal Access

**11.** Which command can be used to set the delay and repeat rate for a keyboard?

    **A.**  `keyboard`

    **B.**  `kbdrate`

    **C.**  `kbd`

    **D.**  `keyrate`

**12.** Which variable is used to indicate the screen on which GUI applications will be shown?

    **A.**  `DISPLAY`

    **B.**  `SCREEN`

    **C.**  `LIST`

    **D.**  `XWIN`

**13.** Users can be added or removed for access to the X server. Which command facilitates this?

   **A.** xauthorization

   **B.** xhost

   **C.** xwin

   **D.** xconnect

**14.** Which option to useradd sets the number of days between password expiration and when the account is disabled?

   **A.** -n

   **B.** -f

   **C.** -e

   **D.** -g

**15.** Which of the following commands displays the current mail aliases known on the server?

   **A.** getent aliases

   **B.** getalias

   **C.** listalias

   **D.** mail aliases

**16.** Which of the following configuration lines in /etc/hosts.deny creates a deny-by-default policy where clients will need to be specifically allowed in /etc/hosts.allow?

   **A.** *.*

   **B.** All: *

   **C.** ALL: ALL

   **D.** LOC: ALL

**17.** Which of the following describes the result of running the atq command as root?

   **A.** The current cron and at jobs for root will be listed.

   **B.** The current at jobs for all users will be listed.

   **C.** The current cron and at jobs for all users will be listed.

   **D.** The last 10 entries in the at log will be shown.

**18.** Which command option can be used to remove all cron jobs for a given user using the crontab command?

   **A.** -d

   **B.** -e

   **C.** -r

   **D.** -l

19. Which option to the `crontab` command enables you to work with a different user's `cron` jobs?

    **A.** -u

    **B.** -m

    **C.** -d

    **D.** -e

20. When deleting a user from the server, you need to maintain their home directory rather than deleting it. Which option of the following commands deletes the user `<username>` but preserves their home directory?

    **A.** `userdel <username>`

    **B.** `userdel -r <username>`

    **C.** `userdel -h <username>`

    **D.** `userdel -p <username>`

21. After deleting a group, you need to search the filesystem for files owned by the group using its group ID. Which option to the `find` command will search using the group ID?

    **A.** -name

    **B.** -group

    **C.** -groupid

    **D.** -gid

22. Which of the following commands changes the group name from `admins` to `serveradmins`?

    **A.** `groupmod -g admins serveradmins`

    **B.** `groupmod -n serveradmins admins`

    **C.** `groupchg -n serveradmins admins`

    **D.** `groupchg admins -n serveradmins`

23. Which command is used to parse log file entries on a systemd-based system?

    **A.** `logger`

    **B.** `journalentry`

    **C.** `jrnctl`

    **D.** `journalctl`

24. Which option to the `ntpdate` command configures the version to use such that an older Network Time Protocol (NTP) server could be queried?

    **A.** -o

    **B.** -v

    **C.** -e

    **D.** -r

**25.** Within which directory are systemd journals stored by default?

   **A.** /var/log/systemd

   **B.** /var/systemd/journal

   **C.** /var/log/journald

   **D.** /var/log/journal

**26.** Which option to the logrotate command specifies the mailer to use?

   **A.** -o

   **B.** -s

   **C.** -m

   **D.** -v

**27.** Which option to date changes the output to Coordinated Universal Time (UTC) regardless of the current time zone?

   **A.** -u

   **B.** -t

   **C.** -s

   **D.** -v

**28.** Which of the following commands can be used to delete a print job on a system that uses the lp print system?

   **A.** lpdel

   **B.** rmprint

   **C.** rm -print

   **D.** lprm

**29.** Which of the following subnet masks represents a /23?

   **A.** 255.255.255.0

   **B.** 255.255.0.0

   **C.** 255.255.255.255

   **D.** 255.255.254.0

**30.** An entry in /etc/nsswitch.conf indicates hosts: files dns. In which order will /etc/hosts be queried for a hostname lookup?

   **A.** The /etc/hosts file will be examined first.

   **B.** The /etc/hosts file is not related to hostname lookup.

   **C.** The /etc/hosts file will be queried second.

   **D.** The /etc/hosts file will be queried last.

**31.** Which port needs to be allowed through the firewall for standard Lightweight Directory Access Protocol (LDAP) traffic to be received by the server?

**A.** TCP port 25

**B.** TCP port 443

**C.** TCP port 143

**D.** TCP port 389

**32.** Which option to ssh changes the username to use for logging in to the server?

**A.** -v

**B.** -i

**C.** -l

**D.** -u

**33.** Which option to ping disables name resolution?

**A.** -d

**B.** -D

**C.** -f

**D.** -n

**34.** Which of the following commands shows various statistics for a network interface such as packets and bytes received and transmitted along with errors and other such conditions?

**A.** ifconfig

**B.** ifstat

**C.** if -s

**D.** ifcond

**35.** When using the host command, which option displays the Start of Authority (SOA) record from each of the authoritative DNS name servers for the given domain?

**A.** -N

**B.** -n

**C.** -C

**D.** -a

**36.** You need to specify an additional localhost address and hostname for a server in order to support a specialized network configuration. Which line in /etc/hosts sets the hostname with a unique IP address in the correct range for localhost?

**A.** 127.0.1.1 host.example.com host

**B.** 192.168.0.1 host.example.com host

**C.** host.example.com 127.0.0.1

**D.** host.example.com 172.16.31.32

**37.** Which of the following options to ifup tells the command to ignore errors and continue?

    **A.** `--continue`

    **B.** `--C`

    **C.** `--ignore-errors`

    **D.** `-h`

**38.** Which option to passwd can be used to unlock an account that was locked with the passwd command?

    **A.** `-S`

    **B.** `-l`

    **C.** `-u`

    **D.** `-w`

**39.** Which of the following is the correct syntax to connect using ssh to host.example.com on port 2200?

    **A.** `ssh -l 2200 host.example.com`

    **B.** `ssh host;example.com`

    **C.** `ssh host.example.com:2200`

    **D.** `ssh host:2200 -d example.com`

**40.** Which option in /etc/sudoers sets the destination address for administrative and security emails related to sudo?

    **A.** `mail`

    **B.** `mailto`

    **C.** `secmail`

    **D.** `adminmail`

**41.** Which of the following commands displays a listing of who is logged in to the server along with the date and time that they logged in?

    **A.** `whois`

    **B.** `who`

    **C.** `loggedin`

    **D.** `curusers`

**42.** Which port should be allowed through a firewall for NTP communication?

    **A.** Port 139

    **B.** Port 161

    **C.** Port 123

    **D.** Port 194

**43.** Which option to nmap causes it to scan using UDP?

   **A.** -sT

   **B.** -sS

   **C.** -sP

   **D.** -sU

**44.** Which of the following options to lsof searches an entire directory tree for open instances of files or directories?

   **A.** -d

   **B.** +D

   **C.** -f

   **D.** -i

**45.** Which option to the ip command displays DNS names rather than merely IP addresses?

   **A.** -n

   **B.** -f

   **C.** -r

   **D.** -a

**46.** Which of the following commands and options enables you to examine timing related to listening sockets?

   **A.** ss -o

   **B.** netstat -rn

   **C.** ping -f

   **D.** ls -l

**47.** Which of the following IP address and subnet mask pairs represents a private network in a /24 size?

   **A.** 192.168.3.0/255.255.255.128

   **B.** 172.16.19.128/255.255.0.0

   **C.** 192.168.2.0/255.255.255.0

   **D.** 10.168.1.0/0.0.0.255

**48.** When viewing the results of a traceroute, you see !H. To what does !H refer?

   **A.** Network unreachable

   **B.** Host available

   **C.** Host unreachable

   **D.** High length

**49.** On which port does the `ping` command operate for Internet Control Message Protocol (ICMP) echo requests?

    **A.** 53

    **B.** 1337

    **C.** 33433

    **D.** No port is used for ICMP.

**50.** When using `netstat -a`, which file is consulted for the port number to name translation?

    **A.** `/etc/portnum`

    **B.** `/etc/services`

    **C.** `/etc/portnames`

    **D.** `/proc/sys/net/ipv4/ports`

**51.** Which of the following commands launches Orca with speech capabilities?

    **A.** `orca --no-setup --disable main-window`

    **B.** `orca --screen`

    **C.** `orca --screen-reader`

    **D.** `orca --no-setup -s`

**52.** Which of the following locations stores the configuration for LightDM?

    **A.** `/etc/lightdm/`

    **B.** `/etc/lightdm.conf`

    **C.** `/etc/lightdm-conf`

    **D.** `/etc/lightdm.d`

**53.** Which of the following commands displays statistics and information about windows in X windows?

    **A.** `xinfo`

    **B.** `xstats`

    **C.** `xwin`

    **D.** `xwininfo`

**54.** Which of the following commands can be used to set the time zone on a Debian system?

    **A.** `tzconfig`

    **B.** `/etc/timeconfig`

    **C.** `timeconfig`

    **D.** `timecfg`

**55.** Which of the following commands displays the available character maps?

  **A.** charmap

  **B.** charmap -l

  **C.** locale -m

  **D.** mapinfo

**56.** Within which directory hierarchy will you find information regarding the available time zones on the server?

  **A.** /usr/zoneinfo

  **B.** /usr/share/zoneinfo

  **C.** /etc/zoneinfo

  **D.** /etc/tz.conf.d

**57.** The driftfile, as specified in /etc/ntp.conf on a Red Hat system, is stored in which location by default?

  **A.** /var/lib/ntp/drift

  **B.** /var/ntp/drift

  **C.** /usr/share/ntpdrift

  **D.** /usr/share/lib/ntpdrift

**58.** Which character combination sets the body of the message to STDIN when using the mail command?

  **A.** <

  **B.** >

  **C.** <<<

  **D.** |

**59.** Which of the following commands deletes a group from a CentOS Linux system?

  **A.** groupdm

  **B.** grouprm

  **C.** groupdel

  **D.** delgroup

**60.** Which of the following syslog facilities captures messages from the lp printing facility?

  **A.** auth

  **B.** messages

  **C.** lpr

  **D.** root

# Appendix

# Answers to Review Questions

# Chapter 1: Topic 101: System Architecture

1. D. The udevadm command is used to work with the udev interface of the kernel, and the monitor subcommand displays kernel uevents and other udev events in real time.

2. B. Current IRQ assignments are contained in the file /proc/interrupts. Therefore, viewing the contents of the file with a command such as cat will work. There is no "view" command, making option A incorrect. Likewise, there is no /dev/irq file, making options C and D incorrect.

3. D. Configuration files for udev are found in /etc/udev, which makes option D correct. The other options do not exist.

4. A. The modprobe command loads the module and its dependencies, if applicable. The lsmod command is used to list currently loaded modules, making option B incorrect. The insmod command will load a given module but not its dependencies. Option D, rmmod, is used to remove a module from memory.

5. B. The lsusb command is used to obtain a basic list of USB devices on a system. The other commands are not valid. In the case of option D, the ls command is valid, but there is no --usb option.

6. B. The info command for udevadm enables querying for additional information about a hotplug device managed with udev.

7. D. The dmesg command displays the contents of the kernel ring buffer. On many Linux distributions, this log is also saved to /var/log/dmesg. The other options shown for this question are not valid commands.

8. C. Runlevel 1, sometimes displayed as runlevel s or S, is single-user mode in which many services are not started. Runlevels 5 and 6 are used for other purposes, and runlevel SU is not a valid option.

9. D. Scripts are stored in /etc/init.d on a system using SysV init. You may sometimes find these linked from /etc/rc.d/init.d as well. The other options are not valid for this question.

10. A. The init command can be used to access different runlevels. Runlevel 6 is used for rebooting the system. Option B will shut down the system entirely, not reboot it. Option C will place the system into single-user mode. Option D is not a valid option.

11. C. The telinit command can be used to refresh the system after changes have been made to /etc/inittab. Notably, option B will reboot the system but that was not an option in the question. Options A and D are not valid commands.

12. D. The runlevel command displays the current runlevel for a system. Option B is not a valid option to the init command, and adding sudo in front of the init command makes no difference. Option A is not a valid command.

**13.** C. Unit configuration files are stored in /lib/systemd/system. The other directory options for this question are not relevant or do not exist by default.

**14.** B. The systemctl command is used to work with services and targets. The list-units command is used to list targets. The other commands are not used for this purpose or do not exist with the required option.

**15.** C. The -nn option displays both numbers and device names, making option C correct. The -n option (option B) displays only numbers. The other two options do not exist.

**16.** D. The lsmod command is used to list currently loaded kernel modules, making option D correct for this question. The insmod command (option A) is used to load modules. Option C is a valid command but not a valid option for that command, and option B does not exist.

**17.** C. The --show-depends option shows the modules that depend on the specified module. The other options do not exist.

**18.** B. The wall command is used to send a message to all users, thereby making option B correct. The cat command is used as a means to concatenate or view files, and tee is used to send output to standard output and a file. Finally, ssh is the secure shell client command and is not used for the purpose specified.

**19.** B. Checking to ensure that the disk is detected in the basic input/output system (BIOS) is a good first step in troubleshooting. Option A, unplugging the disk, won't help it to be detected. Restarting the web server won't help detect the disk, and the disk-detect command does not exist.

**20.** D. The /sys/bus/usb/devices directory contains information about USB devices. The other directories are not valid for this purpose.

**21.** D. The file /var/log/dmesg will typically contain historical messages from the current booting of the system. On some distributions of Linux, this information is also in /var/log/boot.log.

**22.** C. Out of the options given, the systemctl status command and option is the most appropriate. The telinit and sysctl commands are not used for this purpose. Likewise, the --ls option is not valid for systemctl.

**23.** B. The isolate option is used to move the system into the target specified, making option B the correct one. The other options do not exist.

**24.** A. The initctl reload command causes Upstart to reread its configuration files.

**25.** B. The --list option will show all services on a system along with their status for each runlevel.

**26.** C. USB devices are generally considered to be hotplug devices. Hotplug devices describe those devices that can be inserted and removed while the system is "hot," or powered on, whereas coldplug devices are those that must be inserted and removed when the system is powered off.

**27.** B. The umount command is used to unmount drives within a running system. The other commands do not exist.

**28.** D. Of the options presented, running dmesg is a common way to determine the location to which the kernel has assigned the drive. Rebooting the system is not a good option, though it would work. There is no such thing as /var/log/usb.log, and the location of the drive may change regardless of port, depending on how the drive may be detected in the system.

**29.** B. From these options, only B will shut down the system immediately. Option A will cancel a shutdown.

**30.** C. The ExecStart option indicates the command to be executed on startup of a systemd service.

**31.** D. The systemctl get-default command will show the default target. The other commands and options are not valid.

**32.** A. The enable option configures the service to start on boot. The start option, D, is used to start a service immediately. The other options are not valid for this command.

**33.** C. The /proc filesystem contains information about currently running processes and additional information about the kernel and current boot of the system.

**34.** C. The -t option to lsusb will print output in a tree-like format so that you can see which devices are connected to which bus. The other arguments to lsusb are not valid, and the usblist command is not real.

**35.** D. If a working device does not appear in lsmod, it typically means that the kernel has a driver already loaded by virtue of being compiled into the kernel itself rather than loaded through a module. The use of systemd (option A) or initramfs (option B) has no effect.

**36.** C. The -w option causes the module to wait until it's no longer needed prior to unloading. The -f option forces immediate removal and should be used with caution. The other options are not valid for rmmod.

**37.** B. The tune2fs command can be used for this purpose but should be used with care because it can result in data corruption.

**38.** C. Rules related to udev are stored in /etc/udev/rules.d. The /etc/udev hierarchy contains the udev.conf configuration file along with other components related to the configuration of udev.

**39.** B. The -k option shows the kernel driver associated with a given PCI device and can be helpful when planning a new kernel compile. The -t option displays information in a tree-like structure, and -n uses numbers instead of device names. There is no -a option.

**40.** B. The /etc/modprobe.d directory is used for storing configuration information related to modules such as that used for blacklisting purposes but also for other configuration information, such as udev and module options.

**41.** B. The dracut command is used to create the initial RAM disk for newer systems and has replaced the legacy mkinitrd command used for the same purpose.

**42.** D. The file /proc/kallsyms provides a way to view the currently loaded kernel symbols. This can be helpful for resolving module dependencies. Note that on legacy systems, this file might be called /proc/ksyms.

**43.** A. The systool utility can be used to show currently loaded options for a given module. The modinfo -r command is not valid, and though modinfo shows information about a module, it does not include core size and other settings. The lsmod command cannot be used for this purpose, and there is no infmod command.

**44.** B. The /proc/sys/kernel hierarchy contains vital configuration information about a kernel. These settings can be changed on a running system.

**45.** B. The /etc/systemd/system directory is where it is recommended to store unit files for systemd. The other locations are not valid.

**46.** C. The systemctl command will be used for this purpose with the daemon-reload subcommand. The reboot option would work to reload the systemd configuration but is not correct because it requires the entire server to reboot, which is not what was asked in this question.

**47.** B. The /etc/inittab file contains the various runlevels and what to run at the given runlevel. For example, runlevel 1 is single-user, runlevel 6 is reboot, and so on. The other files listed do not exist.

**48.** B. The SYSLINUX boot loader is used for FAT filesystems to create rescue disks and to assist with installation of Linux in general. SYSLINUX also describes an overall project containing other specialty boot loaders. The other options listed for this question are not valid boot loaders, though.

**49.** C. initrd is used for an initial root filesystem for early drivers. initrd is configured to load within the GRUB configuration file for a given operating system.

**50.** B. The fsck command is used to diagnose and repair hard drive problems in Linux. The defrag command is not available in Linux.

**51.** D. The telinit command can be used for this purpose, and passing 1 as the argument will switch the system into single-user mode. The other commands shown are not valid.

**52.** D. The -n option changes the boot order for the next boot only and boots from the specified partition. The -b along with -B modifies and then deletes the option. The -o option sets the boot order. The -c option creates a boot number.

**53.** A. ISOLINUX provides a means by which CD-ROMS formatted as ISO 9660 can be booted. It's very common to have live CDs or rescue/recovery CDs that use ISOLINUX for boot. The other boot loaders are not valid for this purpose or don't exist.

**54.** A. The /usr/lib/systemd hierarchy contains files related to systemd configuration. The user directory within the hierarchy is used for user unit files, and the system files are stored in /usr/lib/systemd/system.

**55.** B. Due to the decidedly insecure decisions made with the design of Microsoft's UEFI, a shim is often needed to enable Linux to boot on a system with UEFI. The shim.efi file can be used as an initial boot loader for this purpose.

**56.** D. Scripts for starting and stopping services are located in /etc/init.d on a SysV init-based system. The other directories listed within this question are not valid.

**57.** C. The systemd-delta command is used to determine overridden configuration files. Of the other commands, diff is valid but not for this purpose. The systemctl command is also valid, but again, not for the purpose described.

**58.** B. The chkconfig --list command displays all services that will be executed on boot along with the setting for each service for each runlevel. Of the other commands, the init command is valid but does not have a --bootlist option. The other commands are invalid.

**59.** B. The bcfg command within the UEFI shell is used to configure boot loaders on a UEFI-based system. The command can accept various parameters to configure how the boot loader and kernel will load on boot. Of the other commands shown, grub-install is valid but not within the UEFI shell.

**60.** D. The pxelinux.0 file must exist within /tftpboot on the TFTP server in order for a system to use PXELINUX for booting. The other files are not valid or necessary for PXELINUX.

**61.** D. The update-rc.d utility can be used to manage SysV init scripts on Debian or Ubuntu and other distributions. When using update-rc.d, you supply the script name and the utility will take care of creating symlinks to the appropriate runlevels.

**62.** B. The e key, when pressed at the right time during boot, will send you into the GRUB shell, where you can change parameters related to boot, such as the kernel options and other related parameters.

**63.** D. The isolate subcommand followed by the desired target is used to switch between runlevels with a systemd-based system. The other subcommands shown are not valid for systemctl.

**64.** C. The runlevel defined as initdefault is the default runlevel for the system. The other options shown do not exist.

**65.** B. The initramfs system is used instead of initrd to create the filesystem-based loading process for key drivers that are needed for boot.

**66.** A. The systemctl command will be used for this purpose, and the set-default subcommand is necessary to affect the desired behavior. The target file is simply called multi-user.target.

**67.** C. The `shim.efi` boot loader loads another boot loader, which is `grubx64.efi` by default. The other options are not valid filenames for the purpose described.

**68.** D. The `/etc/rc.d` hierarchy contains symbolic links to files found within `/etc/init.d`. These symlinks are then used for executing the scripts at the appropriate runlevel. For example, on boot the system will execute the scripts found in the runlevel directory for each runlevel executed at boot time.

**69.** A. The `default.target` is the default target unit that is activated by `systemd` on boot. The default target then starts other services based on the dependencies.

**70.** B. LUNs that contain the characters `fc` are found through Fibre Channel. Therein lies the difference between options B and C, where option C contains the letters `scsi`, which would usually represent a local disk. The other options are not valid.

**71.** B. NVMe-capable drives are named `/dev/nvme*`. No special drivers are needed other than those found in the native kernel on a modern system. The other options do not exist as paths by default.

**72.** D. The `/proc/mdstat` file contains information on RAID arrays, including RAID personalities found on the system, the devices that comprise the array, and other pertinent information. The other files shown are not valid.

**73.** B. The `/sys/class/fc_host` directory contains other directories based on the Fibre Channel connections available. Within those host directories will be found the WWN in a file called `port_name`. The other directory hierarchies are not valid.

**74.** C. The `/dev/mapper` directory contains information about multipath devices such as logical volumes. The other directories are not valid.

**75.** C. The `lspci` command will be used for this purpose. NVMe devices are listed with the name nVME or NVMe; therefore, adding `-i` to grep will make the search case insensitive. You'd use this in order to ensure that the devices are detected. The other commands are not valid, with the exception of the `lspci` command, but you cannot grep for `scsi` in this scenario.

**76.** D. Tape devices are found within `/dev/st*`, making `st0` the first device.

**77.** C. The `/etc/issue` file is used to provide a message to users, such as a login banner, prior to local login. The other files shown are not valid for the purpose described.

**78.** C. The contents of the file `motd`, an abbreviation for Message of the Day, are displayed when a user logs in successfully. Among the other options, the contents of `/etc/issue` are displayed prior to local login. The other filenames are not valid for this purpose.

**79.** B. The `/etc/issue.net` file is used to provide a message for remote logins such as telnet. The other files listed are not valid for the purpose described.

**80.** D. The `poweroff` target of systemd, accessed using the `systemctl` command, is used for halting the system and then attempting to remove power on compatible systems. The `halt` target stops the system but does not attempt to remove power, whereas `reboot` simply restarts the system. There is no `stop` target.

**81.** A. The -r option is needed to specify reboot, and the format for counting time from now is prefaced with a plus sign (+), making option A correct. Of the other commands, specifying +15 without the -r option simply shuts down the computer in 15 minutes, and specifying the time as 00:15, as in option D, will shut down the computer at 12:15 a.m.

**82.** A. The service command is used to work with services, such as starting and stopping them. On newer systems, the systemctl command has replaced the service command.

**83.** A. The journalctl command with the -b option displays boot messages.

**84.** A. The -h option halts the system, including shutting down acpid-related hardware.

**85.** C. The number 9 corresponds to SIGKILL and can be passed to the kill command to issue that signal. The number 1 is SIGHUP. Others can be found within the manual for the kill command.

**86.** C. The /etc/init.d directory contains the startup and shutdown scripts for services on a Debian system that is not running systemd.

**87.** A. Among the options, examining the boot messages would be a first logical step and would prevent having to reboot the system. Rebooting may be a next step in order to examine the status of the peripheral within the BIOS.

**88.** C. The -n option prevents the banner from displaying when using wall. The other options shown are not used with the wall command.

# Chapter 2: Topic 102: Linux Installation and Package Management

**1.** C. SATA disks are addressed as /dev/sdX, just like a Small Computer System Interface (SCSI ) disk. /dev/hdX is a traditional ATA disk. The other options do not exist.

**2.** C. The keyword single, given on the Linux kernel command line, will boot the system into single-user mode. The other options are not valid.

**3.** A. The Shift key, if pressed when control has first been handed to GRUB, will cause the GRUB menu to be displayed.

**4.** B. The root=/dev/sda2 option will cause the given kernel to load /dev/sda2 for its root partition. The rootpartition option is not valid, and the format of the root={hd0,3} is not valid in this context.

**5.** C. You begin an editing session with an e when the boot option is highlighted. You can then make changes and, when done, press b to boot the system.

**6.** D. The root partition is mounted after device initialization. System services, including multi-user mode, start after the root partition is mounted. The other two options, A and C, take place prior to the kernel-initializing device drivers. This process is essentially the same for virtual machines as it is for physical machines.

**7.** D. The ESP is typically mounted at /boot/efi.

**8.** D. The partition containing /var should be the largest for a mail server because mail spools are stored within this hierarchy. The /etc/ hierarchy is usually small, as is /usr/bin. The /mail directory does not exist by default.

**9.** C. The rootnoverify option is used to specify a non-Linux kernel, one that GRUB should not attempt to load. The initrd option is used for specifying the initial RAM disk, making option A incorrect. The remaining options, B and D, are not valid options for GRUB.

**10.** A. The update-grub command sends its output to STDOUT. Therefore, you must redirect using > and send that output to the correct file. The other options are not valid for this purpose. Options C and D are not valid commands, and option B contains invalid options as well as an invalid location for the destination file.

**11.** B. MBR-based disks can be partitioned with up to four primary partitions, one of which can be further partitioned or extended into logical partitions.

**12.** D. The ldconfig command updates the current shared library cache and list. ldconfig reads /etc/ld.so.conf and incorporates any changes found within it. The other commands listed as options for this question do not exist.

**13.** B. The upgrade option for apt-get will upgrade the system to the latest version of software for packages already installed. The apt-update command does not exist, nor does the -U option to dpkg. The apt-cache command is used to work with the package cache.

**14.** C. The yum install command will install a given package. The update option will update a package. The other options listed do not exist.

**15.** C. Root's home directory is /root on a Linux system. While the /home directory does exist, there is no root or su user within that hierarchy by default. The / directory is the root of the filesystem but not the root's home directory.

**16.** A. rpm2cpio sends its output to STDOUT by default, and therefore that output needs to be redirected to a file in most cases.

**17.** B. The /usr hierarchy contains many of the programs that run on a Linux system. Other notable directories for programs are /bin and /sbin.

**18.** B. GRUB begins its count at 0 and in this scenario there are two operating systems. Therefore, because Linux is first in the configuration file its number would be 0, which is then sent to the default= option.

**19.** A. The /etc/default/grub file can be used for this purpose. You may also edit /boot/grub/grub.cfg, but this was not an option given for this question.

**20.** B. The deplist option displays the dependencies for the given package. The list option displays information about a specific package while the other two options are not valid.

**21.** A. The -ivh options will install a file using rpm, displaying both verbose output and hash marks for progress. The other options presented do not exist or do not accomplish the specified task.

**22.** B. The export command is used to set environment variables in BASH. The other commands are not valid for this purpose.

**23.** D. The yumdownloader utility will download an RPM package but not install it. The yumdownloader utility is part of the yum-utils package. The other options listed for this question do not exist.

**24.** A. The apt-cache command is used to work with the package cache and the search option is used to search the cache for the supplied argument, in this case zsh. The apt-get command is used to work with packages themselves, and the apt search command does not exist.

**25.** C. The GRUB_DEFAULT option, when in the /etc/default/grub file, is used to configure the operating system that will boot by default. The other options do not exist in this context.

**26.** A. The ro option, which is the default for GRUB, will initially mount the root partition as read-only and then remount as read-write.

**27.** D. Configuration files related to the repositories for yum are located in /etc/yum.repos.d. Of the other options, /etc/yum.conf is a file and not a directory, and the other directories do not exist.

**28.** A. The -V or --verify option will check the files in a given package against versions (or checksums) in the package database. If no files have been altered, then no output is produced. Note that output may be produced for files that are changed during installation or for other reasons. Note also the use of an uppercase V for this option as opposed to the lowercase v for verbose.

**29.** C. The -o option can be used to specify a destination file to which output will be sent instead of STDOUT. The other options listed in this question do not exist.

**30.** A. The menu.lst and grub.conf files are used in GRUB Legacy, that is, prior to GRUB 2. This therefore makes option B incorrect.

**31.** D. The ldd command will list the libraries on which the command's argument depends.

**32.** B. Swap space is used when there is insufficient RAM memory on a system.

**33.** B. The /etc/lib directory is not typically associated with library files and does not usually exist on a Linux system unless manually created. The other options either contain system libraries or can be used for that purpose.

**34.** C. The `apt-get update` command will cause the package cache to be updated by retrieving the latest package list from the package sources. There is no `cache-update` or `update` option to `apt-cache`. The `upgrade` option is used to update the system's packages and not the cache.

**35.** C. The `sources.list` file located in `/etc/apt` contains the list of repositories for Debian packages. The other file locations do not exist by default.

**36.** A. The `/boot` partition will typically be much less than 500MB but should not be undersized. The used space within `/boot` will increase as more kernels are added, such as during an upgrade process. Therefore, even though the recommended size is up to 500MB, experience proves that a larger partition is helpful, possibly 1GB to 2GB.

**37.** B. The `pvcreate` command initializes a physical partition for future use as a logical volume with LVM.

**38.** D. The `grub-install` command is used to install GRUB onto a disk and the second SATA disk would be `/dev/sdb`, making option D correct.

**39.** A. The `dpkg-reconfigure` program will cause an already installed package to be reconfigured or changed. The `-r` option for dpkg removes a package, making option B incorrect. There is no `reconf` option for dpkg or `reinstall` option for apt-get.

**40.** C. The `lvcreate` command is used to create logical volumes with LVM. The `pvcreate` command initializes physical volumes prior to creating logical volumes. The commands in the other two options for this question do not exist.

**41.** A. Physical volumes are initialized first, followed by volume group creation, and then logical volume creation.

**42.** D. `aptitude` provides the terminal-based interface rather than the standard command-line interface of the other tools listed in this question.

**43.** D. The `search` option performs a search of various fields such as the package name and description.

**44.** B. The `rpm -qa kernel` command will show the kernel version. You can also use `uname -r` for the same purpose.

**45.** C. The `GRUB_DEFAULT` option in `/etc/default/grub` will set the operating system to boot by default.

**46.** A. The `exclude` option can be used to exclude certain packages. The argument accepts wildcards, and therefore excluding all `kernel*` updates will create the desired behavior.

**47.** B. The `grub-mkconfig` command should be run after making a change to the `/etc/default/grub` file so that a new configuration file can be created with the changed option(s).

**48.** B. The `-s` option to dpkg searches for the given package and provides information about its current status on the system. The `apt-cache` command is not used for this purpose, and the `-i` option for dpkg installs a package. The `apt-info` command does not exist.

**49.** C. The lvmdiskscan command looks for physical volumes that have been initialized for use with LVM.

**50.** B. The --resolve option will download the dependencies of the package being downloaded. The other options shown within this question are not valid for the yumdownloader command.

**51.** A. The -i option to dpkg will install a previously downloaded package. The other commands don't exist, and the -U option for dpkg does not exist.

**52.** D. GRUB Legacy begins counting at 0 and separates disk letter and partition with a comma, making 0,0 the first partition on the first disk. Options A and C are not the first disk on the system, and option B contains a nonexistent partition.

**53.** A. ESP uses the legacy FAT filesystem type for its underlying format. There is a specification for how the ESP partition must be created on top of the FAT format for boot loaders and kernel images. Note that the partition is typically FAT32 but can be FAT16 if only Linux systems will reside on the drive.

**54.** A. The --install option is used followed by the partition to which extlinux will be installed for boot.

**55.** C. The format for the mount command is [partition] [target], making option C correct. The other options are not valid because the arguments are in the wrong order.

**56.** B. The master boot record (MBR) is the first sector on a disk and contains information about the structure of the disk. If the MBR becomes corrupt, all data on the disk may be lost. The other options shown for this question are not valid.

**57.** D. The --boot-directory option enables you to specify an alternative location for GRUB images rather than the default /boot. The other options shown for this question are not valid.

**58.** D. The /etc/mtab file lists the currently mounted filesystems. The /etc/fstab file lists overall filesystems for the computer but does not distinguish between mounted or unmounted filesystems. The other options listed for this question do not exist.

**59.** B. The swapon command enables swap space, making it available for use as virtual memory. The mkswap command formats the space. The other two commands are not valid.

**60.** C. The pvdisplay command shows information about a given physical volume. You can use pvdisplay to view the device on which the PV is built along with the extent size of the PV. The other commands shown are not valid.

**61.** B. The lvcreate command is used to create a logical volume from previously created physical devices and volume groups. Using lvcreate is the final of three steps in the process for using LVM prior to actually using the logical volume.

**62.** A. The vgscan command looks for both physical volumes and volume groups related to an LVM configuration. The vgscan command is run at system startup but can also be run manually. The other commands are not valid.

**63.** C. The pvscan command displays a list of physical volumes on a given server. The PVs displayed are those that have been initialized with pvcreate for use with LVM.

**64.** A. The -a or --activate option sets whether or not the logical volume can be used. There is no -b or -c option, and the -d option is used for debugging.

**65.** C. The script is using a relative path to look for srv/vhosts rather than /srv/vhosts with an absolute path back to the root directory of the system.

**66.** B. Application containers share kernel and other resources with the underlying OS and use a container daemon to communicate between the host OS and the application container. Virtual machines have their own kernel and are self-contained machines running on top of a host OS or host kernel. Linux containers also provide a containerized virtual machine–like experience but are distinct from application containers.

**67.** D. The /etc/ld.so.conf directory is used in addition to /lib and /usr/lib to configure library locations. The other paths and files shown do not exist.

**68.** A. Among these options, compute resources, such as adding more CPUs, would be the most likely option. Adding RAM might also be warranted, but that was not one of the available options for this question. There is no indication in the question that the network is slow, and there is no indication that adding disk space or block storage (which are essentially the same thing in this context) will help.

**69.** A. GRUB 2 uses grub.cfg whereas GRUB uses menu.lst and grub.conf, making option A the correct choice.

**70.** B. The MAC address will be unique for each virtual machine deployed using the image. Guest drivers would usually not be unique to an individual virtual machine but might be unique on a per-template or per-image basis. System directories are not unique per virtual machine, and there is no such thing as pilot homing in this context.

**71.** B. The cloud-init program is available on Ubuntu and other distributions and can be used to deploy images to popular cloud providers.

**72.** C. The yum package manager configuration file is /etc/yum.conf. The other files listed do not exist.

**73.** B. The -L option to dpkg lists the files included with a given package. The -f option to dpkg shows a field from a package entry, and the other options do not exist.

**74.** A. The public key is deployed to the authorized_keys file on each image, and the private key is used from the host to connect to each virtual machine. There is no reason to deploy the private key to the virtual machine in order to make a connection to it.

**75.** A. The /boot/efi partition needs to exist for the EFI partition and is typically sized 100MB to 250MB, though that size can vary.

**76.** A. The install option, or simply in, will install a package on a system that uses zypper for package management. Among the other options listed, the ref option refreshes the repository. The other options are not valid with zypper.

**77.** D. A system running Fedora 22 will use the dnf package manager by default. The yum package manager is used on CentOS and Red Hat, and apt and dpkg are used on Debian.

**78.** A. The repoquery command with the -l option is used for this purpose. The dpkg -L command is appropriate for this purpose on Debian systems. The other commands do not exist.

**79.** C. Home directories for normal users are in /home and the home directory for root is at /root, making option C correct.

**80.** A. The /etc/machine-id file contains the unique identifier for a given machine.

**81.** A. The -n option tells ldconfig to process only the directories given on the command line. The -i option ignores the auxiliary cache file. The -v option is verbose, and -r changes the root directory from which to begin processing.

**82.** C. The stats option shows total package names along with other information about the package cache. The other options are not valid for use with apt-cache.

**83.** D. The --efi-directory option is used to specify the location of the EFI partition, typically /boot/efi.

**84.** A. The /etc/fstab file contains a list of partitions for the system. The /etc/mtab file contains currently mounted partitions. The other files do not exist.

**85.** B. The options qlp list the files in an rpm package. The other options are not valid for the purpose described in the question.

**86.** B. Among the commands and options shown, the info option to yum is used for this purpose. The dpkg and apt package managers are used on Debian systems and thus would not be appropriate for a CentOS system.

**87.** A. The presence of the string vmx in the flags section indicates that an Intel processor is capable of virtualization. This extension is called svm on an AMD architecture.

**88.** A. The lvm.conf file is a primary configuration file for LVM. Within lvm.conf, typically found in /etc/ or /etc/lvm/, you can set things like filters for devices to include or exclude from the vgscan process. The other files shown are not valid.

**89.** C. The --show option displays information about the swap spaces on the computer, including how much swap is currently being used. The -a option activates all swap spaces. There is no --list option, and -h displays help.

# Chapter 3: Topic 103: GNU and UNIX Commands

1. D. The set command can be used for a variety of purposes to change how the shell environment works. One such option is –C, which prevents output redirection such as that done with > from overwriting a file if the file already exists.

2. B. The env command will print the current environment variables from Bash. The printenv command will perform the same operation. The other commands listed in this question do not exist.

3. C. The man command displays documentation for the command given as the argument. The other options listed for this question do not exist.

4. D. The uname command is used to print system information, and the -a option prints all information available to uname.

5. A. The g option, also known as global or greedy, will apply the matched operation to the entire line rather than just the first instance of the match. The other options apply as they would for a Perl-Compatible Regular Expression. Note also the tr command that provides some of the same functionality as sed.

6. C. The -l option provides the number of lines given as input. For example, wc -l /etc/passwd would print the number of lines in the /etc/passwd file. The other options given in this question are not valid for the wc command.

7. C. Both head and tail print 10 lines of output by default.

8. B. The -rf options to rm will recursively remove the contents of a directory, including other directories. The -f option alone will not work in this case because of the additional directories. The other options given for rmdir do not exist.

9. D. The -type option causes find to limit its search to directories only, whereas the -name option limits the names of returned elements. Note the use of the wildcard due to the phrasing of the question. Also note the use of ./ to denote beginning the search in the current directory.

10. A. The cat command will display the contents of file /etc/passwd and then pipe that output to the awk command. The awk command then parses its input, splitting along the specified separator for /etc/passwd, which is a colon (:). The output is then printed and piped to the sort command. The sort command in option B will not work because the cut command requires an argument. Likewise, the echo command in option C will only echo /etc/passwd to STDOUT.

11. C. The -l option for ls produces long or listed output and -t sorts by time stamp. The -r option reverses the order, and -a is needed to include hidden (dot) files, making option C correct.

**12.** A. The time stamp of the file will change when touch is run on a file that already exists.

**13.** D. The -i option will cause both cp and mv to be interactive, that is, prompt before overwriting. The -f option will force the command to run, whereas -r is recursive.

**14.** C. The tee command will send output both to STDOUT and to the specified file, making option C correct. Option A will redirect output to the correct file but not to STDOUT simultaneously. The other options will not work for this question.

**15.** A. The -p option will cause mkdir to create additional levels of directories without error. Running mkdir without options will not work in this case. The -r and -f options to mkdir do not exist.

**16.** B. The -R option will copy directories recursively. Note that if the -i option is not enabled, the recursive copy will overwrite files in the destination. The -v option adds verbosity but does not cause any recursion, and the -Z option does not exist.

**17.** C. The file command can be used to determine which type of file is being used. This can be particularly helpful for files without extensions where you are unsure if you should view the contents of the file. Option A, grep, is used to look within files but would not be helpful in this case. The telnet and export commands are not used for this purpose.

**18.** C. The dd command is used to create disk images, among other things. In this case, the input file is /dev/sda1 and the output file is output.img. It's also common to add the blocksize option by using the bs argument, such as bs=1M.

**19.** B. The cut command uses Tab as its default delimiter. This can be changed with the -d option.

**20.** A. The -z option will unzip the file, -x will extract from the tar archive, and -f is used to indicate the file on which to perform the aforementioned operations. It's typical to add -v for verbose output as well.

**21.** D. The fg command will bring a command to the foreground if it has been backgrounded with either & or with the bg command.

**22.** B. While the ps auwx command combined with grep will provide information on the running Apache instances, it will provide much more information than is required or useful for this problem. The pgrep command provides only the process IDs and therefore meets the criteria presented in the question.

**23.** D. The top command is used to continuously monitor things like CPU and memory usage, and the -p option monitors a single process. By using the runquotes with the pidof command, the process ID is provided as input to the -p option.

**24.** D. The free command displays overall memory usage for both RAM and swap and can be used to determine when additional memory might be needed.

**25.** A. You need to write the changes to the file; therefore you'll need :w. The addition of q will also quit. Note that you could use ZZ to write and quit as well. The dd command deletes a line, and x deletes a single character.

**26.** D. The -n option changes the number of lines of output for both head and tail to the number specified. The other options listed in this question are not valid for head, and the -f option follows a file with tail as the file grows.

**27.** A. The uptime command shows basic information such as that described along with the number of users logged into the system and the current time. The bash command is a shell environment, and the ls command will not display the required information.

**28.** D. The screen command starts a new terminal that can be disconnected and reconnected as needed. Processes running from within the screen session do not know that they are running in a screen session and therefore meet the criteria needed to satisfy this question. The fg and bg commands will not meet the criteria, and the kill command will stop a process.

**29.** C. The -9 option invokes SIGKILL, which will force the process to end. The 15 signal is the default, and the -f and -stop options do not exist.

**30.** C. Within Bash, the number 1 represents STDOUT and 2 represents STDERR. Redirecting both means combining them in the manner shown in option C.

**31.** B. The nice command, when run without arguments, will output the priority for the currently logged-in user, which is normally 0. The renice command can be used to change the priority of running processes. The other two commands shown as options for this question do not exist.

**32.** D. Within a regular expression, * represents 0 or more characters. In this case, it doesn't matter whether a person is using /bin/bash or /usr/bin/zsh. Likewise, a . matches a single character, but in the case of bash and zsh, we need to look at the first and then optionally a second character. The ? character makes the second . optional. Finally, the $ anchors the pattern at the end of the string and is also the key for this regular expression.

**33.** A. The different levels of the manual are accessed by preceding the argument with the desired level. The other options, such as --list, do not exist in this context.

**34.** C. The o command opens a new line below the current cursor location. The a command begins an insert mode session at the character after the cursor, not the line. The i command begins an insert mode session at the current cursor location.

**35.** A. Sending -HUP as part of the kill command will restart a process. Of the other options, a -9 will kill the process completely. The other two options do not exist as valid means to kill a process.

**36.** B. The history command will display your command history, including commands from the current session. You can specify how many lines of history to display, as shown in the answer for this question. Note that .bash_history will not show the current session's history.

**37.** C. The jobs built-in command shows the list of jobs running in the background. Its output includes a job number and the status of the job.

**38.** B. The `find` command, beginning with the path and then the -name argument, will locate all of the files called `.bash_history`. The output from the `find` command should be piped to `xargs`, which can then build further commands from standard input. Note that this question and solution assumes that all users use the Bash shell and are keeping history.

**39.** C. The `tail` command provides the end portion of the file given as an argument. Adding the -f option will cause the output to update as new lines are added to the file being tailed.

**40.** D. The `nl` command will prepend line numbers onto the file given as its argument. The output is then sent to STDOUT. Of the other options, `wc -l` will print the number of lines in the file but not prepend those numbers onto each line, as was asked for in this question.

**41.** A. The `xz` command can compress and decompress files in a variety of formats, one of which is `lzma`.

**42.** A. The `find` command will be used for this purpose. Adding -type f will limit the search to only files and the -mtime option will limit to modification time in day format.

**43.** C. The `mv` command is used to move files, and `*.txt` will look for all files with a .txt extension. Note the fully qualified destination with a / preceding the name `tmp`.

**44.** D. The `pwd` command prints the current working directory. The `cd` command changes directory.

**45.** A. The file needs to first be sorted to group common ZIP codes together. After that, piping the output to `uniq` will display the unique ZIP codes, and the -c option provides a count.

**46.** A. Preceding the command with a ! will search history and execute the specified command. For example, !vi will start your last Vi session.

**47.** C. The `killall` command is used to terminate processes using their name.

**48.** C. The ? key will search backward in a file within Vi. The / is used for searching forward. The h key moves the cursor to the left one character, and the x key will delete a character.

**49.** D. The export command makes an environment variable available to subsequent child processes. The other commands shown are not valid.

**50.** B. The echo command sends output and $0 is the parameter that contains the current script name. Of the other options, $PS1 is the shell prompt and the other two options do not exist by default.

**51.** B. The gunzip command is typically used for decompressing files with a .gz extension. The other options are not valid commands.

**52.** C. The -i option causes `rm` to use interactive mode, where the command will prompt for confirmation prior to taking action. See the (1) `rm` man page for additional information on the other options.

**53.** A. The find command can be used for this purpose. When used with the size option, various size-related options can be used. The option +1G searches for files greater than or equal to 1GB.

**54.** B. The -v or verbose option lists files as cpio is working with them. Of the other options, -s is swap bytes and –l is used to link files. The -k option is included for compatibility purposes.

**55.** B. The bzcat command sends output to STDOUT from a bzip2 archive.

**56.** C. The jobs command is actually a shell built-in command, meaning that more information is available by using the man page for bash itself. The other options either are not valid or will not show information about the jobs command/built-in.

**57.** B. The nohup command can preface another command when starting so that the process or command will not accept a SIGHUP.

**58.** D. The watch command runs a command repeatedly and displays the output and errors from the command. The pgrep command does not fulfill the needs of this scenario. The mon and procmon commands are not real.

**59.** B. The tmux command creates two (or more) sessions within the same physical terminal window and thus enables this scenario. The screen command can be used to create an additional session, but the screen command does not meet the criteria specified in this scenario, because the scrollback buffer does not capture enough lines by default. The other commands shown are not valid.

**60.** A. The pkill command can be used for the scenario described. The other options are not valid commands.

**61.** A. The -f option matches against the full path. The -d option is used to set the delimiter, the -o option matches the oldest process, and the -i option sets the search to be case insensitive.

**62.** B. The which command is used to determine the command that will be run based on the current environment settings such as the path. The find and ls commands will not work for this purpose.

**63.** B. The unset shell built-in is used for the purpose described. Both the reset and clear commands do not accomplish the task described, and there is no undo command.

**64.** A. The type shell built-in displays information about a given executable. For example, the command type alias shows that alias is a shell built-in as well.

**65.** C. Double quotes help to ensure that variables are interpolated within a shell script. Runquotes are not used for this purpose, and the other options are not valid types of quotes.

**66.** C. The less pager fits the scenario described. The more pager does not have as much flexibility as less. The other options shown are not valid.

**67.** C. The od command converts a file to octal format. The other options shown all have invalid commands.

**68.** B. The -b option for sha256sum and sha512sum reads the file in binary mode as opposed to text mode, which is the default.

**69.** B. The h, j, k, and l keys enable movement of the cursor in command mode Vi.

**70.** C. The decompress and stdout options to xz are functionally equivalent to the xzcat program. There is also a related program called zcat for outputting files compressed with gzip to STDOUT.

**71.** A. The EDITOR environment variable controls the editor that is used. Typical choices include nano, Emacs, Vi or enhanced Vi, known as Vim.

**72.** D. The seventh manual section for regex is found by specifying the level after the command and prior to the manual page to examine.

**73.** B. The renice command changes the priority of a running process. The nice command is not capable of altering running processes, and the other commands shown are not valid.

**74.** B. The fgrep command is equivalent to running the grep command with an -F option. The -f option specifies a file, and the -E option utilizes an extended regular expression and is equivalent to the egrep command. The -a option is important in its own right and causes grep to process a binary file as if it were a text file.

**75.** A. All of the options shown use regular expressions. In the correct answer, the strings Steve and steve will match due to the use of a character class. Option B would match only Steve but, due to the quantifier *, would also match strings like Siwejfiwjfheteve. Option C uses anchoring and thus would only match Steve or steve at the beginning of a line. Option D also uses an anchor to indicate end of line and thus does not make sense in this context.

**76.** C. The top command shows running processes, typically sorted by CPU usage and updates every few seconds. The ps command shows processes but does not auto-update. The nice command sets priority, and there is no procs command.

**77.** A. Files compressed with the gzip utility can typically be read by other operating systems, though it may require additional software for certain operating systems. Compression utilities like bzip2 and xz almost certainly require additional software. The tar command in option D is not a compression utility.

**78.** A. The question mark can be used as a wildcard for such a scenario. An asterisk would also work for file globbing.

**79.** B. The split command can break up a file into multiple pieces. The cut command would split an individual line but does not meet the criteria in this scenario. There is no dice or rem command.

**80.** C. The scheduling priority of the process is shown in the PR column. The process ID is displayed in the PID column. The top command shows CPU utilization in the %CPU column and does not display information about the processor cores.

**81.** A. The d key will be used for this and the number 7 used in order to cut or remove eight lines. Other keys to work with text for cut, copy, and paste in Vi include p, y, dd, and yy. The other options shown for this question are not valid.

**82.** A. The unxz command decompress a file that has been compressed with xz.

**83.** D. The md5sum command creates a 128-bit MD5 message digest. The sha256sum command produces 256-bit values, whereas sha512sum produces 512-bit values.

**84.** A. The paste command fits the scenario described and separates the lines from each file by a tab. The other commands are not valid.

**85.** A. Using a fully qualified path meets the scenario in the most typical manner. You could add the command path to the PATH environment variable, but that is unnecessary given the scenario. Restarting the shell or computer would not have any effect.

**86.** B. The SIGTERM signal is used by default by the pkill command. This can be changed using the --signal option.

**87.** D. Running jobs are listed with the -r option. The -s option displays only stopped jobs, whereas -l shows process IDs. There is no -a option to the jobs built-in command.

**88.** C. The -c option outputs to STDOUT. See the bzip2(1) man page for additional details.

# Chapter 4: Topic 104: Devices, Linux Filesystems, Filesystem Hierarchy Standard

**1.** A. The listing shows a symbolic linked file located in the current directory, linked to .configs/fetchmail/.fetchmailrc. The file is owned by the root user and root group and was created on July 8, 2014.

**2.** A. The mount command is used to mount drives in Linux. The source and destination mount points are expected as arguments. Drive partitions begin at the number 1, making the first partition number 1.

**3.** C. The noexec option will prevent programs from being executed that reside on the partition. The noexec option is used frequently for mounting the /tmp partition.

**4.** B. 0x82 is Linux swap, and 0x83 is Linux. NTFS is 0x07, and FAT is 0.0c.

**5.** B. The partition type 0x83 should be created for a normal Linux partition. Type 82 is used for swap; 84 is an OS/2 partition. There is no L type.

**6.** A. The `which` command returns the full path to the given command and is useful for determining both whether a given command is available and the location from which the command will run.

**7.** A. The `chgrp` command can be used to change group ownership of a file. The order is `chgrp <groupname> <target>`.

**8.** C. The file is almost certainly a hard link to the original script. Although `ls` won't show this information, the `stat` command will show that it is a link and also show the inode to which the file is linked.

**9.** A. The `-i` option to `df` produces information on inodes across all filesystems. The `ls -i` option will produce inode listings, but only for the current directory. The `-i` option is invalid for `du`, and `dm` does not exist as a command.

**10.** C. The `-y` option will attempt to repair automatically, essentially answering y or yes instead of prompting. Of the other options, only `-V` is valid and will produce verbose output.

**11.** B. The addition of journaling in ext3 increased filesystem reliability and performance.

**12.** C. The `-S` option displays output in a format such as `u=rwx,g=rx,o=rx`. The other options listed do not perform the desired operation.

**13.** B. The `-s` option to `ln` creates a symbolic link, or symlink.

**14.** C. The `whereis` command displays pertinent information about the command given as its argument. For example, entering `whereis apache2` on a Debian system will show the binary location, configuration file location, and other relevant details.

**15.** A. The PRUNEPATHS option accepts a space-separated list of paths to remove from the results. The other options listed do not exist.

**16.** D. The `/srv` hierarchy is used for data for server programs. The `/etc` hierarchy is configuration information; `/var` is also data files but variable, such as mail files. The `/tmp` directory is for temporary files.

**17.** C. The `chmod` command is used for this purpose, and the u+s option sets the sticky bit for the user on the specified target.

**18.** B. The `-a` option mounts all filesystems in `/etc/fstab` that are currently available. This option is typically used if the mount points are not mounted at boot time or another mount point is added to the system after it has been booted.

**19.** B. The `mkswap` command formats a swap partition. The `fdisk` command is used to create the partition itself but not format it. The other two options do not exist.

**20.** A. The `tune2fs` command displays a lot of information about filesystems, and when used with the `-l` option, the output includes the number of times that the filesystem has been mounted.

**21.** A. The -g option displays progress of the dump. The other options listed do not exist.

**22.** A. The du command will report on disk usage in a recursive manner, unlike the other commands shown here.

**23.** C. The /etc/fstab file is used to store information about the filesystems to mount within the system.

**24.** D. The /media mount point is used for removable media. See https://wiki .linuxfoundation.org/lsb/fhs-30 for more information on the FHS.

**25.** A. The /etc/mtab file contains currently mounted filesystems. Note that /etc/fstab contains filesystem information but doesn't report which filesystems are currently mounted.

**26.** B. The -r option causes umount to attempt to remount in read-only mode. The -v option is verbose mode, and the -f option forces the operation. The -o option does not exist.

**27.** A. The 022 umask will translate into 644 permissions on a new nonexecutable file.

**28.** C. The updatedb command will update the database used by the locate command.

**29.** A. The type built-in returns the location that the shell will use in order to run the given command. The find command cannot be used for this purpose, and the other commands do not exist.

**30.** B. The -R option will perform the change ownership in a recursive manner.

**31.** D. The proper order is the device (UUID or partition) or filesystem to mount, followed by the mount point or directory to mount that device, followed by its type and options, and then the dump and pass settings.

**32.** A. The blkid command will show partition UUIDs. You can also get this information with the lsblk -no UUID <partition> command. The other commands shown in this question do not accomplish the required task.

**33.** A. Priority order for systemd configuration files are those within the /etc/ hierarchy, followed by files in the /run/ hierarchy, followed by files in the /lib/ hierarchy.

**34.** A. The -y option causes fsck to assume yes instead of prompting when repairing a filesystem. The -v option is verbosity. There is no -m or -x option for fsck.

**35.** C. The -t option sets the filesystem type as ext2, ext3, or ext4. The mke2fs command is typically symlinked from /sbin/mkfs.ext2, /sbin/mkfs.ext3, and /sbin/mkfs.ext4. The -F option forces mke2fs to create a filesystem, and the -a and -e options do not exist.

**36.** B. The file /etc/auto.master contains the configuration for autofs. The other files listed as options are not valid for this scenario.

**37.** C. The mkisofs command creates an ISO filesystem, which can then be written to a CD or DVD. The other commands listed are not valid.

**38.** B. The -c option sets the maximum mount count. The -C option sets the current number of mounts. The -b and -a options do not exist.

**39.** D. The -f option, also known as fake, is helpful for situations where you need to debug the mount process or when you need to add an entry to /etc/mtab for a previously mounted filesystem. The -l option shows labels, and -v is verbose. There is no -q option.

**40.** C. The letters ro indicate that the filesystem has been mounted read-only, meaning that it is not possible to perform a write to the filesystem. The other possible option is rw, indicating that the filesystem has been mounted read-write.

**41.** C. Bad blocks are shown with the -b option. The -f option forces dumpe2fs to perform the requested operation, and the other command options do not exist.

**42.** D. Btrfs is based on the copy-on-write principle and is generally considered more advanced than ext4 and its predecessors. FAT is a legacy filesystem primarily used for DOS and its follow-ons like Windows.

**43.** B. The xfs_info command, which is functionally equivalent to xfs_grow -n, displays information about an XFS-formatted filesystem.

**44.** A. The blkid command shows information about partitions including their type, their UUID, and other basic information. The other commands shown do not exist.

**45.** C. The -t option, which can accept a comma-separated list of types, specifies that only filesystems of the listed type are to be unmounted. This is useful in conjunction with the -a option, which unmounts all filesystems except /proc. The -v option is verbose, and -f forces the operation to continue.

**46.** D. The sync command writes unwritten data to the disk immediately and is useful to run just prior to attempting an unmount operation.

**47.** C. The -f option specifies that xfs_check should check the contents of the named file for consistency. The -v option sets verbosity, and there is no -d or -a option.

**48.** B. The -w option causes debugfs to open the filesystem in read-write mode. There is also a -c option to open in catastrophic mode for filesystems with significant damage. The -rw, -r, and -n options are not valid.

**49.** D. The smartd daemon monitors SMART-compatible disks for notable events and can be configured to send alerts when events occur. The other commands listed are not valid for this scenario.

**50.** A. The -f option forces fsck to run on an otherwise clean filesystem for ext3 filesystems. This can be helpful for times when you suspect there is an error on the filesystem and need to verify the integrity of the filesystem as part of the troubleshooting process. This can also be helpful to prepare the filesystem for conversion, such as might be the case with a tool like btrfs-convert.

**51.** A. The block size for import or restore must match the block size used on export or dump. Block size is specified with the -b option, making option A correct. The other options are not valid for xfsrestore.

**52.** B. A filesystem with the word defaults for its mount options will be mounted read-write (rw), suid, with the ability to have executables (exec). The filesystem will be auto-mounted (auto), but users will not be able to mount it (nouser). Character and block special devices will be interpreted (dev), and operations on the disk will be performed in an asynchronous manner (async).

**53.** B. The btrfs subvolume create command creates a btrfs subvolume. The other commands are not valid.

**54.** C. The -z option sets the maximum size for files to be included in the dump. The -b option sets the block size but is not related to what is being asked for in this scenario. The -s option sets the path for inclusion in the dump, and -p sets the interval for progress indicators.

**55.** C. The -e option sets the behavior, such as continue, remount read-only, or panic, when an error occurs at the filesystem level. The -f option forces whatever operation you're requesting to continue even if there are errors. The -d and -k options are not valid.

**56.** D. The -n option causes mount to not write to /etc/mtab and is particularly useful for the scenario described. The -a option mounts all filesystems in /etc/fstab. There is no -b or -a option.

**57.** A. The swapoff command deactivates swap space, thereby making it unavailable as virtual memory on the system. The other commands shown as options are not valid.

**58.** A. The Where= directive specifies the location for the final mounted filesystem.

**59.** A. The mkfs.fat or mkfs.vfat commands are valid for creation of FAT filesystems. There is no -f option to mkfs, and there is no mkfat command.

**60.** D. The tune2fs command is used for working with ext2, ext3, and ext4 filesystems. The -j option adds a journal. The other commands are not valid.

**61.** A. The snapshot subcommand of btrfs subvolume creates a snapshot. The other commands shown are not valid.

**62.** A. The -L option forces the log to be cleared or zeroed out, which may cause a loss of data. The -v option sets verbose output; -V prints the version. The -d option performs a dangerous repair, which can be used on a read-only filesystem.

**63.** C. The -o option enables the setting of one or more options for the mount command, and ro is read-only. Note that the -r option will also mount as read-only. The other options shown are not valid.

**64.** B. The -E option signals that an extended option follows, such as stripe_width. The -f option forces an operation but should not be necessary for this solution, and the -e option sets the behavior on error. There is no -extend option.

**65.** A. The gdisk utility is the equivalent of fdisk for working with GPT partitions. Later versions of fdisk can also be used to manage GPT partitions.

**66.** A. The maximum size for a partition on an MBR disk is 2 terabytes. GPT has largely replaced MBR on newer Linux systems.

**67.** C. The -m option with 0 will format the partition with no reserved blocks for superuser or system use. The -r option sets the filesystem revision.

**68.** B. The default time for filesystem reorganization is two hours, or 7200 seconds.

**69.** C. The file permissions are 640, meaning that the group owner can read the file. Therefore, changing group ownership should have the fewest side effects. Granting root access is not preferred, especially noting that the problem statement indicated that granting sudo wasn't preferred. While using chown on the file to change the owner would also work, it's likely to have additional side effects that could prevent the owner of the file from reading and writing, and there isn't enough information in the problem for that. Finally, running chmod 777 is almost never the correct solution to any problem on Linux.

**70.** B. The -a option shows all devices, even those that are empty. The -r option is for raw devices, and the other options do not exist.

**71.** D. USB devices and others removable media can typically be found within the /media/ mount point.

**72.** C. The mkfs-related commands are typically used for formatting filesystems on Linux. In this case, mkfs.exfat is the correct option for formatting exFAT filesystems.

**73.** C. The xfs_db command is used for debugging XFS-formatted filesystems.

**74.** C. The -b option is used to specify an alternate superblock and helps in the scenario described, where the superblock has been damaged. The -B option specifies the block size. There is no -s or -o option for e2fsck.

**75.** A. The -h option is the flag for human-readable formatting and shows numerical output in larger size increments rather than bytes. The other options are not valid for df.

**76.** B. The /etc/profile file is one of a few locations in which default options can be set for users of Bash. The other file locations shown do not exist.

**77.** A. A symbolic link will not work. The users would be editing the same file and, without saving as a different filename, would not be able to keep their own edits.

**78.** B. The find command will be used for this purpose, and the -uid option will need to be used because the user has already been deleted. If the user had not been deleted, then the -user option would still work.

**79.** A. The updatedb command is used to update the locate database. The other commands are not valid.

**80.** B. The -f option shows the UUIDs of the filesystems mounted on the system. The -a option shows all devices, the -o option enables specification of output columns, and the -u option does not exist.

**81.** C. The -c option checks for bad blocks before formatting. The other options are not valid with mkswap.

**82.** D. The sticky bit has been set on the file as denoted by an uppercase S.

**83.** C. Using octal form, 4 is user, 2 is group, and 1 is sticky bit. Therefore, 2755 would have setgid for the file.

**84.** C. The -name option is used for this purpose, and / indicates the root of the system. A * wildcard is used to indicate all filenames ending in .sql, as described in the scenario.

**85.** B. The UUID=<UUID> syntax is correct for the /etc/fstab file.

**86.** C. The --inodes option shows inode usage with du. The -h option is human-readable, and -d sets the maximum depth. There is no -i option for du.

**87.** A. The -size option is used with find for this purpose, and the +1G argument will look for files greater than 1 gigabyte. Note that if the + is omitted, only files of the exact size are found.

**88.** B. A symbolic link is the preferred method because it does not require additional maintenance that a script would or that copying would in order to keep the libraries current. Moving the libraries may have unintended consequences if another program is dependent on the libraries in that location.

# Chapter 5: Topic 105: Shells and Shell Scripting

**1.** B. The PS1 variable usually has its default set in /etc/profile and is used as the shell prompt. Users can customize the prompt to include hostname, working directory, and other elements.

**2.** C. The source command is used to execute commands from a file. A typical use case is to create functions or variables that are then available for use within the current session. The other commands listed do not exist.

**3.** B. While it's true that every user has a .bash_logout in their home directory, that file can still be edited by the user. Therefore, to ensure that the required command is executed at logout, the /etc/bash.bash_logout file must be used.

**4.** B. The env -u command will unset an environment variable for the current session. The unset command can also be used for this purpose.

**5.** C. The -v option, which is the default, tells unset that the name given is a shell variable rather than a function. The other options shown do not exist.

**6.** A. The alias command is used for this purpose and its format is name=value, making option A correct. The ln command cannot be used for this purpose because it will not accept command-line arguments for the target in such a format, as shown in the options.

**7.** B. User-based configuration files are located in the order .bash_profile, .bash_login, and .profile. Only the first file found is executed and the others are ignored.

**8.** C. The $1 variable is automatically available within Bash scripts and represents the first command-line argument. The other variables listed in this question do not exist by default.

**9.** D. The fi construct is used to indicate the end of an if conditional within a Bash script. In many languages, if conditionals are scoped by braces such as { }, but in shell scripting, fi is used to denote the end of the condition.

**10.** B. The seq command is used to print a sequence of numbers in a variety of formats. The answer for this question provides a starting point (0), and increment (1), and the final number (5), resulting in six numbers being displayed as output.

**11.** B. The echo command is used to display its argument, regardless of whether the command is used inside a shell script or from the command line itself. The env command is used to display environment variables and therefore does not meet the need specified in the question. The var_dump command is used within PHP, and ls is used to display contents of directories.

**12.** A. The suid bit enables the program to run as the user who owns the file regardless of who executes the program. Using SUID is typically not recommended for security reasons.

**13.** D. The exec command executes the command given as its argument and will then exit the shell. The source command does not exit the shell.

**14.** C. The double-ampersand sequence executes commands only if the previous command exited cleanly.

**15.** C. The read command awaits user input and places that input into the specified variable. The exec command is used to execute commands, and the other options are not valid for the purpose described.

**16.** A. Parentheses are used to denote a function, such as myFunction(). The parentheses are optional but are then followed by curly braces containing the commands to be executed when the function is called.

**17.** C. The || sequence indicates an alternate command to run if the initial preceding command does not exit cleanly. The && sequence executes only when the preceding command exits cleanly, so it's just the opposite of what the question was asking.

**18.** C. The elif keyword is used to create an alternative execution path within a shell script. The other constructs, such as else if and elsif, are used in other languages.

**19.** C. The `unalias` command is used to remove a previously defined alias. The `rm` command will remove regular files but not aliases. The other commands do not exist.

**20.** D. At a minimum, you need to be able to read the file being sourced; therefore, `chmod 400` will correctly set the permissions. Any `chmod` that gives additional permissions is not necessary.

**21.** C. The `for` loop construct in this case will require the variable name `LIST` to be preceded with a dollar sign ($),making option C correct. The other options will not work for the purpose described.

**22.** C. The `-lt` operator is used to test for "less than" conditions within a script. The other operators are not valid for use in a shell script.

**23.** B. The `-e` test checks to ensure that a file exists and is typically used in the context of a conditional within a shell script. The other options may work within shell scripts but are not tests for file existence.

**24.** C. The `/etc/skel` directory contains files to be copied to the user's home directory. The other directories listed for this question do not exist by default.

**25.** C. The `--norc` option causes `bash` to execute without reading the `/etc/bash.bashrc` file or the local `~/.bashrc` file. The other options listed do not exist as options for `bash`.

**26.** A. Array creation in a shell script involves parentheses when used in this manner. You can also use square brackets to define individual elements, as in `ARRAY[0] = "val1"`.

**27.** C. The `-p` option to `declare` displays fully qualified shell statements such that the statements could then be used as input for another command, either through piping or redirection to a script.

**28.** A. The `.bash_profile` file, if it exists in your home directory, will be executed on login. Note that placing the function in `/etc/profile` would technically work but then the function would be available to all users, which is not what the question asked for.

**29.** B. The `readonly` command displays the list of read-only variables that have been declared in the current session. The other commands listed for this question do not exist.

**30.** C. Square brackets are used to denote the beginning and end of the test portion of a `while` loop in a shell script. Other languages generally use parentheses for this purpose.

**31.** B. The `test` built-in will return `true` and can be used to test for the value existence of a variable not being null. Note that the behavior of the `test` built-in differs depending on the number of arguments.

**32.** C. The `HOME` environment variable, set automatically to the user's home directory, is consulted when the command `cd ~` is entered. The other paths beginning with `HOME` do not exist by default, and the `MAILPATH` environment variable shown contains a list of locations where mail is checked when using the shell interactively.

**33.** B. The TMOUT variable can be set in a given user's shell and that user will be logged out after the value given (in seconds) of inactivity. The other environment variables listed here do not exist.

**34.** B. Just as with an if statement where the statement is ended with fi, so too is a case statement ended with the word *case* spelled backward. The curly brace shown as option D is used to close case statements in many languages, but not for shell scripts.

**35.** A. The provided answer performs command substitution and places the value from the resulting command into a variable. Note the use of +%s formatting on the date, which then formats the output as seconds since the epoch, as specified in the question. Option C will provide the date within the DATE variable but will not format it as specified.

**36.** B. Wrapping a variable in curly braces, such as ${FILEPATH}, will ensure that the variable is interpolated or expanded correctly even when used in a place where it might not normally be expanded, such as within a quoted string.

**37.** B. In shell scripts, the commands to execute begin at the do keyword and end at the done keyword. Other languages generally use either curly braces or tabs.

**38.** D. The -r test determines whether a given file exists and can be read by the current user. The -e test only checks to see if the file exists.

**39.** A. The -r option to declare will create or mark the variable as read-only. The -p option prints output in a format that can be reused. The -x option declares the variable for export.

**40.** D. The *) sequence is used to denote a default set of statements that will be executed if no other case matches within the set.

**41.** A. Backquotes can be used for command substitution within a Bash script. The other options shown are not valid for command substitution.

**42.** B. The character sequence done denotes the end of a while loop in Bash.

**43.** B. Greater than or equal to is tested with >=. Of the other operators shown, != tests for inequality.

**44.** C. The execute bit is not set on the script, resulting in the permission denied error, making option C correct. The file extension does not matter, so option A is incorrect. Likewise, option B is not correct because the script isn't even executing. Lowercase or uppercase letters do not matter, making option D incorrect.

**45.** D. The -f option exports names as functions to child processes. The other options shown do not exist with the export command.

**46.** D. The unset command removes a variable from being set. The other options shown do not exist.

**47.** A. The /etc/bash.bashrc file is a systemwide configuration file for the Bash environment. Another systemwide file used for similar purposes is /etc/profile.

**48.** D. The +x option enables debugging output and is frequently used when debugging shell scripts. The -x option is used to disable debugging. The -d and +d options do not exist.

**49.** D. The `.bashrc` file in a given user's home directory is executed for interactive logins. The other files shown do not exist.

**50.** A. The `function` keyword declares a block of code to be a function in Bash. It's worth noting that the `function` keyword can be omitted in most cases. The other options are not valid.

**51.** B. The syntax shown in option B is the correct syntax to add a path to the current environment. Option A does not include the existing path (and will, in fact, overwrite the existing path). Option C contains spaces, and option D uses a semicolon as a delimiter.

**52.** D. The `$0` variable is automatically defined and contains the name of the script itself. The other options shown do not exist by default.

**53.** A. The `-s` argument enables setting of a delimiter. When used, the numbers will be printed in a sequence rather than one per line. The `-m` and `-d` options do not exist.

**54.** D. The `-O` option is used to determine if the user currently running the test is the owner of the file being tested. The `-k` option checks to see if the sticky bit has been set. There is no `-m` file test.

**55.** A. A successful return from a command executed within a Bash script is `0`. A `1` or higher typically indicates an error condition. There is no C condition.

**56.** A. The file is not copied to directories for existing users, making option A correct. There is nothing in the question to indicate that the file is too big or that it already exists. File extensions don't matter in Linux, so option D cannot be correct.

**57.** C. The `find` command begins the search in the current directory, which is problematic in a scripted scenario like the one presented. The `find` command can find directories, and those directories can begin with a dot character.

**58.** B. The `-i` option ignores the environment. The other options are not valid for use with env.

**59.** A. The `-x` option enables debugging when passed on the interpreter line of a Bash script. The other options are not valid for this purpose.

**60.** C. Doing math in Bash requires a special syntax. The `bc` command can also be used for such operations and is frequently used for math within Bash scripts.

**61.** A. The `read` command will be used, and option A shows the correct syntax. Option C is incorrect because it does not prompt the user. There is no `prompt` command, making options B and D incorrect.

**62.** D. The `-n` option removes a variable from being exported. The other options do not exist.

**63.** A. The exit code from the previous command is captured automatically in the `$?` variable, thus ruling out any option that did not have this value. A test for the value is done with `-eq` in a Bash script, thus making option A correct.

**64.** D. The `source` command is frequently used for the purpose described. The `function` command can be used to create functions but would not be used for the purpose described. The `include` and `require` commands are not valid.

**65.** B. Adding the execute bit for the user can be done in a non-octal format, as shown in option B. The only other valid chmod option is 644, which does not grant execute permission.

**66.** B. The problem statement specified files, making option B the best answer. Option A will also find directories.

**67.** C. The -f option removes a function. The other options do not exist for the unset command.

**68.** A. The env command, when used as #!/usr/bin/env bash, will determine the location of the Bash interpreter automatically. This makes the resulting script more portable for systems where Bash may not be located in /bin/.

**69.** B. The front slash, or forward slash, is used for division. Of the other options, an asterisk is used for multiplication and the other options are not valid.

**70.** B. The mailx command can be used to send mail from the command line. The other options shown are not valid commands.

**71.** D. The -s operator tests if a file is not zero size. The -d operator looks for directories, whereas -e merely checks if the file exists.

**72.** A. An alias exists only for the length of the current session, making option A correct. If the alias or command was invalid, you would have seen it immediately when you created or used the alias.

**73.** D. The correct syntax is shown in option D for the scenario described.

**74.** B. The user is most likely not using Bash but is rather using another shell like Tcsh. The user could be logging into a different system, but hopefully by having them log out and log in again that would have been noticed, as would their manual removal of the environment variables.

**75.** A. The LOGNAME environment variable contains the currently logged-in user. The other variables do not exist by default.

**76.** A. The -h test determines if the file is a symbolic link. The -p option tests if the file is a pipe, and -S returns true if the file is a socket. The -t test determines if the file is a terminal.

**77.** C. The -f option marks a function as read-only. The -p option prints a list of read-only identifiers. The -a option assumes that the name is an array, and there is no -r option to the readonly command.

**78.** B. Option B is the best answer because it will find files where the user permission includes the execute bit. It's worth noting that options A and C will find the execute bit but only with the exact permissions specified.

**79.** A. The /usr/local/bin directory is the location specified for local binaries according to the FHS. It's also a typical place for scripts as well. The /usr/bin and /usr/sbin directories are for system binaries, and /home/scripts does not exist by default.

**80.** D. Ctrl+c is used to terminate a script and is usually used for terminating programs as well.

**81.** B. The -0 option follows each environment variable with a null byte rather than a newline. The other options shown are not valid for use with env.

**82.** D. In all likelihood, the cp command has been aliased with the -i option. Running unalias cp will correct the issue. It is possible that the cp command has been recompiled to always ask for confirmation, but this is not the most likely cause.

**83.** C. An exit code of 1 usually means error, but in the case of grep it means that the search pattern was not found.

**84.** B. The -d test checks if a file is a directory. The -e option checks for existence, and the -a option is no longer used. The -w test checks to see if a file is writable by the current user.

**85.** B. The command shown prepends /usr/local/bin on to the existing path. Option A uses $PATH, which is the incorrect identifier for the left side of the assignment. Option C appends /usr/local/bin rather than prepends, and option D uses a semicolon as a delimiter.

**86.** C. The until loop construct will execute at least once before the condition is evaluated. The while and for loops both evaluate the condition first. The case statement is not a loop construct.

**87.** B. The single dot, ., can be used as a means to source environment variables. The other characters and character sequences do not work for the purpose described.

**88.** A. The -p option displays all exported variables. The other options shown do not exist.

**89.** D. The word do indicates the beginning of a while loop in a Bash script. The other options shown are not valid for the purpose described.

# Chapter 6: Topic 106: User Interfaces and Desktops

**1.** A. The greeter is configured through /etc/lightdm/lightdm.conf using the greeter-session option. The other options provided here are not valid.

**2.** B. The Screen section of xorg.conf is used to logically bind a given graphics card and monitor, each of which would be defined in its own respective section in the configuration file. The other options shown for this question do not exist.

**3.** A. Frequency options are Hz, k, kHz, M, or MHz, making uHz an unavailable option.

**4.** C. The systemctl set-default command will be used for this purpose, and the target of multi-user is used to boot to the command line. You will also need to remove the word splash from /etc/default/grub and run update-grub as well.

5. A. The DISPLAY variable can be used to remotely send the windows of an X session to another computer when using protocols like SSH. There is no XTERMINAL or XDISP environment variable, and XTERM is typically a terminal window and not an environment variable.

6. D. The Welcome option sets the message to be displayed to users within the display manager when they log in. For remote users, the RemoteWelcome message can be used for the same purpose.

7. C. The Shift key can be used to enable and disable sticky keys within GNOME and other operating systems for accessibility purposes.

8. A. The Disable keyword is used to ensure that a given module is not loaded. Note that a Load statement for the same module takes precedence over the Disable statement, but Disable can be used to unload modules that are loaded by default.

9. A. The Orca project provides assistive screen reading capabilities within GNOME. Of the other options given, the screen program is valid but is not used for this purpose.

10. C. The xrandr command can be used to change resolution, and changing the resolution to something like 800×600 would make icons and other items appear larger.

11. D. The allow-guest option changes the behavior of guest login for LightDM, and disallowing guest login would generally make the computer somewhat more secure. However, if someone has physical access to the device, they might be able to get access in other ways.

12. C. The XFree86 -configure command tells the XFree86 server to query for hardware and create a configuration for the recognized hardware. Note that you may still need to edit the resulting configuration file because of unrecognized hardware or to account for specific configuration items.

13. B. The XkbModel configuration option is used to set the type of keyboard being used, such as pc105 for a 105-key keyboard. The XkbLayout option defines the layout of the keyboard such as US for United States–style keyboards.

14. B. The VertRefresh option is used for this purpose and accepts a range of values in the manner shown. The other options given for this question are not valid for the purpose described.

15. D. The file ~/.xsession can be used for commands that run X clients. The other files are not valid for the purpose described.

16. C. The linear acceleration profile is enabled by setting AccelerationProfile to 6 within xorg.conf. The 0 setting is known as classic, whereas -1 provides constant acceleration (no profile) and 7 is known as limited, which performs the same as linear but with a maximum amount of speed and acceleration.

17. A. The /usr/share/fonts hierarchy is used for storage of fonts. Another path that might contain font information is /usr/share/X11/fonts, but that was not among the choices given for this question.

**18.** C. Kernel versions beginning with 2.6.26 include native support for Braille displays in Linux.

**19.** A. The DontZoom option prevents the specified key combinations from changing the video mode. Of the other options, the DontZap option changes the behavior of the Ctrl+Alt+Backspace key combination. The other options don't have any effect and are not valid in xorg.conf.

**20.** C. The xauth program looks for the configuration file in the user's home directory in the file .Xauthority. The other files do not exist by default.

**21.** C. The Xaccess file is used to control access when using XDMCP. The other files are not valid for this purpose.

**22.** D. The kmag program magnifies items on a desktop and is used as an assistive technology. In general, kmag can be used with other window managers as well.

**23.** A. The SIGTERM signal causes the X server to exit cleanly. SIGKILL would not be a clean exit. The other signals shown as options are not valid signals.

**24.** B. The Appearance section of GNOME Control Center is used to set many aspects of how the desktop appears and behaves, including the choice of a high-contrast theme.

**25.** B. Mouse gestures are commonly associated with assistive technologies and help to facilitate uses of programs by moving the mouse in a certain way. Mouse gestures could be used for login and to capture screenshots, but those are not adequately or generally descriptive of their use.

**26.** D. The Alt+Super+S keyboard shortcut activates the screen reader in GNOME 3.9 or later. The Super+S shortcut enters Overview, and the other shortcuts provided do not have a special meaning by default. Note that the Super key is also called the Windows key or the Command key.

**27.** D. The startx command kicks off the display manager after login to a local terminal. The other commands shown do not exist or will not work for the purpose described.

**28.** B. The BlankTime option, which is set to 10 minutes by default, causes the monitor to go blank but not actually go into standby or other power-saving modes.

**29.** C. The xwininfo command displays information about a given window within an X session. The other commands listed for this question are not valid.

**30.** A. The Mouse button displays keys to move the mouse. The Compose button shows a compose keyboard, and the other options are not valid.

**31.** C. The xhost command is used to control access to the X server. A host is added with the + sign.

**32.** B. The ForwardX11 option must be enabled on the client in order for X connections or windows generated from the X server to be sent over an SSH connection.

**33.** D. The FontPath directive provides another location in which the server can find fonts. The other options do not exist within the context of an xorg.conf configuration file.

**34.** D. With an on-screen keyboard, users can utilize a pointer such as a mouse to select keys on the keyboard.

**35.** C. The XAUTHORITY environment variable can be used to specify the location of the xauth authority file.

**36.** B. The Alt+Ctrl+F1 key combination is used to get to a terminal prompt and is helpful in situations where the X server won't start properly.

**37.** B. The autologin-user option is used to define a user who will be automatically logged in to the system. The other options given in this question do not exist.

**38.** C. The AccessX utility is used on legacy or older systems to set many of the accessibility options. The functionality provided by AccessX can typically be found in one of the utilities provided by the native X window manager, dependent on the window manager in use.

**39.** A. The export shell command sets an environment variable. In this case, the DISPLAY environment variable needs to be set. The env command shown will not set the variable.

**40.** A. The Menus option displays the menu options for a given application so that those options can be manipulated with the keyboard. The Activate option helps to work with the desktop and other applications. The other options shown for this question are not valid.

**41.** B. The /etc/lightdm/lightdm.conf.d directory contains individual *.conf configuration files for various settings and is typically parsed along with the /etc/lightdm/lightdm.conf file.

**42.** B. The COLUMNS environment variable specifies the width in characters of a terminal device. The other environment variables are not valid.

**43.** C. The VideoRam option, which can be expressed in bytes, configures the amount of RAM available to the video card.

**44.** B. The Depth option sets the color depth for a given monitor display. A typical value might be 24 for this option.

**45.** B. The Identifier option provides a unique description of each of the server layouts in an X configuration. The other options shown for this question do not exist.

**46.** A. The mkfontscale command will create a fonts.scale file, which describes the outline fonts on the system and is used for configuration of fonts that are manually added to the system.

**47.** A. Display Power Management Signaling (DPMS) enables additional power-saving modes, such as a full sleep mode, that enable further energy efficiency for the display.

**48.** B. The emacspeak program provides another visual assistive technology as an alternative to Orca. The other technologies listed here are not related to visualization or assistive technologies.

**49.** B. Weston is a reference implementation of the Wayland protocol.

**50.** C. The SuspendTime sets the time, in minutes, for the monitor to go into standby mode. The other options shown are not valid.

**51.** C. The files in /etc/X11/xorg.conf.d/ are included when X is starting.

**52.** B. XDMCP, which is typically disabled by default, uses no compression or transport security. XDMCP is therefore not usually preferred for remote access. Of the other options, SSH offers encryption of the session, and XR and RD are not valid protocols.

**53.** D. The Xfce desktop environment uses xfwm4 as its window manager. The other options are not desktop environments.

**54.** B. The disable-ticketing option turns off simple authentication for clients with Spice.

**55.** B. Simon is the speech recognition software that is part of the KDE project.

**56.** D. The only valid panel listed in the options for this question is called Universal Access, making option D correct.

**57.** A. The setxkbmap command can be used to enable Xkboptions when X is already running. The other commands shown do not exist.

**58.** B. The xrdp program is an open source implementation of an RDP server. The other programs shown are not valid.

**59.** A. Changing the VISUAL environment variable to an editor that can run over an SSH session will fix the issue. In this case, /bin/vim was used.

**60.** B. The -passwd option is used to set the password on the server for x11vnc.

**61.** D. The xauth utility is used for working with the X authority file. The other options shown are not valid.

**62.** C. Bounce keys cause the interface to not react when keys are accidentally pressed in succession or held down.

**63.** B. The TMPDIR environment variable is used if the normal home directory location, ~/.xsession-errors, cannot be opened. The other environment variables are not valid.

**64.** D. The xdpyinfo command displays various elements about the current display(s) along with information about X itself.

**65.** B. The Weston configuration file is called weston.ini and is located in ~/.config. The other files are not valid.

**66.** A. The x11vnc program, an implementation of VNC, offers built-in SSL/TLS capabilities. The other programs shown are not valid.

**67.** B. The brltty program enables a text-mode braille display. The other programs are not valid.

**68.** B. The xzoom program is used for screen magnification. The other programs shown are not valid.

**69.** D. The GRUB_INIT_TUNE variable can be used within the GRUB configuration in order to beep when GRUB is ready for input.

**70.** B. The xhost command will be used for this purpose, and the minus sign removes a host from being able to connect.

**71.** B. The Xsession script is executed as the user logging in, making option B correct. The Xstartup script is executed as root prior to the execution of Xsession. The other files are not valid as part of the xdm login process.

**72.** A. The -nolisten tcp option disables listening for TCP connections for an X server. The other options are not valid.

**73.** B. SIGHUP is used for the purpose described, typically when a user logs out. SIGKILL does not restart the server or prepare for a new connection. The other signal names given as options are not valid signals.

**74.** C. The greeter-show-manual-login option, when set to true, will require the user to enter a username for login rather than select the username from a list.

**75.** B. The -n option disables hostname lookups. The other options shown are not valid.

**76.** C. In runlevel 3, accessed through the telinit command, the X server is not typically executed. Runlevel 6 will shut down the system. Runlevel 1 switches to single-user mode, and runlevel 5 is a multi-user mode in which X is usually running.

**77.** C. According to the X server documentation at https://www.x.org/releases/X11R7.7/doc/man/man1/Xserver.1.xhtml, the default location is within the /usr/lib path, but it's worth noting that Linux distributions may change this location to be within the /var/log/ hierarchy.

**78.** B. The ~/.xinitrc file can be used for per-user initialization. The other files are not used by default for this purpose.

**79.** C. The -nolisten local option can be added to prevent the X server from listening on abstract sockets.

**80.** D. The -broadcast option for XDMCP enables sending of BroadcastQuery packets. The other options shown are not valid options with XDMCP.

**81.** C. The gdmsetup program is used to configure various options for the login window and environment, including those for local and remote users. The other options are not used for this purpose or do not exist.

**82.** C. Any host within the example.com domain can connect.

**83.** C. The family inet6 enables the specified host to connect with IPv6. The other methods shown will not work.

**84.** B. The ~/.xsession-errors file is the default log file for Xsession and X clients. The other files are not valid for this purpose.

**85.** A. The gok command, short for GNOME On-screen Keyboard, is the program to start the on-screen keyboard. The Caribou program will be the successor to GOK.

**86.** B. The -f option enables file specification for the X authority file. The -v option enables verbose output. The other options are not valid.

**87.** B. Slow keys is the name used to describe this assistive technology.

**88.** C. RDP listens on port 3389 by default. Port 389 is LDAP, and 3306 is usually MySQL.

# Chapter 7: Topic 107: Administrative Tasks

**1.** A. The best option among these choices is to change the group to www-data and change the permissions such that the group can write into the directory. Option B should never be used because it enables world-writing to the directory. The other options will not allow the web server group to write into the directory.

**2.** B. The format for cron is [minute hour day-of-month month-of-year day-of-week], thereby making option B the correct option for this question.

**3.** C. The /etc/localtime file, which can be an actual file or a symbolic link, is used to indicate the local time zone. The other files listed as options do not exist.

**4.** D. The LDAP Data Interchange Format (LDIF) is an open format, defined in Request for Comments (RFC) 2849, that enables import and export of LDAP entries. The file formats TXT and CSV are valid but not for the purpose described; there is no specific file format known as LDAP.

**5.** B. The chage command will be used for this purpose, specifically with the -E option. When provided with a date, chage will expire the account on that date. When provided with -1, the expiration will be removed.

**6.** D. Within the /usr/share/zoneinfo hierarchy, you will find information on the various regions and time zones available. The files within this hierarchy can be symlinked to /etc/localtime. The file /etc/timezone is also sometimes used by Linux systems and, notably, by Java in certain situations.

**7.** B. The at command is used to run a series of commands that you enter. Unlike with cron, you can schedule commands from the command line to be executed in the same order entered rather than having to create a specific script for the commands. The syntax shown in option B sets the time to be one hour from now.

**8.** B. The userdel command is used for this purpose, and the -r option (lowercase) deletes both the home directory and mail spool files. The -R (uppercase) option tells the userdel command to use a chroot directory.

**9.** B. The /etc/shadow file contains usernames, UIDs, and encrypted passwords and is not readable by any non-root user on the system due to the sensitive nature of the encrypted passwords. The /etc/passwd file contains usernames and UIDs but not encrypted passwords. The other two files listed for this question do not exist.

**10.** C. Use anacron when you need to schedule a job on a computer that might be off when the job is scheduled. anacron will take care of running the job at its next available time.

**11.** B. The +%s option will format the date as seconds since January 1, 1970. This option is used frequently in scripting and elsewhere for obtaining a unique time stamp that can be parsed easily as an integer. The other options will not work.

**12.** C. The --list option shows the available character sets on the system. The other options given for this question do not exist.

**13.** C. The LC_TIME environment variable is used to control the display and behavior of the date and time and can be changed to a different locale in order to achieve the desired display and behavior of date and time formatting. The other options shown for this question do not exist.

**14.** D. Beginning with OpenLDAP version 2.3, slapd-config is used for configuration of OpenLDAP, as documented at http://www.openldap.org/doc/admin24/slapdconf2 .html. The other commands are not valid.

**15.** A. The @daily shortcut schedules a job to run at midnight every day. The other options shown do not exist.

**16.** B. UTF-8 provides multibyte character encoding and is generally accepted as the standard for encoding moving forward. ISO-8859 is single byte encoded. The other options are not valid.

**17.** A. The groupmod command will be used for this purpose, and the -n option is used to change the group name. The other commands listed do not exist.

**18.** D. The /etc/group file contains information on groups on a Linux system. The other files are not valid for the purpose described.

**19.** C. The slapcat command dumps the slapd database in LDIF format to STDOUT. The output can then be redirected into a file. The other commands are not valid.

**20.** C. The /etc/cron.d/ directory can contain scripts that have scheduling information within them along with jobs to run. The other locations given as options are not valid.

**21.** B. The getent command is used to display entries based on the /etc/nsswitch.conf file. One use case for getent is when integrating with Microsoft Active Directory or another LDAP service to check if the connection can be made to the LDAP server. The usermod command is valid but is not used for this purpose, and the other commands shown for this question are not valid.

**22.** B. The /etc/login.defs file contains various configuration items such as the minimum and maximum user and group IDs to be used on the system.

**23.** C. The LC_MEASUREMENT environment variable is used to indicate the measurement units that should be used.

**24.** D. The TZ environment variable is used for this purpose and the general format is as shown, making option D the correct answer.

**25.** A. The /etc/cron.daily directory contains files such as scripts that are executed daily. There are corresponding cron.hourly, cron.weekly, and cron.monthly directories that run on their respective schedules, as indicated by the name of the directory.

**26.** C. Setting LANG=C is an alias for Portable Operating System Interface (POSIX) compatibility and will cause programs to bypass locale translations. The other options shown for LANG are not valid.

**27.** B. The -m option causes the user's home directory to be created. By default, if this option isn't specified and CREATE_HOME has not been set, the home directory won't be created. The –h option displays help text, and the other options shown are not valid.

**28.** A. The usermod -L command locks an account by placing a ! in the encrypted password. If the user has another means to log in, such as with an SSH key, using usermod -L will not prevent their login.

**29.** C. The LC_ALL variable can be used to set environment variables to the current locale and will override others. This can be used when there is a need for a temporary change. The other variables listed here are not used for this purpose and are not created by default.

**30.** A. The format when adding a username places the username between the schedule and the command to run, making option A correct. The other options shown for this question are invalid. In the case of option B, there is no schedule. In the case of options C and D, the schedule is incorrectly formatted.

**31.** C. The passwd command will be used for this purpose. The -a option displays all users but requires the use of -S to indicate status. The -S option alone will not produce a report for all users, and the --all option is an alias for -a.

**32.** D. The chage command is used for this purpose. The -d option sets the days since the last password change and is measured in days since January 1, 1970. The -W option is the days of warning for changing a password, and the -l option displays a list of the various settings related to the account.

**33.** B. The /etc/anacrontab file contains information about the jobs such as the job name and delay, among other information. The other files listed do not contain anacron-related information about jobs.

**34.** D. The ldapadd command is used to add entries to the OpenLDAP database.

**35.** B. The /etc/cron.deny file contains a list of users who cannot create cron scheduled tasks. The other files do not exist by default.

**36.** B. The system uses shadow passwords if an asterisk shows up in the password field of the /etc/passwd entries. There is no indication that the system has been compromised, making option C incorrect, and there is no password scheme called "forward password aging," making option A incorrect as well.

**37.** D. There is no direct relationship between the UIDs and GIDs on a system. UIDs represent users, whereas GIDs represent group IDs. On some systems, the UID and GID number will match for regular users, but this is not a requirement and is more of a coincidence.

**38.** C. The slapindex command generates indexes based on slapd databases. The other commands are not valid.

**39.** A. The usermod command is used for this purpose. The -d option changes the home directory, whereas -m moves the contents. The other commands shown for this question are not valid.

**40.** D. The -G option is a list of supplemental groups to which the user will be added. A lowercase -g option provides the primary GID. The -l option causes the user to not be added to the lastlog and faillog databases. There is no -x option.

**41.** A. The crontab command can be used for this purpose, and the -l option is used to list the crontab entries. The -u option is needed to specify a user other than the current user.

**42.** A. The -r option creates a system user that will typically entail no expiration, no home directory, and a UID below 1000. The -s option defines the shell and is not typically used for this purpose. The -a and -S options do not exist.

**43.** B. The /etc/gshadow file contains secure information such as an encrypted password for groups, where applicable. The /etc/group file contains general information on groups. The other two files listed as options do not exist.

**44.** D. The slapd_db_recover command can be used to help recover an OpenLDAP database that has become corrupted or otherwise invalid. The remaining options for this question are not valid commands.

**45.** B. The groupdel command cannot delete groups unless there are no users who have the given group as their primary GID. There is no -f or -r option.

**46.** A. The id command shows the username, UID, primary group, and GID, along with supplemental groups. The passwd and chage commands are not used for this purpose. There is no getid command.

**47.** D. The -c option changes the comment field in /etc/passwd. The comment field is typically associated with the real name of the account. The -R option indicates a chroot directory, whereas -d indicates a change of home directory. There is no -n option.

**48.** D. The find command will be used for this purpose. The correct syntax is shown in option D. The group command will merely look in the specified files for the number 1501, and the -u option to grep includes byte offsets, which is not applicable for this question.

**49.** A. The standard port for unencrypted LDAP is 389, and that is the port on which slapd listens for connections. Port 3389 is RDP, whereas 3306 is MySQL. Finally, 110 is POP3.

**50.** A. The ln command is used for this purpose, and the -s option creates a symbolic link, and -f forces or overwrites the destination. The other options or order of commands are not valid.

**51.** C. The LC_MONETARY variable is used by certain programs to determine the localization for currency.

**52.** C. The --on-calendar option adds a timed event with systemd-run. The other options shown are not valid for use with systemd-run.

**53.** B. The /etc/cron.allow file is a list of users who have permission to create and remove their own cron jobs. The /etc/crontab file is used to store cron jobs, and the other files do not exist.

**54.** B. Debug level 64 provides configuration processing debug information. Debug level 1 traces function calls, whereas level 8 shows connection management. Debug level 0 is no debug.

**55.** C. The atrm command removes jobs given their IDs. The ID can be obtained with the atq command. The at -l command shown will list jobs but not delete them. The rmat command is not valid.

**56.** B. The dpkg-reconfigure command is used to cause the configuration questions to be asked again. The tzdata package is the name of the package on Debian-based systems. The two apt- commands shown are not valid.

**57.** D. There are multiple ways to specify loglevels and debugging for slapd, including by keyword, by integer, or as shown in the question, by hex. All of the values shown are valid for loglevel. No debugging is 0, trace is 1, stats logging is 256 or 512 depending on type, and packets sent and received is integer 16, or hex 0x10.

**58.** A. The /etc/skel directory contains files that are automatically copied to a user's home directory when that user is created. The other directories listed for this question do not exist by default.

**59.** B. The atq command shows a list of jobs that have been scheduled with the at command. The other commands don't exist with the exception of option D, which shows the at command but with an invalid option, --jobs.

**60.** C. The port for LDAPS or LDAP over SSL is 636. Port 389 is standard, non-SSL, LDAP. Port 443 is used for HTTPS, and 3128 is used for Squid proxies.

**61.** A. The at command runs a command at a specified time. While cron can be used to run a command, it will run the command repeatedly according to the schedule set for the command. The other commands are not valid.

**62.** D. The /etc/at.allow file is used to specify users who can create at jobs. The other files are not valid.

**63.** B. Systemd timer files have the extension .timer and are used for scheduling service unit files or events. The other file extensions are not used for systemd timer units.

**64.** A. The /var/spool/cron/crontabs directory contains a file for each user who currently has one or more cron jobs or entries. Note that the other files listed here are not valid for this purpose.

**65.** D. The -j option enables specification of a line from which the import will be started. It is useful in the scenario described where the import needs to be restarted due to error. The -f option specifies an alternate location for the slapd configuration file. The -q option is quick mode, with less checking, and -l specifies the input file.

**66.** B. The -a option shows all locales currently available on a system. The other options do not produce the output specified in this scenario.

**67.** A. The --adjust-system-clock option sets the system clock when used with set-local-rtc. The other options are not valid.

**68.** A. The -i option displays information that can help determine the character set such as ISO-8859, ASCII, or Unicode for the given file. The -m option specifies a list of magic files, -l shows a list of patterns, and -a is not a valid option with the file command.

**69.** B. The LC_PAPER variable is used to set the paper size for printing. The other variables are not available by default.

**70.** C. The /etc/crontab file is a plain-text file that is treated as a systemwide cron file. As such, the file is generally not associated with any single user and it's not necessary to run a special command after editing this file.

**71.** D. The tzselect command will, by default, display a step-by-step menu to select a time zone. The eventual output will include a region/time zone line, such as America/Chicago, as output.

**72.** A. The OnBootSec option is used for this scenario and option A has the correct syntax. The other options shown do not exist.

**73.** B. GECOS is the legacy name for information stored in /etc/passwd such as full name and other contact information.

**74.** A. The -g option sets the group ID for the newly created group. The -h option is help, and neither -k nor -a exists as an option for groupadd.

**75.** C. The list-timers option shows the currently active timers with systemd. The other options are not valid.

**76.** B. The weekly shortcut means that systemd will execute the event once a week. The other shortcuts given as options are not valid.

**77.** A. The -r option removes the current crontab. The -i option can be added so that the user is prompted prior to removal.

**78.** B. The `SKEL` variable controls the location of the skeleton home directory, which is normally `/etc/skel/` by default. The other options shown are not used for the purpose described.

**79.** C. The `passwd` option is used to list the password database on a system. The other options do not exist.

**80.** A. The directory `/var/spool/cron/atjobs` contains the jobs. The other directories shown do not exist.

**81.** C. The `GID_MIN` variable contains the minimum GID to use on the system. The other variables are not used for the purpose described.

**82.** D. The `MAIL_DIR` variable contains the directory where a user's mail spool is located. The other options shown are not valid variables for this purpose.

**83.** C. The `/etc/passwd` file contains various information about users on a system such as username and real name, along with user ID (UID) and login shell. The file is world-readable.

**84.** C. The `@reboot` shortcut indicates that the `cron` job will be executed when the system starts up.

**85.** A. The `-r` option specifies that the group being added will be a system group.

**86.** A. The directory `/var/lib/ldap` stores database files related to the OpenLDAP deployment on a given server. The other directories shown are not valid for this purpose.

**87.** A. Only active units are shown by default, so the `--all` option displays all units.

**88.** B. The `/etc/at.deny` file contains a list of users who cannot create `at` jobs.

# Chapter 8: Topic 108: Essential System Services

**1.** C. The `journalctl` command is used to work with the `systemd` journal. On `systemd`-based systems, `journalctl` is a central command for debugging and troubleshooting.

**2.** C. The kern facility receives messages from the kernel for logging purposes. Of the other options, syslog is used for logging messages about syslog itself. The other two options shown are not valid syslog facilities.

**3.** D. `ntp.org` provides a free service for time synchronization. When you use `pool.ntp.org` as the target, you will typically receive an NTP server that is geographically close to your location, or at least as close as possible. Setting your address to 127.0.0.1 or 192.168.1.100 will use a local server but only if that server has an NTP service.

**4.** A. The service used for logging on a computer managed by systemd is called systemd-journald. You use the journalctl command to view logged entries rather than the standard Linux toolset.

**5.** B. The create option is used for this purpose and accepts arguments such as those shown to set the permissions and ownership. The other options shown are not valid within a logrotate configuration.

**6.** D. Configuration files for CUPS are found in /etc/cups. However, it is also common to manage CUPS through its web interface. The other directories listed are not valid.

**7.** A. The Allow directive is used for this purpose and the addresses 192.168.1.1 through .127 signify a /25 in Classless Inter-Domain Routing (CIDR) notation, making option A correct. Note that option B, with a /24 netmask, would allow the addresses too but would also allow 192.168.1.128 through .255, which is larger than should be allowed.

**8.** B. The ntpdate command provides a command-line interface that immediately changes or sets the time according to the NTP server given as its argument. The ntpd option provided in option A will run the NTP daemon and would not be appropriate for a script. The other two commands are not valid. It is worth noting that ntpdate has been deprecated in favor of ntpd, but you will likely find ntpdate available on many systems.

**9.** B. Typically, the Connection refused message from an NTP-related command means that the daemon is not running. There is no indication that the ntpq command is querying a different server; therefore, whether the network is up or down is irrelevant. The permission-based options are not valid based on the error message indicated.

**10.** D. The hwclock command is used to both query and set the hardware clock, such as the one maintained by the system firmware or basic input/output system (BIOS). The ntpdate command is used to set the local system time but is not related to the hardware clock. The other commands are not valid.

**11.** C. The /usr/share/zoneinfo directory and its child directories contain information on time zones on a Linux system. The other files and directories do not exist by default.

**12.** D. The info severity level provides information messages for a given facility. Of the options given, emerg is used for emergency messages and not normally used by applications, whereas debug is the highest or most verbose level of logging available through syslog.

**13.** B. The driftfile configuration option sets the location of the driftfile for ntpd. The drift file helps to maintain time accuracy. The location shown is the default for Red Hat Enterprise Linux.

**14.** A. The mail option is used to send the log to the specified email address on completion of the logrotate process. The others shown do not exist as options in /etc/logrotate .conf.

**15.** C. The journalctl command is used for this purpose, and the --disk-usage option displays the disk space used by journal log files, which are typically stored in /var/log/ journal.

**16.** D. The `mailq` command is used on Postfix servers in order to view a summary of the current mail queue. Details of the queue include the ID of the mail being sent along with one or more of the email addresses involved in the transaction. The `mailq` command may also work with newer versions of `sendmail`.

**17.** C. The `ntpq` command provides an interactive, menu-like interface into the NTP server. You can use `ntpq` to check statistics on peers, for example. The `ntpdate` command shown as option B is used as a command-line means to set the time. The `ntpd` command shown as option A would execute the NTP daemon itself.

**18.** D. The format is *user: destination for the aliases file*, making option D correct. The other options are not valid syntax for the aliases file.

**19.** B. The `-f` option indicates the file to which messages will be logged. The `-d` option is used for debugging, whereas `-v` prints the version of `klogd`. There is no `-l` option for `klogd`.

**20.** A. The `chrony` package is used for the scenario described and helps with systems that are frequently offline or disconnected from the network. The other packages listed as options are not valid for the purpose described.

**21.** A. The `lpr` command places a file (or standard input) into the print queue for `lpd` to work with. The `lpq` command prints the current queue. There is no `lpx` command.

**22.** C. The `-bp` option to the `sendmail` command prints information about the current queue. There is no `-queue` or `-f` option that is relevant for this question. The `-bi` option is used to work with the aliases database.

**23.** A. The `-w` option sets the hardware clock to the current system time. The `-s` option does the opposite, setting the system time to the hardware clock. There is no `-a` or `-m` function for `hwclock`.

**24.** D. TCP port 631 is used as the administrative interface into CUPS. Visiting an active CUPS server on that port will show the administration website for working with print queues and other configuration items related to CUPS.

**25.** A. The `-q` option causes `sendmail` to attempt to deliver messages from the queue. Add the `-v` option to display verbose output.

**26.** B. The requirements of multiple email addresses prevent the use of `.forward`; therefore, it will need to be accomplished in `/etc/aliases`. The format for multiple email addresses is to separate them with a comma, making option B correct.

**27.** A. The `--systohc` command will set the hardware clock according to the current system time. The use of `--utc` is required in order to ensure that the time is set to UTC. If `--utc` is omitted, the time will default to whatever was used last time the command was run, which could be UTC but might also be localtime instead. Therefore, the best option is A.

**28.** D. The `postsuper -d` command deletes messages from the queue. The `ALL` keyword causes all messages to be deleted from the queue. Care should be taken when performing this action because it is irreversible. There is no `-remove` option to `postqueue`, and the `-f` option for Postfix is not relevant. The `rm -rf` command shown is not specific enough, and it is generally not recommended to manually remove files from a mail queue.

**29.** A. The URL shown will display the jobs area of the local CUPS server with a query string name of which_jobs and a value of completed. The other URLs shown are not valid.

**30.** C. Just as the tail -f command will continuously update the display as new content is added, so too does the -f option display new entries for journalctl. The -t option shows messages for the given syslog identifier. There is no -tail or -l option.

**31.** B. The $UDPServerRun option is used for the purpose described. The port on which the server should listen is then provided as the value for this option. The other options shown are not valid configuration items for rsyslogd.

**32.** A. The postqueue -f command is used to flush the queue. The command will process all of the emails that are awaiting delivery. The other commands are not valid for this purpose.

**33.** C. The -g option specifies the maximum offset or skew that can be adjusted for when synchronizing time. When set to 0, there is no offset check.

**34.** A. The SystemMaxFileSize option controls the size of the journal log file to ensure that a log does not cause problems related to disk usage. The SystemMaxUse option controls overall size of journal files, and the default for SystemMaxFileSize is one-eighth of the SystemMaxUse setting to allow for rotation of files.

**35.** C. The lpstat command is used for this purpose. The lpstat command displays information about printers, print jobs, and related information. The -W option specifies which jobs to display, complete, or not complete. The lpq command shown as an option is used to view the queue, and the other options are not valid.

**36.** D. The postrotate option within a configuration for log rotation can be used for this purpose. After postrotate, a line typically follows with the script or commands to execute. The other options shown for this question are not valid.

**37.** B. SMTP operates on TCP port 25, and if other servers are contacting your SMTP server, then you'll need to listen on this port and allow traffic to it as well. Port 23 is used for telnet, port 110 is POP3, and port 143 is Internet Message Access Protocol (IMAP), none of which are necessary for SMTP traffic.

**38.** A. The makemap command is used to create the hashed database in the correct format for sendmail to use. The other commands are not valid for sendmail.

**39.** A. The configuration file for syslog-ng is stored in /etc/syslog-ng and is named syslog-ng.conf. There is not typically an /etc/syslog directory, even on systems without syslog-ng.

**40.** C. The application could theoretically use any of the logging facilities, depending on the type of application being developed. However, the requirement to log to a custom log file means that the logs will have a different name and possibly location than the standard logs. Therefore, logging to any of the standard or system-level facilities is not appropriate for this scenario, making one of the local (local0 through local7) facilities appropriate.

**41.** B. The usermod command with the -aG option is used to append a group onto the user's list of groups. In this case, the user needs to be a member of the lpadmin group.

**42.** D. The `nocompress` option is used to prevent the log file from being compressed or zipped as part of the rotation process. This might be needed on systems where compression negatively affects performance or where additional processing is necessary.

**43.** C. The `cupsctl` command should be used with the `--share-printers` option to enable printing for remote clients within the same subnet. You would then also flag each printer for sharing with the `lpadmin` command, setting the `printer-is-shared` option to `true`.

**44.** B. The `mailstats` command is used for the purpose described. Of the other options, the `mailq` command will display the current mail queue but not statistics on mail that has been processed. The other two options are not valid commands.

**45.** B. The `--disk-usage` option shows the amount of space consumed by active and archived journals. The other options shown are not valid.

**46.** A. The `systemctl` command is used for controlling services. In this case, restart should be sent to the CUPS service as denoted by the name `cups.service`.

**47.** D. The `-p` option is used to filter based on priority and the loglevel given in the scenario is debug, making option D correct. The other options are not valid for the purpose described.

**48.** A. The `Port` configuration option is used for this purpose and is used as an alternative to the `Listen` directive. With the `Listen` directive, you will specify `address:port`. However, option C, while valid syntactically, will listen only on the localhost IP of 127.0.0.1 and not all interfaces.

**49.** A. The `postsuper` command is used for management of various items with Postfix, including deletion of individual messages from the mail queue. The other commands will not work for the purpose described.

**50.** B. The `--vacuum-time` option will be used for this scenario. Time can be specified in seconds, minutes, hours, days, months, weeks, and years.

**51.** B. The file `.procmailrc`, found in a user's home directory, is used by Procmail for processing messages on a per-user basis. The other files are not used by Procmail in a default configuration.

**52.** D. The format is *local-address: destination-address*. Each destination address is separated by a comma. The difference between options C and D is that the question specifically asked for addresses `@example.com` and since the question didn't specify whether this server was the server for `@example.com`, the destination addresses needed to be fully qualified.

**53.** D. The `postcat` command shows the contents of a message from the Postfix queue. The other commands shown are not valid.

**54.** C. The `/var/log/mail.err` file contains errors related to mail delivery. However, on some systems, mail-related errors may go to a different log, such as `/var/log/mail.log` or `/var/log/mail.info` or similar.

**55.** D. The EHLO command indicates Extended Hello syntax and is followed by the host from which communication has been initiated. Of the other options, the HELO option is valid but is not the Extended Hello syntax specified in the question.

**56.** A. The list-timezones option to timedatectl shows the names of time zones and is useful for obtaining the correct time zone name. The other options are not valid with timedatectl.

**57.** A. The /etc/localtime file is a symlink to /usr/share/zoneinfo/America/Chicago, making option A correct. Some systems also link /etc/timezone for the same purpose.

**58.** A. The date command shows the current time zone. The other options shown will not work.

**59.** C. The /etc/chrony.conf file is the configuration file used by the Chrony package. The other files do not exist by default.

**60.** C. The -k option shows kernel messages only when used with journalctl. The other options shown do not query the journal.

**61.** B. The newaliases command re-creates the aliases database on servers running Postfix, sendmail, and qmail. There is no need to restart the mail server after running newaliases. The alias command shown in option C will create an alias for the command shell but is not related to Postfix.

**62.** D. The systemd-cat command logs to the systemd journal. When given a parameter such as a command, both STDOUT and STDERR are logged. The other commands shown as options are not valid.

**63.** A. The lprm command is used to help manage printer queues by removing jobs. The other commands shown are not valid.

**64.** D. The logger command is used to send messages to syslog and can be executed in a shell script context in order to take advantage of the robustness of syslog without having to write separate log management into the script.

**65.** C. The mailq_path parameter contains the path to the mail queue for Postfix. You can use this to diagnose problems with the queue directories. The other parameters shown are not valid in Postfix.

**66.** D. The _SYSTEMD_UNIT filter can be used to show messages related to a single service. Multiple _SYSTEMD_UNIT arguments can be given to show messages for multiple services. The other options shown for this question are not valid.

**67.** C. The lp command, usually used with the -d option to specify the queue name, is used to add a job to the specified print queue. The other commands shown as options are not valid.

**68.** B. When the .forward file is found within a user's home directory, forwarding of email will typically occur when mail is destined for that user.

**69.** B. The -s option sets the subject for the email to be sent. The -E option informs mail to not send messages that have an empty body. The -c option enables setting of carbon-copy (CC) addresses. The -f option specifies an alternate mailbox and would not be used for this scenario.

**70.** D. The -s option sets the date and time as specified within the command. If there is another means to automatically set the date, it may override the change. For example, if ntpd is running, that process may alter the date even after it has been set with date -s.

**71.** B. The --vacuum-size option to journalctl will trim the journal data files so that they consume the specified size. It is worth noting that the size may not be exactly that specified because journalctl deletes only archived files.

**72.** A. The --since option filters journal messages based on the time elapsed since that specified. There is also a corresponding --until option that enables further time filtering.

**73.** C. The use of - indicates that syslog does not need to sync to disk for every log entry. This can greatly improve performance for busy systems but may cause log entries to be lost if the sync process has not been run prior to a system crash or other issue.

**74.** A. The -P option sends a print job to the specified destination. Of the other options shown, -h disables banner printing, and the remaining options do not exist for lpr.

**75.** C. The qshape command displays information regarding the number and age of the messages in the Postfix incoming and active queues. Other queues can also be viewed using the command as well. The other commands shown as options for this question are not valid.

**76.** D. The SystemMaxUse configuration option configures how much space journal files can take on the system. The other options shown are not valid, but it is worth noting that there are several options for controlling journal sizes and these options should be examined as part of preparation.

**77.** C. The /var/spool/postfix directory contains directories and files related to the mail queue for Postfix. The other directories listed are not valid for this scenario.

**78.** D. The --directory or -D option can be used to specify an alternate location for the journal data and would support the scenario described. The other options are not valid with journalctl for the scenario described.

**79.** C. The /var/log/ directory is the normal location for system logs, and daemons will typically use this hierarchy for logs as well. For example, some Linux distributions use /var/log/journal/ for systemd journals. The other directories shown as options do not exist by default.

**80.** C. The :blackhole: option can be used as a destination to prevent Exim from delivering the mail for that particular user or email account. The other options shown for this question are not valid.

**81.** C. The <DefaultPrinter printerName> stanza, where printerName is the name of the printer, configures a printer for CUPS.

**82.** C. The lprm command can be used for this purpose and, when given a single dash, will delete all jobs from the queue if run as root. The other options given for lprm are not valid.

**83.** B. The -r option enables setting the From header of the email to be sent rather than the currently logged-in user. The -f option specifies a different mailbox and is not useful for this scenario. The -o and -m options do not exist.

**84.** B. The @@ symbol specifies that TCP should be used rather than the default @ that normally precedes a host using UDP for remote logging.

**85.** C. The Storage=Persistent key/value pair within the [Journal] stanza of the configuration file enables persistent storage for the journal. The other key/value pairs are not valid.

**86.** A. The chronyc command can be used for monitoring the status of time updates. The other options shown are not valid commands.

**87.** C. Individual configuration files for various log file rotation policies are found in /etc/logrotate.d. This directory is included in the primary configuration file /etc/logrotate.conf.

**88.** A. The postqueue -p command and option view the pending queue. The postqueue -f command causes the queue to be flushed. The other commands shown are valid, but their options are not.

# Chapter 9: Topic 109: Persistent Network Configuration

**1.** A. The netstat command can be used for this purpose, and the -r option displays the current routes. The addition of -n prevents DNS lookups, which can help with performance.

**2.** A. The ifconfig command will be used for this purpose and requires the addition of the -a option because the adapter is currently down. The ifup command can be used to bring up an interface but does not display information by default. The netstat command displays information about the network but not with the -n option.

**3.** D. Private IP addresses are found within the 10.0.0.0/8, 172.16.0.0/12, and 192.168.0.0/16 ranges, making an address in the 143 range a public IP.

**4.** C. The route command is used for this purpose, and adding a route is done with the add option. The default gateway is added using the default gw keywords followed by the IP of the gateway and the adapter.

**5.** A. The host command enables changing of the query type with the -t option. Using ns as the type will query for the name servers for a given domain. There is no all type, and the other options are also invalid.

6. B. Traditionally, udp/53 is used for DNS queries, but with a primary and secondary server it is assumed that zone transfers may occur. DNS zone transfers typically take place over tcp/53.

7. B. The -I option enables the choice of interface. A lowercase -i option sets the interval, whereas -a indicates an audible ping. Finally, -t enables a time-to-live (TTL)-based ping only.

8. D. A /27, with a netmask of 255.255.255.224, splits a subnet into four segments of 32 addresses, thus enabling 30 usable addresses.

9. A. The host or dig commands can be used for this purpose by setting the type to mx. The mx type will query for the mail exchanger for the given domain. There is no smtp type.

10. B. The localhost address for IPv6 can be written as ::1. Addresses shown like 127 represent the IPv4 localhost range but are not written properly for IPv4 or IPv6.

11. A. The -T option causes traceroute to use TCP packets. This option, which requires root privileges, can be helpful for situations where a firewall may be blocking traceroute traffic. The -i option chooses the interface, whereas -s chooses the source address. A lowercase -t option sets the Type of Service (ToS) flag.

12. C. The ifup command is used to bring up network interfaces, and the -a option brings up those interfaces marked as auto. Likewise, ifdown can be used to turn off network interfaces. The ifconfig -a command displays information on all interfaces, and there is no ifstat command.

13. D. The hostname command is used to return the hostname and domain. When given the -d option, just the domain name is returned to STDOUT, thereby making it appropriate for use in a script.

14. A. The ip command with the monitor option/subcommand will display netlink messages as they arrive. There is no netlink subcommand for ip, and the route command will not work for this purpose.

15. D. The -6 option, as in traceroute -6, executes an IPv6 traceroute. The other options shown for this question are not valid. It would be rare for the traceroute6 command to not be available and still have the traceroute -6 command available.

16. A. The syntax is database: databasename with additional database names separated by spaces, as shown in the correct option for this question.

17. A. The @ symbol is used to indicate a server to which the query will be sent directly. This can be quite useful for troubleshooting resolution problems by sending the query directly to an authoritative name server for the domain. Of the other options, -t sets the type and the others are not valid.

18. D. SNMP traffic takes place on ports 161 and 162. Though the traffic is usually on UDP, the TCP ports are also reserved for SNMP. Ports 110 and 143 are used for POP3 and IMAP, respectively, whereas 23 and 25 are telnet and SMTP. Finally, ports 80 and 443 are HTTP and HTTPS.

**19.** A. The getent command is used for working with NSS databases, and getent hosts will display the available hosts using the databases configured in /etc/nsswitch.conf.

**20.** D. A /25 in CIDR notation represents half of a /24 in address space, therefore making 255.255.255.128 the masked bits. The 255.255.255.0 option is /24, whereas 255.255.255.192 is a /26. Finally, 255.255.0.0 is a /16.

**21.** C. The configuration option is called nameserver, and the value for the option is the IP address of the desired name server. There are several options that affect how name resolution is performed, such as the number of attempts and timeout. Also, the order in which name servers appear affects in which order the name servers are queried. See resolv.conf(5) for more information.

**22.** D. The /etc/services file contains standard port-to-protocol information based on the well-known and assigned ports from the Internet Assigned Numbers Authority (IANA). If you'd like to provide a custom name for the service, you can do so by editing this file. There is no /etc/ports or /etc/p2p file by default, and /etc/ppp is usually a directory for the Point-to-Point protocol daemon and related services.

**23.** A. The route command can be used for this purpose, and the syntax includes the network range, denoted with the -net option, followed by the word netmask and the masked bits, followed by the lettersgw and the IP of the gateway. The other options shown are invalid for a variety of reasons, including missing keywords and options and order.

**24.** C. The -a option displays statistics for each socket, both listening and non-listening. Included in this information is the send and receive queues. This information can be used to gauge performance and potential bottlenecks.

**25.** A. The correct format is the IP address followed by canonical hostname followed by any aliases for the host. You can use entries in /etc/hosts to override DNS lookups, which can be useful to prevent those names from resolving or to provide a different resolution.

**26.** C. The ifconfig command for configuring interfaces begins with the device followed by the IP address, which is then followed by the netmask keyword and the netmask you want to add. Because this is a /24, the netmask is 255.255.255.0.

**27.** C. IPv4 addresses are 32 bits in length and IPv6 addresses are 128-bits. Both IPv4 and IPv6 can be used on internal and external networks alike, and subnetting is indeed necessary with IPv6.

**28.** D. ICMP is a layer 3 protocol, meaning that it does not use ports for communication. TCP/43 is used for whois whereas port 111 is used for sunrpc. UDP/69 is used for the TFTP protocol.

**29.** B. The ip route command can be used for this purpose, and its syntax uses a change command and the via keyword. The same operation could be completed with the route command but would require deleting the existing gateway first and then re-adding a new default gateway.

**30.** C. Secure Shell (SSH) operates on TCP port 22 by default. TCP/23 is used for telnet, TCP/25 is used for SMTP, and TCP/2200 is not associated with a well-known service.

**31.** B. The nc command is used to start netcat and the -l option causes it to listen. The -p option is used to specify the port on which netcat will listen. The -s option specifies the local source address and is not used for this scenario.

**32.** A. The soa type is used to query for Start of Authority records for a domain. Note that in many cases, dig will attempt to look up the domain within a given command and may not appear to have had an error. For example, when running option D (dig -t auth example.com) you will receive information about example.com and there will be a line in the output that dig has ignored the invalid type of auth.

**33.** A. The search option is used for this purpose and can be provided with multiple domain names, each separated by a space or tab. The domain option is valid within /etc/resolv.conf but does not allow for multiple domain names. On newer systems, systemd-resolved has taken over for the /etc/resolv.conf file.

**34.** C. The ping6 command is used to ping IPv6 addresses. Unique local addresses are the IPv6 equivalent of RFC 1918 private addresses in IPv4. In IPv6, fc00::/7 is the unique local address space. Note that there is no -6 option to the normal ping command.

**35.** A. The route command can be used for this purpose, and in the scenario described, a reject destination is used for the route. The other options shown are incorrect because they use invalid options to the route command.

**36.** B. The tracepath command provides the maximum transmission unit (MTU) of the hops where possible. Both traceroute and tracepath can be used internally or externally, and both provide IPv6 capabilities, though traceroute6 and tracepath6 provide IPv6 capabilities as well. Certain options with the traceroute command can require root privileges, but not enough information was given in the question for that to have been the correct option.

**37.** D. The -c option provides the count of the number of pings to send. The -n option specifies numeric output only, whereas -p specifies the pattern to use for the packet content. Finally, the -t option sets the TTL.

**38.** A. The nmcli command provides a command-line interface suitable for working with NetworkManager through a terminal or SSH connection. The nmtui command provides a curses-based interface that also works through a terminal or SSH connection.

**39.** A. The syntax for ifconfig uses the device—in this case followed by the protocol inet6— and then the keyword add to indicate that an additional IP address is being added, followed finally by the address itself.

**40.** C. LDAP over SSL, or LDAPS, operates on port 636. Port 53 is used for DNS, port 389 is used for normal, non-SSL LDAP, and port 443 is used for HTTP over SSL.

**41.** D. The best option for this question is to add an entry for the host in /etc/hosts. Doing so will always cause DNS queries to resolve to 127.0.0.1. The other options are not as robust because they rely on www.example.com always having the same IP address, or the solutions require additional maintenance to constantly add new IP addresses if www.example.com's IP address changes.

**42.** A. The `ip route flush cache` command should be executed after changing the routes. The other commands shown for this question are not valid.

**43.** A. SPF records are stored in the txt record type in DNS, making `-t txt` the correct option for this. Of the other options, only `-t mx` is valid and returns the mail exchangers for the given domain.

**44.** B. TCP is a connection-oriented protocol that uses a three-way handshake to establish a connection. ICMP does not use ports for communication, and UDP is connectionless. IP is the core Internet Protocol and does not use a handshake.

**45.** D. There are 1,048,576 IP addresses in the 172.16.0.0 private range. There are 16,777,216 in the 10.0.0.0 range and 65,536 in the 192.168.0.0 range.

**46.** C. The only viable possibility of those listed is that ICMP traffic is blocked. TCP traffic is obviously passing because of the ability to get there using HTTP, and DNS must also be working.

**47.** C. The G signifies a gateway within the route table.

**48.** A. The `axfr` type is a zone transfer, and the @ symbol signifies the server to which the query will be sent. There is no xfer type, and option B is just a normal query for the domain sent to the specified server.

**49.** D. The `netstat -s` command displays aggregate statistical information for networking, including the total packets received and the number of packets forwarded. The `ifconfig` command does not show packets forwarded. The `ls` command is not used for networking, and the `ipstat` command does not exist.

**50.** C. The `ip` command defaults to the `inet` family if not otherwise specified with the `-f` option. The command will attempt to guess the correct family and fall back to `inet`. The other families listed as options for this command are not valid for use with the `ip` command.

**51.** B. The `ifconfig` command will be used for this purpose, followed by the interface. The `hw` keyword is used for the hardware address, which is then followed by the hardware class, in this case `ether`. That is followed by the new MAC address (not depicted in the options). The other commands are not valid.

**52.** D. The `-n` option causes route to use numeric values only, performing no name resolution. This option is useful for the scenario described. The `-e` option causes the output to be in `netstat` format. There is no `-d` or `-f` option for the `route` command.

**53.** A. Because we're working with MAC addresses, the `arp` command will be used. The `-d` option removes or deletes an Address Resolution Protocol (ARP) entry, which would be appropriate here so that the MAC address resolution occurs again. The `netstat` command will not be used for this purpose. The `hostname` and `dig` commands work with name resolution but not for MAC addresses or the ARP table.

**54.** A. The iw command will be used for this purpose. When using iw with a specific device, the dev keyword appears next, followed by the device name and then the command you want to execute on that device. In this case, the link command is used.

**55.** B. The iwconfig command, which is similar to the ifconfig command, works with an individual wireless interface to set and display parameters. Of the other commands, the ifconfig command is valid but not used for wireless. The other commands are not valid.

**56.** C. The iwlist command will be used for this purpose, and the scan subcommand is used to look for local access points and wireless networks. Superuser privileges are required for a full scan. The iwconfig command does not have a scan subcommand. Likewise, there is no subcommand called get for the iwlist command, and there is no iw-scan command.

**57.** B. NTP listens on UDP port 123 by default. Ports 20 and 21 are used for FTP services, port 139 is used by NetBIOS, and port 5150 is not usually used.

**58.** B. The mtu can be used to set the value for the maximum transmission unit (MTU) for a given interface. The metric option sets the interface metric. The other options are not valid.

**59.** A. The -s option creates an ARP table entry. The -d option removes an entry. The -c and --add options do not exist.

**60.** A. The ss command provides many of the same functions as netstat but can show some extended information, such as memory allocation for a given socket. The free command shows memory usage but not by socket, and the other two commands do not exist.

**61.** D. The -f option is a flood ping. This will effectively cause the interface to send and receive large amounts of traffic, usually making it easier to find on a switch. The -a option is an audible ping, emitting a sound on ping. The -c option sends a certain count of pings, and there is no -e option.

**62.** B. The netcat command provides a method for opening and communicating on both sides, server and client, for a TCP connection. The netcat command avoids some of the issues with telnet capturing characters specific to the Telnet protocol. The netstat command does not test connectivity, and ping does not do so at the TCP level. There is no nettest command.

**63.** C. The -D option lists the interfaces on a given computer. The -d option dumps compiled matching code, and -i selects an interface. There is no -a option.

**64.** A. The ping6 command performs the same as the IPv4 ping command but does so for IPv6. The other commands are not valid on Linux.

**65.** B. The ip command can be used for this purpose. When using it with the addr object and the -6 option, only information about IPv6 addresses will be shown. The first option, simply ip addr, will show all addresses, including IPv4. The other commands are not valid.

**66.** A. The ifconfig command will be used for this purpose, and ARP can be disabled by preceding the word arp with a minus sign, as shown. If no minus sign is present, then ARP will be enabled. The other commands will not work for this scenario.

**67.** C. The dev option specifies the device to use for the route being specified. This is a typical use case for many routes to reduce the chance of the kernel guessing incorrectly. The other options shown for this question are not valid.

**68.** C. The -p option shows the process IDs associated with a given socket within the ss output. The -a option is all sockets, whereas -l is listening sockets. The -f option is used to specify the protocol family.

**69.** C. The -I option tells traceroute to use ICMP for requests. The -T option is TCP SYN. The -A option performs AS path lookups, and the -i option configures traceroute to use the specified interface.

**70.** C. Internally, the hostname command uses gethostname. This can be useful to know when troubleshooting address resolution issues such as conflicting results for host naming. The other functions are not valid.

**71.** A. The grep command used with the -i option makes the grep case insensitive. When used with the -v option, grep will exclude the argument, thus doing the opposite of what's needed here. The kernel ring buffer will probably not contain information about DHCP, making dmesg an incorrect option.

**72.** B. Only alphanumerics, minus/dash, and dot are valid for hosts in /etc/hosts.

**73.** B. Options within /etc/resolv.conf are preceded with the options keyword followed by one or more options, such as debug.

**74.** D. The journalctl command will be used for this purpose. Adding the -u option specifies the unit for which journal entries are desired.

**75.** A. The /etc/hostname file typically contains only the hostname of the local computer rather than the hostname and domain name. This is then read at boot time to set the hostname for the computer. The /etc/hosts file contains information on various hosts for name resolution purposes. The other files do not exist.

**76.** B. The traceroute6 command is used for tracing IPv6 routes. The other commands do not exist.

**77.** D. The axfr type can be used with dig to request a zone transfer. The client from which you request the zone transfer will need to be authorized to initiate a transfer.

**78.** A. Setting -a as an option to the host command sets the query type to ANY. The -c option sets the class, and -d turns on debugging. There is no -b option.

**79.** C. The .digrc file, when created in a user's home directory, can be used to set defaults for use of the dig command. There is no dig configuration file found in /etc.

**43.** B. The `pubring.gpg` file, found in `~/.gnupg/`, contains the public keyring.

**44.** C. The `.gpg-v21-migrated` file, when present, indicates that gpg version 2.1 or later is in use and that the files have been migrated for that version or a later one.

**45.** D. The `find` command will be used for this purpose, and the `-perm` option is needed, specifically as the 2000 permission to indicate `setgid`. Note the use of / to indicate that the entire server will be searched. The `grep` command shown cannot be used for this purpose because it looks for the presence of the string `'setgid'` within files located in the current directory only.

**46.** C. The `update-rc.d` command creates symbolic links from a service file in `/etc/init.d/` to the appropriate locations in `/etc/rc.d/*` for each runlevel. The other commands shown are not valid.

**47.** A. Single-user mode is typically runlevel 1. In runlevel 1, no network services are started. Runlevel 2 has networking but typically not services. Runlevel 5 is full multiuser with networking, and runlevel 6 is reboot.

**48.** C. The - option is the typical option passed to `su` for login. There is no `-u` or `-U` option, and the `-login` option does not exist. There is a `--login` option with two dashes, but that is not what's shown.

**49.** A. The `netstat` command is used for this purpose, and the `-a` option displays all sockets, listening and nonlistening. Note that it's frequently helpful to add the `-n` option, or combine them as in `netstat -an`, in order to prevent name lookup. Doing so can significantly improve the performance of the command.

**50.** C. This solution will require a way to filter out the bind user; therefore, options that `grep` for `bind` or specify `bind` as the user are incorrect. However, the `lsof` command allows for negation with the caret (^) character. Therefore, listing all files except `bind` requires the syntax shown.

**51.** B. The `-R` option requires an attempt at name resolution be performed. The `-n` option does the opposite; it disables name resolution. There is no `-b` or `-a` option.

**52.** C. The `PARANOID` wildcard specifies that the hostname and IP must match. The `ALL` keyword is also a valid wildcard in `TCPWrappers` for use in both `/etc/hosts.allow` and `/etc/hosts.deny`.

**53.** A. The `PermitRootLogin` directive, set to `yes` or `no`, determines whether the root user can log in directly. The other options shown are not valid.

**54.** B. The `nmap` command will be used for this purpose, and the `-sT` option performs a TCP connect to the specified host or network. The other commands are not valid.

**55.** C. The `-X` option enables X11 application forwarding through an SSH connection. The `-A` option is used for authentication agent forwarding, and `-F` indicates a per-user configuration file. There is no `-X11` option.

**56.** B. The `--output` option is used with `--encrypt` to send the output to a specified file. The other options shown are not valid for gpg.

**57.** B. The `ssh-add` command adds keys to `ssh-agent`. The other commands shown are not valid.

**58.** B. The `-x` option sets the maximum password age until the password needs to be changed again. The `-l` option locks the account, and the other options do not exist.

**59.** A. The `-l` option sets the maximum amount of memory that can be locked. The `-t` option sets the maximum CPU time, and the `-x` and `-b` options do not exist.

**60.** B. The command shown to display the password file and pipe the output into cut will display the usernames from the password file, /etc/passwd. The /etc/shadow file would also produce the same output.

**61.** B. The `access_times` configuration item sets the times in which access is allowed. The other configuration options shown are not valid.

**62.** A. The `.socket` file extension is used for interprocess communication, network sockets, and first-in, first-out (FIFO) queues controlled by systemd. For more information, see `systemd.socket`.

**63.** C. The `-N` option provides the "new" passphrase, and when generating a key, it can be used to generate an empty password. The `-p` and `-P` options both work with passwords but would do so on an existing key. The `-d` option does not exist for `ssh-keygen`.

**64.** A. The MD5 algorithm has been used if the password in /etc/shadow begins with $1$. Of the other options, shadowed passwords beginning with $2a$ or $2y$ would indicate the Blowfish algorithm. There is no RIN or PIK algorithm for shadow passwords.

**65.** B. The `--detach-sig` option creates a detached signature file so that the original file remains unchanged. Both the original file and detached signature file are needed in order to verify the signature. The other options do not exist.

**66.** C. The server host key provides a means by which clients can verify that the server host key has not changed.

**67.** B. The `IdentityFile` option specifies the key that will be used to connect to the host. The other options do not exist for client configurations in SSH.

**68.** C. The `gpg-agent` command is a daemon process to manage private keys. The gpg program and other GnuPG-related utilities use `gpg-agent`. The other options shown for this question are not valid.

**69.** D. The sudoedit editor, part of the sudo package, can be used for the purpose described. Of the other commands, only nano is a real command, but it would also present the same possibility of shell escapes as vim would in this scenario. While there may be ways to prevent a shell escaping with both vim and nano, sudoedit is typically the preferred option.

**70.** A. The -l option changes the login name for a connection with ssh. Among the other options, only -a and -m exist and are not used for the purpose described.

**71.** A. The -l option for usermod changes the username. It is worth noting that the user's home directory and mail spool file do not change and would need to manually be changed following the usermod command. The other options are not used for the purpose described.

**72.** C. The send-keys option followed by the name of the key sends the key to the key server specified by the key server option. This is a typical scenario for sending a locally generated public key to a public server for others to use. The other options do not exist.

**73.** D. The % is used to denote a group within /etc/sudoers and provides an excellent way to facilitate an administrative privileged group.

**74.** D. The fsize option is used within the limits.conf file to control the maximum size of a file that can be created by a user for whom the limit applies.

**75.** B. The ServerAliveCountMax option is used to set the number of keepalive messages that can be sent by the client but not responded to before the client will terminate the connection.

**76.** C. The /etc/nologin file prevents login when present and can also contain a message that is displayed to users when attempting to login.

**77.** A. The -t option specifies the lifetime for the key and is usually given in seconds but can also be given in minutes, hours, days, and weeks with qualifiers. The other options shown do not fulfill the scenario described.

**78.** A. The -R option sets up a remote forward so that remote users can also connect to the tunnel being set up. The other options are not valid for the remote forwarding scenario.

**79.** B. The -W option sets the number of days to warn a user before their password expires. The other options do not exist for chage.

**80.** B. The /etc/shadow- file contains the state of the shadow file before the last change and would likely be the first place to begin recovery. The next would likely be a backup, though /var/backups/ does not hold backups unless manually created.

**81.** B. Integration with the libwrap library is an indicator that a given service or daemon will be able to utilize TCP wrappers for access control.

**82.** A. The User_Alias option enables specification of a group of users for use elsewhere within the sudoers file.

**83.** A. Setting -P0 will allow no ping requests to precede the scan and is useful for the scenario described. There is an -s option, but it is not used for this purpose. The other options are not valid.

**84.** C. The UserKnownHostsFile configuration option enables specification of the location and filename for the known hosts file for users.

**85.** C. The -t argument sets the type of key to generate, and dsa creates a key with the dsa algorithm. Other types includes rsa and ecdsa. The files are normally placed in /etc/ssh and assigned names such as ssh_host_[algorithm]_key and ssh_host_[algorithm]_key.pub, where [algorithm] is one of rsa, dsa, ecdsa, or ed25519.

**86.** C. The -q option prints the users who are logged in along with a count of those users. The -l option prints the login processes, the -t option prints the last system time change, and the -e option does not exist.

**87.** B. The -u option unlocks an account while setting the password. The -l option locks the account, and the -t and -r options do not exist for the passwd command.

**88.** C. The maxlogins option is used to control the number of times that a user can log in. The only other limit-related option shown is maxsyslogins, which sets the maximum number of logins for the entire system.

# Chapter 11: Practice Exam 1

**1.** B. The /proc filesystem stores information about running processes on the system. The /etc filesystem is used for configuration information, and /dev is used for device information. The /environment filesystem does not exist on a default Linux system.

**2.** C. The /etc/modprobe.d directory contains information related to the modprobe configuration. This can be overridden with the -C option on the command line.

**3.** A. The -g option to wall sends the input to the specified group. Answer B will send the output to all users, whereas answers C and D will not work.

**4.** B. The -e option to dmesg displays the time in a localtime and the delta in a format that is typically easier to work with. The -rel option does not exist. The -f option specifies the logging facility, and -t does not display time at all.

**5.** B. The init process is typically associated with the initial process ID of 1 to indicate that it is the process from which others are spawned. Killing PID 1 will typically and immediately halt the system.

**6.** C. The lspci command shows the PCI devices in the system, and the -k option shows the kernel driver being used by the given device. The lsusb command will not accomplish the task requested and the ls command with -pci will not display the correct information. There is no showpci command.

**7.** C. The --no-wall option will cause telinit to not send a wall command to logged-in users about the state change. The other options listed in this question do not exist.

**8.** A. The class/net hierarchy within /sys contains information on the network configuration for the computer. It is a symlink to the devices hierarchy, where the device will be listed by its address rather than the logical eth0 name.

**9.** B. The SIGTERM signal is the default signal sent with the systemctl kill command.

**10.** D. A logical location to begin troubleshooting is within the system BIOS to ensure that the drive is being detected by the computer.

**11.** C. The dbus-monitor program, which requires an X display, can be used to monitor dbus. The other programs and options listed for this question do not exist.

**12.** A. The udevd service is called systemd-udevd.service within a systemd environment.

**13.** A. The system can be scheduled to shut down at a certain time, and that time should be entered in 24-hour format, as shown in the answer.

**14.** C. The -s option changes the signal to be sent from its default of SIGTERM. The new signal must be one of the main signal types, such as SIGINT or SIGSTOP.

**15.** D. The list-unit-files command will show the files available, whereas --type=service will limit those files to the services, in the same way that chkconfig --list returns a list of services.

**16.** A. The -C option sets the location of the cache to be updated instead of the default /etc/ld.so.cache. The lowercase option, -c, changes the format of the cache, whereas -v sets verbose mode. The --f option does not exist.

**17.** C. The -P option to dpkg will purge a package from the system, including the configuration files associated with the package. The apt-cache clean command cleans the package cache but not an individual package, and the apt-get remove command removes a package but not the associated configuration files.

**18.** C. The deb-src prefix is used to indicate that a given repository contains source packages. The deb prefix in option A would indicate normal packages. The other options are not valid.

**19.** B. The -U option is used to upgrade a package. Adding -v for verbose and -h for hash marks will print additional information and progress, as requested by the problem.

**20.** A. The -y or --assumeyes option will do what it says: Assume that you will answer "yes" and therefore not prompt. The other options do not exist.

**21.** A. The exclude option within /etc/yum.conf is a space-separated list of packages that accepts wildcards and is a list of packages that cannot be installed or upgraded. The other options listed in this question do not exist.

**22.** C. The ldconfig command is used to work with the library cache, and the -p option prints the directories and libraries in the cache. The -C option tells ldconfig to use a different cache. The ldd command prints the library dependencies for a given command, but the options given don't exist for ldd.

**23.** D. The baseurl option is used to set the URL and must be fully qualified, meaning that it must include the protocol, such as http:// or file://.

**24.** B. The `apt-cache dump` command will display a listing of the available packages and their respective dependencies. The other commands and options listed in this question do not exist.

**25.** A. The `/boot` directory almost certainly exists but has not been partitioned into its own space. The `/boot` partition would not be hidden from `lsblk` if it was indeed a separate partition.

**26.** B. The `/var/cache` hierarchy contains cached data for both package management tools—in the case of yum, in `/var/cache/yum`, and in the case of a Debian-based system, in `/var/cache/apt`.

**27.** A. The master boot record (MBR) is the typical location for the boot loader to be stored on a BIOS-based system.

**28.** D. The `/` filesystem is the root filesystem. If separate partitions have not been created, the `/` filesystem will be the beginning of the hierarchy and will contain all other directories in the same partition.

**29.** A. The `--output` option configures the location for output of the command instead of STDOUT.

**30.** A. The `dd` command is used for this purpose, and for this case it takes an input file with the `if` option and an output destination with the `of` option. The `bs` option signals that the block size for writing should be 1 megabyte.

**31.** D. The `history` command displays history from the current session and can be used for the purpose described. The `.bash_history` file is written on session close, by default.

**32.** C. The `--boot-directory` option will install the boot images into the directory specified. This might be helpful for nonstandard installs or at times when you need to mount the boot partition separately. The other options listed in this question do not exist.

**33.** A. The `update-grub` command should be executed in order to make changes take effect in the menu and when changes have been made to the GRUB configuration. The other commands listed in this question do not exist.

**34.** B. The `export` command is used for this purpose and accepts a `name=value` pair, as shown in the answer. The other commands are not valid with the exception of the `echo` command, which will simply echo the argument to the console.

**35.** C. The `HISTFILESIZE` option configures the number of commands to keep in the history file. The other variables are not valid within Bash.

**36.** D. The `-b` option configures the body numbering format for `nl`, which by default will not number blank lines. The `a` format option will number all lines, including blanks. The `-a` option is not valid for the `nl` command, and the `-n` option configures the numbering format and would require an additional argument in order to be valid.

**37.** D. The `od` command is used to create octal output. The `cat` command will show the file as it exists on disk. The other two commands are not valid.

**38.** A. The pr command formats text for printing, including the date and page numbers at the top of each page. Adding the -d option causes the output to be double-spaced. The cat command will display output but not paginated in such a way. The other two commands are not valid.

**39.** A. The -n option is used to change the number of lines. Adding the +N after the -n option begins the tail process at the Nth line within the file.

**40.** C. The -i option causes the unique test to be done while ignoring the case of the element to be matched.

**41.** C. The awk command shown can be used for this purpose. The -F option sets the field separator, and the OFS option sets the output field separator.

**42.** C. The -a option is equivalent to the -d and -R options, which preserve links and copy recursively, respectively. The -b option creates a backup, and -f forces the copy.

**43.** A. When in command mode, typing a number followed by an uppercase G will immediately move the cursor to that line number. The /23 option will search for the number 23 in the file. The i23 option will insert the number 23, and finally ZZ will exit Vi.

**44.** A. The -d option changes the update interval and can be helpful on a busy system where top may be affecting performance. The -n option sets the number of iterations to run. There is no -t or -f option for top.

**45.** B. The ps -e command is used to display all processes, and the -o option configures the columns to display.

**46.** A. The grep command will be used for this purpose. Note the difference between grep -r and grep -ri. The question did not ask for case insensitivity, and therefore the use of -i in option B makes it incorrect.

**47.** B. The find command will be used for this purpose. Setting the directory from which to begin the find is required, along with the expression, which in this case, are files beginning with DB.

**48.** B. Load average information is gathered from /proc/loadavg, whereas uptime information is stored on /proc/uptime.

**49.** D. Interactive repair is the default, so no option is required. The -f option forces the operation, and -y and -a are both variations of noninteractive repair.

**50.** D. The /etc/mtab file is updated dynamically as filesystems are mounted and unmounted. The /etc/fstab file is not dynamically updated.

**51.** B. The -B option changes the format, and T sets the scale to terabytes. The -T option alone prints the filesystem type. The other options do not exist.

**52.** A. The e2image program can be used to create an image of metadata that can help with drive recovery. The resulting image file can be used with programs like dumpe2fs and debugfs.

**53.** C. The -c option checks for bad blocks. The -b option sets the block size. There is no -a or -d option.

**54.** B. The chown command is used for this purpose and can be used to set both the user and group for ownership.

**55.** A. The ssh-keyscan command can be used for the purpose described and can help with virtual machine deployment by obtaining the SSH host key and adding it to the known_hosts file.

**56.** C. The GRUB_RECORDFAIL_TIMEOUT option is used to configure the behavior of the system in the event of a failed boot. Setting the value to -1 will display the GRUB menu and not continue booting. Setting the value to 0 will cause the menu to not display. Setting to a value greater than or equal to 1 will cause the menu to display for that many seconds.

**57.** A. The -s option displays a summary, and -h displays it in a human-readable format.

**58.** D. The -L option tells find to follow symlinks. The -H and -P options are both variations to tell find not to follow symlinks, and the -S option does not exist.

**59.** A. The -a option appends to the file rather than overwriting when using tee. The other options do not fulfill the needs of the problem statement.

**60.** C. The /etc directory and its subdirectories typically contain configuration files that would be necessary in order to re-create the system in a restoration scenario. The /var directory usually contains variable information, whereas /opt may be used for several other purposes. The /bin directory contains binaries that can usually be reinstalled.

# Chapter 12: Practice Exam 2

**1.** A. The /etc/hosts.deny file is part of TCP wrappers along with /etc/hosts.allow. Both provide a basic mechanism for configuration of access from remote hosts to network services.

**2.** C. The alias command uses the alias name followed by an equal sign followed by the command to be aliased. In this case, because the command to be aliased contains spaces, it needs to be contained in quotation marks.

**3.** C. Shell scripting syntax uses the format shown, with square brackets around the condition to the tested and double-equal signs for a string test. Variables are preceded by a dollar sign as shown.

**4.** A. The export command is necessary so that any variables that are manually defined in your current session become available to child processes. The source command executes the file and can be used for the purpose described but requires an additional argument. The let and def commands are not valid.

**5.** C. The source command is the functional equivalent of a single dot (.). The set command exists but is not used for this purpose. The other commands are not valid.

**6.** A. The syntax for setting the PATH separates the new path with a colon, as shown in the correct option. A primary difference between the correct and incorrect options for this question was in how the actual specified path was shown.

**7.** A. The correct syntax is as shown. Note that a semicolon is required when the commands are included on one line, as displayed in the answer.

**8.** C. The mail command with -s for the subject is necessary, followed by the email address for the mail. Then, input is redirected to the mail command using /etc/hostname.

**9.** C. The /etc/skel directory contains files that are a skeleton of a user's home directory when their account is created. The other directories listed do not exist by default.

**10.** D. The Universal Access section, which can be found by typing **Universal Access** from within an Ubuntu GUI interface, enables configuration of accessibility options.

**11.** B. The kbdrate command is used for the purpose described and can help with accessibility. The other commands shown are not valid.

**12.** A. The DISPLAY variable controls the destination and screen for displaying GUI applications. Setting this variable facilitates forwarding of X applications over ssh.

**13.** B. The xhost command is used to control who can make connections for both users and hosts to a given X server. The other commands are not valid.

**14.** B. The -f option sets the days between expiration and disabled for an account. The -g option is used to set the group ID, whereas -e is used to set the overall expiration date.

**15.** A. The getent command can be used for the purpose described and will display the aliases on the server by examining the aliases database. The other commands are not valid and, in the case of the mail command shown, will simply attempt to send mail to an address known as aliases.

**16.** C. The ALL: ALL syntax will cause all hosts to be denied. This means that you must explicitly authorize hosts and networks using /etc/hosts.allow.

**17.** B. The current at jobs for all users are shown when atq is executed as superuser.

**18.** C. The -r option to the crontab command removes all cron entries for a given user. The -l option lists cron jobs, whereas the -e option edits the crontab. There is no -d option.

**19.** A. The -u option specifies the user. The -l option lists the cron jobs and -e edits them. There is no -d or -m option.

**20.** A. The userdel command, given no other options, does not delete the home directory. When given the -r option, the command will delete the home directory and mail spool file. There is no -h or -p option for the userdel command.

**21.** D. The -gid option is used to specify group ownership for the find command. The -group option does exist, but since the question specified that the group had already been deleted, the gid must be used instead. There is a -name option, but it searches by name and not group ID.

**22.** B. The groupmod command will be used for this purpose, and the -n option followed by the new group name is used to change the name. There is no groupchg command.

**23.** D. The journalctl command is used to view and parse log file entries on systemd-based systems that maintain logs in a special format. The logger command can be used to create log entries, and the other commands shown do not exist.

**24.** A. The -o option followed by either 1 or 2 enables ntpdate compatibility with older NTP servers. The default, when no -o option is specified, is version 3. The -v option tells ntpdate to be verbose, whereas the -e option sets the authentication timeout.

**25.** D. The /var/log/journal directory is used to store journal log files for systemd-based systems. The other directories do not exist by default.

**26.** C. The -m option sets the mail program to use when mailing logs. It is set to /usr/bin/mail -s by default. There is no -o option, and -v is verbose. The -s option to the logrotate command sets the state file to use.

**27.** A. The -u option configures the output to UTC regardless of the time zone. The -s option sets the time, and there is no -v or -t option.

**28.** D. The lprm command is used to remove print jobs on a system that uses the lp system for printing. There is no lpdel or rmprint command. There is an rm command, but it's not used for working with print queues.

**29.** D. The 255.255.254.0 subnet mask is equivalent to /23. The 255.255.255.0 subnet mask is /24. The subnet mask 255.255.255.255 is /32, and 255.255.0.0 is /16.

**30.** A. The /etc/hosts file will be examined first, and then a Domain Name System (DNS) query will be sent based on the configuration shown.

**31.** D. Standard LDAP traffic is TCP port 389 on the server. TCP port 25 is SMTP, 443 is HTTPS, and 143 is IMAP.

**32.** C. The -l option to ssh changes the username sent for authentication. This can be useful for scripting scenarios where the @ notation cannot be used. The -v option is verbose mode, and -i is the identity file to use. There is no -u option.

**33.** D. The -n option disables name resolution for addresses involved in the ping request/reply. The -D option returns a time stamp, whereas -d sets the SO_DEBUG option. Finally, -f is a flood ping.

**34.** A. The ifconfig command shows various statistics about the interfaces on a Linux system, including whether the interface is up or down, its packets and bytes, queue length, and other information. The other commands listed do not exist.

**35.** C. The -C option shows the SOA for each of the DNS name servers listed as authoritative for the domain. The -a option sends an ANY query, whereas -N sets the number of dots for the domain to be considered absolute. There is no -n option.

**36.** A. The entire 127.0.0.0/8 range is available for local host addresses. Therefore, an answer would need to be in this range. The proper format for /etc/hosts is IP address followed by name, followed by optional aliases, which makes option A correct.

**37.** C. The --ignore-errors option tells ifup to continue even if there are otherwise fatal errors. The -h option outputs help. There is no -C or --continue option.

**38.** C. The -u option unlocks an account that was locked using the -l option. The -w option sets the warn days, and -S prints the status.

**39.** C. When connecting to an alternate port, you can use the -p option to set the port or use a colon to separate the host from the port.

**40.** B. The mailto configuration option sets the destination for emails related to sudo. The other options listed are not valid for sudo.

**41.** B. The who command displays who is currently logged in and the date and time they logged in. The whois command displays information about domains. The other commands are not valid.

**42.** C. Port 123 is used for NTP communication by default. Port 161 is SNMP, 139 is NetBIOS, and 194 is IRC.

**43.** D. A UDP scan can be initiated with -sU. A scan of -sT is a normal TCP scan, and -sS is a SYN scan. There is no -sP option.

**44.** B. The +D option is used to search an entire directory tree for files that are open by processes. The -d option does essentially the same thing but does not go into subdirectories. The -f option is typically used in combination with other options to control path name interpretation. The -i option lists files or processes with open ports.

**45.** C. The -r option causes the ip command to attempt to resolve IP addresses. The -f option specifies the protocol family. There is no -n or -a option to the ip command.

**46.** A. The ss command will be used, and when given the -o option, timer information is displayed. The netstat -rn command shows route information but not sockets or timing, and ping -f is a flood ping and not related. The ls -l command displays files in a long listing format.

**47.** C. All of the addresses shown are in private ranges. The only one with the correct netmask is 255.255.255.0, which is equivalent to 24 masked bits.

**48.** C. The !H sequence indicates host unreachable. Network unreachable is !N.

**49.** D. There is no port for ICMP. The protocol itself does not use ports.

**50.** B. The /etc/services file contains the port number to name translation for a given server. The file contains well-known ports and can be customized on a per-server basis.

**51.** A. The command shown launches speech output for Orca. The other commands contain options that are invalid and thus will not work.

**52.** A. The configuration files can be found in the /etc/lightdm hierarchy or in /usr/share/ lightdm. The other directory locations do not exist by default.

**53.** D. The xwininfo command is used to gather information about windows. The other commands shown are not valid.

**54.** A. The tzconfig command can be used on a Debian system to set the time zone. The other commands listed do not exist.

**55.** C. The locale command will be used for this purpose, and the -m option displays the available character maps. There is no charmap or mapinfo command.

**56.** B. Time zone information is found within the /usr/share/zoneinfo hierarchy. The other directories listed do not typically exist by default.

**57.** A. The default location on a Red Hat system is /var/lib/ntp/drift. The other locations shown do not exist by default. Within /etc/ntpd.conf, the location of the drift file can be changed with the driftfile option.

**58.** C. The <<< character combination reads input from STDIN or standard input and uses it as the body of the message for the mail command.

**59.** C. The groupdel command is used to remove a group from a system. No members of the group can remain or the command will fail.

**60.** C. The lpr syslog facility sends messages from the lp subsystem to syslog. The auth facility is used for security-related messages. The other listed options are not syslog facilities.

# Index

# R

# Comprehensive Online Learning Environment

Register to gain one year of FREE access to the online interactive learning environment and test bank to help you study for your LPIC-1 certification exam—included with your purchase of this book!

The online test bank includes the following:

- **Practice Test Questions** to reinforce what you've learned
- **Bonus Practice Exams** to test your knowledge of the material

Go to `http://www.wiley.com/go/sybextestprep` to register and gain access to this comprehensive study tool package.

## Register and Access the Online Test Bank

To register your book and get access to the online test bank, follow these steps:

1. Go to `bit.ly/SybexTest`.
2. Select your book from the list.
3. Complete the required registration information, including answering the security verification to prove book ownership. You will be emailed a PIN code.
4. Follow the directions in the email or go to `https://www.wiley.com/go/sybextestprep`.
5. Enter the PIN code you received and click the "Activate PIN" button.
6. On the Create an Account or Login page, enter your username and password, and click Login. A "Thank you for activating your PIN!" message will appear. If you don't have an account already, create a new account.
7. Click the "Go to My Account" button to add your new book to the My Products page.

SYBEX®
A Wiley Brand